GW00502891

VISUAL QUICKSTART GUIDE

MOTION

FOR MAC OS X

Mark Spencer

 **Peachpit Press**

Visual QuickStart Guide
Motion for Mac OS X
Mark Spencer

Peachpit Press
1249 Eighth Street
Berkeley, CA 94710
510/524-2178
800/283-9444
510/524-2221 (fax)

Find us on the World Wide Web at www.peachpit.com.
To report errors, please send a note to errata@peachpit.com.
Peachpit Press is a division of Pearson Education

Copyright © 2005 by Mark Spencer

Editor: Cheryl England
Production Editor: Lupe Edgar
Copyeditor: Rebecca C. Rider
Compositor: Owen Wolfson
Indexer: Lynne Grimes, Interactive Composition Corporation
Cover Design: The Visual Group

Notice of rights
All rights reserved. No part of this book may be reproduced or transmitted in any
form by any means, electronic, mechanical, photocopying, recording, or otherwise,
without the prior written permission of the publisher. For information on getting permission for reprints and excerpts, contact permissions@peachpit.com.

Notice of liability
The information in this book is distributed on an "As Is" basis, without warranty.
While every precaution has been taken in the preparation of the book, neither the
author nor Peachpit Press shall have any liability to any person or entity with respect
to any loss or damage caused or alleged to be caused directly or indirectly by the
instructions contained in this book or by the computer software and hardware prod-
ucts described in it.

Trademarks
Visual QuickPro Guide is a registered trademark of Peachpit Press, a division of
Pearson Education.

Throughout this book, trademarks are used. Rather than put a trademark symbol in
every occurrence of a trademarked name, we state that we are using the names in an
editorial fashion only and to the benefit of the trademark owner with no intention of
infringement of the trademark.

ISBN 0-321-29458-0

9 8 7 6 5 4 3 2 1

Printed and bound in the United States of America

To my incredible wife Renée, for her unwavering support of my decision to follow my heart. And to our newborn son Elliott, who is my daily reminder of the wonder and mystery of life that surrounds us all.

Acknowledgments

First, thanks to Sharon Franklin, outstanding Final Cut Pro editor, one of the founders of the San Francisco Cutters, and the person who recommended me for this book.

To Marjorie Baer of Peachpit, for taking a chance on me. To my editor, Cheryl England, whose humor and encouragement lifted my spirits—you were always willing to do whatever it took to support me. To the rest of the Peachpit team, notably Rebecca Rider and Lupe Edgar, thanks for your excellent work.

Michael Wohl, thanks for your thorough technical editing—it's an honor to have an accomplished filmmaker, editor, and Motion expert reviewing my book. And to Dion Scoppettuolo at Apple Computer, thanks for tackling my numerous, convoluted, and occasionally arcane questions.

Damian Allen, thanks for your excellent instruction at the very first Apple Train the Trainers training—you opened my eyes to the possibilities of this amazing application.

To the moderators and contributors of the online Motion forums at Apple, 2-pop and Creative Cow for teaching me something new every day.

To the local San Francisco editing and motion graphics community, especially Kevin Monahan and the SF Cutters, as well as the folks at BAMG.

And finally, thanks to Apple Computer for making the hardware and software that allow me to make a living doing something I enjoy so thoroughly.

This Book Is Safari Enabled

The Safari® Enabled icon on the cover of your favorite technology book means the book is available through Safari Bookshelf. When you buy this book, you get free access to the online edition for 45 days.

Safari Bookshelf is an electronic reference library that lets you easily search thousands of technical books, find code samples, download chapters, and access technical information whenever and wherever you need it.

To gain 45-day Safari Enabled access to this book:

- Go to http://www.peachpit.com/safarienabled
- Complete the brief registration form
- Enter the coupon code AQG7–ZEZF–XUZK–DSFE–F5A8

If you have difficulty registering on Safari Bookshelf or accessing the online edition, please e-mail customer-service@safaribooksonline.com.

TABLE OF CONTENTS

TABLE OF CONTENTS

TABLE OF CONTENTS

TABLE OF CONTENTS

TABLE OF CONTENTS

INTRODUCTION

Are you in for a treat!

Motion, Apple's revolutionary new addition to its Pro Applications lineup, takes motion graphics creation to an entirely new level. With procedural animations, Final Cut Pro HD and DVD Studio Pro integration, a library of presets and templates, and amazing real-time performance, Motion offers a powerful new way to create professional motion graphics. And the streamlined interface coupled with Apple's legendary ease of use puts the ability to translate imagination into reality within anyone's reach.

What is Motion?

Motion is a *behavior-driven motion graphics application*. *Motion graphics* refers to the process of compositing different elements together (such as graphics, photos, video, and text) and animating various properties of those elements over time (such as position, scale, or opacity). Whenever you turn on your TV and see a station ID, a promo for a new show, or the introduction to your favorite sitcom, you are seeing motion graphics in action. And just about any DVD you watch these days employs motion graphics for menus and transitions.

Traditional motion graphics applications use a process called *keyframing* to animate properties of elements over time. In addition to including powerful keyframing tools, Motion introduces a new way of quickly and easily animating objects without keyframes called *behaviors*. Behaviors are deceptively simple, yet very powerful devices you can use to create complex animations that are virtually impossible to make with traditional keyframe techniques.

Motion also contains a powerful particle system generator that you can use to simulate natural phenomena like fog, smoke, and water; compositing tools such as masks, keys, and blend modes; an array of filters for manipulating the look of objects; and an extensive set of tools for creating and animating text.

One of the most amazing and enjoyable aspects of Motion is its real-time capability. Motion is built to take advantage of the latest advances in CPU speed, increased RAM capacity, and, most importantly, graphics card muscle. With Motion, you can combine video, text, and graphics with behaviors, filters, and particles, and you can adjust parameters to your heart's content while you watch your project play in real-time. Combined with the intuitive and flexible interface, Motion enables a completely new approach to motion graphics design that is spontaneous, interactive, and downright addicting.

Motion was designed to integrate easily with other Apple Pro Applications for a complete production workflow. For example, you can export sequences from Final Cut Pro HD into Motion, retaining all tracks, in and out points, composite modes, markers, and motion attributes. Changes you make in Motion update automatically in Final Cut Pro.

Who is Motion For?

Anyone who needs to create professional motion graphics can benefit from the simplicity and power that Motion brings to the creative process. In particular:

- **Final Cut Pro editors** can enhance their editing projects with professional motion graphics for opening title sequences.

- **DVD Studio Pro authors** can use Motion to create compelling menus and transitions.

- **Broadcast facilities** can create station IDs, promos, and interstitials.

- **Post-production facilities** can incorporate Motion into their production workflow.

- **Motion graphics designers** will find Motion makes a strong complement to their arsenal of motion graphics tools.

- **Graphic artists** who work with Adobe Photoshop and/or Illustrator and are interested in adding movement to their work will find Motion an intuitive, easy-to-learn way to step into the world of motion graphics.

Who Should Use This Book

Motion for Mac OS X: Visual QuickStart Guide is designed for intermediate to advanced Mac users who have basic knowledge of video editing and graphics terminology and processes. Although not required, experience with other Apple Pro Applications such as Final Cut Pro HD and DVD Studio Pro will make readers feel at home quickly. Experience with graphics applications such as Photoshop is also helpful. Readers who have experience with other motion graphics applications can use this book as a reference to quickly dive deep into concepts that may be new to them, such as behaviors.

What's in This Book

At a high level, this book is organized around a common workflow used to create motion graphics.

First, I cover system requirements, installing Motion, and an overview of the interface to get you oriented.

Next, I dive deeper into the interface by introducing the process of compositing: browsing, selecting, and placing different types of media elements and applying basic transformations. I then cover compositing and arranging elements over time by using the Timeline.

Then I introduce the world of animation, first by working with behaviors and then by introducing keyframes.

The book then goes a step deeper: it explores filters, generators, and Motion's particle system. It explains drawing shapes and masking objects, and covers Motion's extensive text manipulation capabilities. Working with audio is explained, as is how to work with Motion's professional templates.

Finally, the book deals with finishing your project: various export options, including using the bundled Compressor application; and how to move between Motion and both Final Cut Pro HD and DVD Studio Pro.

How to use this book

This book is designed as a reference guide with an emphasis on step-by-step descriptions of specific tasks. Although you can read it straight through to get a comprehensive understanding of Motion, you may find it most useful if you keep it by your side while you are working for quick reference on how to perform specific tasks. It is structured so that you can use it in a completely non-linear fashion: to learn or review how to complete a task, you can go directly to the task description and get the information you need. In addition to step-by-step task descriptions and illustrations, this text includes:

Sidebars, which explain certain concepts, give examples of applications, or provide suggested processes.

Tips, which are juicy bits of information: a faster, easier way of doing something, a cool trick, a neat feature, or a warning about a potential pitfall.

Appendices, which provide detailed information on Motion's preferences and editing project properties.

Welcome to the new world of Motion! Let's get started!

To Learn More About Motion

Mark Spencer, author of this book, maintains a listing of Motion tips, tricks, and resources on his Web site at www.applemotion.net.

Michael Wohl's Motion PowerStart is a comprehensive DVD training course for Motion, which contains three clear, fun, and practical hands-on tutorials plus a section on integrating Motion with other Apple programs. All source material and project files are included plus bonus materials to use in your own projects.

The DVD was created by Michael Wohl, an award-winning filmmaker and a member of the official Motion documentation team, along with Josh Mellicker of DVcreators.net. Wohl has also written books on Final Cut Pro for Peachpit Press, including *Editing Techniques with Final Cut Pro*. You can find the $79.95 DVD as well as reviews and more information at www.dvcreators.net.

BEFORE YOU BEGIN

Okay, I know you are chomping at the bit, just hankering to jump into behaviors and particles and filters. But hold on! Let's cover a few basics first so that you'll be sure to have the best possible experience as you step into the amazing world that is Motion.

This chapter covers the nitty-gritty of system requirements and real-time performance; walks you through installing and launching Motion for the first time; and touches on Motion's integration with other Apple Pro applications that you may be using as part of your overall workflow.

System Requirements

First, the hard fact: Motion takes some serious hardware muscle to perform its magic. It was designed to take advantage of Apple's dual G5 processors, lots of RAM, and perhaps most importantly, a powerful graphics card. Although it runs on the minimum system I'm about to describe, the beefier the system you have or can afford, the greater the performance you'll get from Motion.

Here are the minimum requirements:

◆ Macintosh computer with 867 MHz or faster PowerPC G4 or G5 processor

◆ 4X AGP slot

◆ 512 MB of RAM (2 GB or more recommended)

◆ Mac OS X v10.3.5 or later

◆ QuickTime 6.5.1 or later

◆ Display with 1024 by 768 resolution or higher (1280 by 1024 resolution recommended)

◆ One of the following graphics cards:
ATI Radeon 9800 XT (R360)
ATI Radeon 9800 Pro (R350)
ATI Radeon 9700 Pro (R300)
ATI Radeon 9600 XT (RV360)
ATI Radeon 9600 Pro (RV350)
ATI Mobility Radeon 9700 (RV M11)
ATI Mobility Radeon 9600 (RV M100)
NVIDIA GeForce 6800 Ultra DDL (NV40)
NVIDIA GeForce FX Go5200 (NV34M)
NVIDIA GeForce FX 5200 Ultra (NV34)

◆ 10 GB of disk space for the application, templates, and tutorials

◆ DVD drive for installation

Here is the system Apple recommends:

◆ Dual 2 GHz Power Mac G5

◆ 2 GB of RAM or more

◆ Mac OS X v10.3.5 or later

◆ ATI Radeon 9800 Pro graphics card or better

Real-Time Capabilities

Motion's capacity to play back your project in real-time as you make adjustments such as adding filters and behaviors is one of its most compelling features. It also takes some real horsepower.

Most important is the graphics card, which stores the frames of your composition in VRAM and calculates the composition of all your elements in its graphics processor unit (GPU).

Second in importance is the amount of RAM you have; Motion uses it to cache and play back video.

Third, Motion uses the central processing unit (CPU) to perform the massive calculations required for behaviors and particle systems.

Figure 1.1 To find out which graphics card is installed in your Mac, first select About This Mac from the Apple menu.

Figure 1.2 Click the More Info button to launch System Profiler.

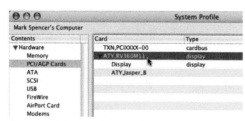

Figure 1.3 Select PCI/AGP Cards and check the model number.

To determine which graphics card is installed in your Mac:

1. Under the Apple menu, select About This Mac (**Figure 1.1**).

2. Click More Info to launch System Profiler (**Figure 1.2**).

3. In the System Profiler, click PCI/AGP Cards and match the number under the Card column to the number in parentheses in the list of approved cards (**Figure 1.3**).

   In this example, RV360 indicates the ATI Radeon 9600 XT graphics card.

✔ Tips

- Don't post that G4 on eBay just yet! Because Motion depends heavily on the graphics card and the amount of RAM you have, even on an older Mac you can improve Motion's real-time performance by updating your graphics card and adding more RAM. Check Apple's Web site (www.apple.com/motion) for up-to-date information on appropriate graphics cards for you computer.

- Got a PowerBook? Motion will run on 15- and 17-inch 1.25/1.33 GHz PowerBook G4s with the ATI Mobility Radeon 9600 graphics card. Unfortunately, if you do not have this model PowerBook with this card, you cannot upgrade the PowerBook to run Motion.

- As of the date of this book's publication in late 2004, Apple has a small application called Motion Compatibility Checker on its Web site. You can download and run it to determine if your computer will run Motion.

SYSTEM REQUIREMENTS

Installing Motion

Once you've confirmed that your Mac meets the minimum requirements (or you've used your purchase of Motion as an excuse to finally get that brand-new G5 you've had your eye on), you can install the application.

To install Motion:

1. Locate the two DVDs that come with Motion: Motion Install, which contains the application itself and Motion Content, which contains the media and files for Motion's Library, templates, and tutorials.

2. Insert the Motion Install DVD into your DVD drive and double-click the Install Motion icon (**Figure 1.4**).

3. Follow the on-screen instructions.

4. Read and accept the license agreement and then choose an install location (**Figure 1.5**).

   When the installation is complete, eject the DVD and store it in a safe place.

   Keep the serial number handy because you'll need it when you launch Motion the first time.

5. Insert the Motion Content DVD.

6. Double-click the Install Motion Content icon and follow the on-screen instructions (**Figure 1.6**).

   This DVD installs all the content in Motion's Library, including graphics and movies for use in particles systems, tutorial elements, and the files for all the templates.

✔ Tip

■ You may want to read through the Before You Install Motion document to make sure you meet all the system requirements before you get started.

Figure 1.4 Click the Install Motion icon and follow the installation instructions.

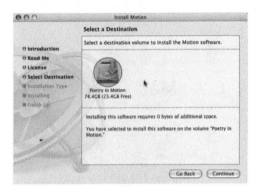

Figure 1.5 Choose an install location.

Figure 1.6 Click here to install Motion content.

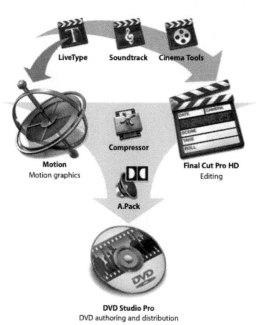

LiveType   Soundtrack   Cinema Tools

Compressor

Motion
Motion graphics

Final Cut Pro HD
Editing

A.Pack

DVD Studio Pro
DVD authoring and distribution

Figure 1.7 Together, Motion and other Apple Pro Applications offer a complete production workflow.

Integrated Applications

Although you can use Motion quite effectively as a standalone application, Apple has designed it to integrate tightly into its other Pro Applications as part of a *production workflow* (**Figure 1.7**).

A typical production workflow may include editing video in Final Cut Pro HD; creating motion graphics elements for the video in Motion; creating animated menus for the final DVD in Motion; and then designing the DVD in DVD Studio Pro. The tight integration between these applications means you can quickly and easily create motion graphics elements for your video and DVD menus, and those elements will update automatically within Final Cut Pro HD and DVD Studio Pro when you make changes in Motion.

You can also export clips from a Final Cut Pro HD sequence to Motion for enhancing it with titling, filters, and other effects. When you open the sequence in Motion, it retains all of its edit points, composite modes, transformations, and markers.

For the step-by-step process of moving between Final Cut Pro HD, Motion, and DVD Studio Pro, see Chapter 17.

WELCOME TO MOTION

2

It's time to get acquainted.

The Motion interface is as flexible as it is elegant. If you've used Final Cut Pro or DVD Studio Pro, you'll feel right at home. If not, no worries—Motion is incredibly welcoming.

In this chapter, I explain how to launch Motion and start a new project. Then I introduce the Motion interface and take you on a walking tour to get you familiar with your newfound motion graphics friend.

Launching Motion

Now's a good time to locate your Motion serial number if you don't already have it handy. You'll need it before you can get started on your first project.

When Motion launches, you are presented with a Welcome screen that contains four buttons (**Figure 2.1**):

View the Quick Tours launches your Web browser and provides access to online QuickTime movies that walk through the basics of using Motion. You need an Internet connection to view these movies.

Begin with a Tutorial walks you through a series of screens that help you learn Motion.

Start with a Template presents you with different preset template options that you can use as a starting point for your project.

Start with a New Project allows you to choose a project preset and work with a brand new empty project.

To launch Motion:

1. Navigate to the Applications folder (or the folder where you installed Motion) and double-click the Motion icon (**Figure 2.2**).

2. Enter your serial number when prompted.

✔ Tips

■ If you drag the Motion icon to your Dock, you'll have quick access to it.

■ By unchecking the check box at the bottom of the Welcome Screen, you can skip this dialog when you launch the application and instead go directly to a new project.

■ Once you have told Motion to bypass the Welcome window, you can bring it back by going to the General tab under Motion > Preferences and setting the At Startup drop-down menu to Show Welcome Screen.

Figure 2.1 The Motion Welcome Screen appears when you launch the program. You can skip it, however, and go directly to a new project by unchecking the check box at the bottom.

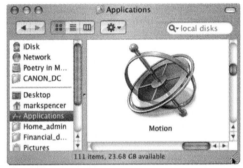

Figure 2.2 Double-click the Motion icon to launch the program.

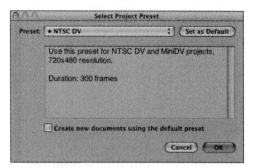

Figure 2.3 The Select Project Preset window lets you choose presets that come included with Motion.

To start a new project:

1. Click the last button in the Welcome Screen—Start with a New Project.

2. In the Select Project Preset window that appears, choose a preset from the Preset drop-down list (**Figure 2.3**). A description of the currently selected preset appears in the window below the Preset drop-down list.

✔ Tip

- Choose a project preset based on the destination of your project. For example, if you are planning to bring your project into Final Cut Pro HD to use in a DV-NTSC Timeline, choose DV-NTSC.

Introducing the Motion Workspace

When you launch Motion, the interface fills your entire monitor with what looks like one large window (**Figure 2.4**). In fact, it consists of two separate windows that you can see, and two additional panes, which are hidden.

The two windows are the Utility window on the left and the Canvas window, or simply the Canvas, on the right. Just like a real window, a window in Motion can have several panes. The Canvas contains a Project pane and a Timing pane. Unlike real windows, these panes slide open like drawers. They are hidden by default.

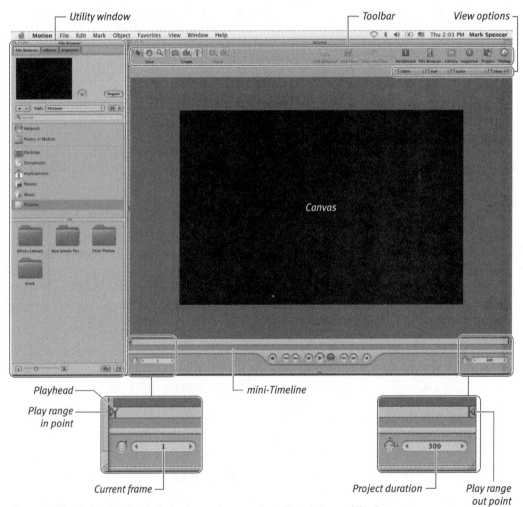

Figure 2.4 The Motion interface includes two main areas: the Utility window and the Canvas.

Working with the Utility Window

The Utility window appears to the left of the Canvas. You use this window to find, select, and make changes to media files, effects, and other content in your project.

The Utility window contains three tabs: File Browser, Library, and Inspector. You use the File Browser to locate, preview, and select files to add to your project. The Library tab contains a variety of effects, templates, and other content you can use in your project. You use the Inspector to manipulate the attributes, called *parameters*, of objects in your project. Note that the name of the currently displayed tab is repeated at the top of the Utility window.

✔ Tip

- You can use the following key combinations to select each tab in the Utility window: Command-1 for the File Browser, Command-2 for the Library, and Command-3 for the Inspector.

What Are Objects?

We've been using the term objects rather loosely, so let's define it. *Objects* are the fundamental building blocks of your project. Media files that you select in the File Browser, such as graphics and video, are objects. Shapes and text that you create directly in Motion are also objects. Particle emitters and particle cells are objects. Masks are objects. Even the computer-generated elements called generators found in the Library are objects. *Effects,* on the other hand, such as behaviors and filters, are *applied to* objects to change the object's characteristics. The bottom line—everything in Motion starts with an object.

The File Browser

Now that you're familiar with the general landscape of the Utility window, let's dig deeper into each of the tabs to learn how to work with them. The File Browser is located on the first tab in the Utility window (**Figure 2.5**). It operates much like the Finder in Mac OS X in that it provides a view of all the files on your computer. It is here that you peruse your hard drive(s) in search of files to add to your project.

The File Browser makes it simple to add files to your project because you don't have to first import files to gain access to them—any file on any connected drive is immediately available.

To reveal the File Browser:

Do one of the following:

◆ Click the File Browser tab in the Utility window.

◆ Click the File Browser icon in the Toolbar of the Canvas.

◆ Choose Window > File Browser.

◆ Press Command-1.

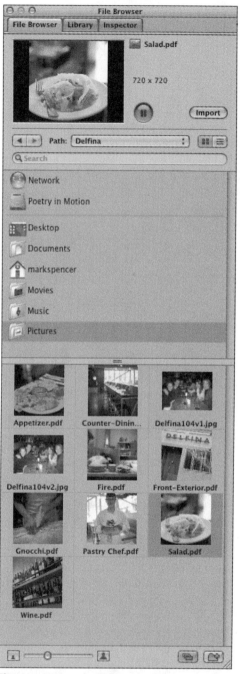

Figure 2.5 You use the File Browser to locate, preview, and select files to add to your project.

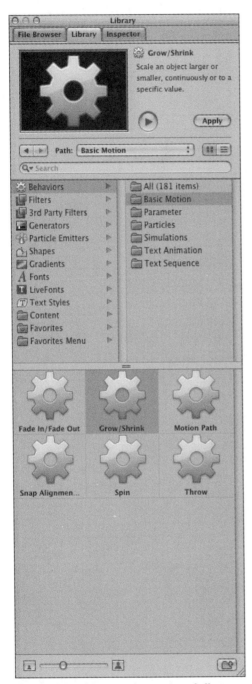

Figure 2.6 The Library contains a variety of effects, templates, and other content you can use in your project.

The Library

The Library is located on the second tab in the Utility window. and it provides access to all the behaviors, filters, generators, particle presets, fonts, and templates that are available in Motion (**Figure 2.6**).

To reveal the Library:

Do one of the following:

◆ Click the Library tab in the Utility window.

◆ Click the Library icon in the Toolbar of the Canvas.

◆ Choose Window > Library.

◆ Press Command-2.

WORKING WITH THE UTILITY WINDOW

The Inspector

The Inspector is located on the third and final tab in the Utility window (**Figure 2.7**). Here is where you view and make changes to the parameters of a selected object, mask, or effect.

The Inspector tab contains four tabs of its own. The first three, Properties, Behaviors, and Filters, always have the same names. The fourth, called the Object tab, is *context-sensitive*—it changes its name depending on what type of element you have selected, such as an image, a behavior, or a filter.

To reveal the Inspector:

Do one of the following:

◆ Click the Inspector tab in the Utility window.

◆ Click the Inspector icon in the Toolbar of the Canvas.

◆ Choose Window > Inspector.

◆ Press Command-3.

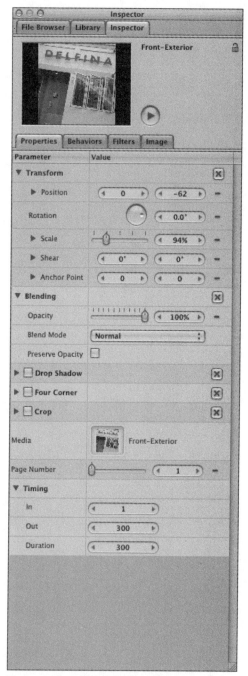

Figure 2.7 You use the Inspector to manipulate the parameters of objects in your project.

To reveal the tabs in the Inspector:

Do one of the following:

◆ Click the appropriate tab (Properties, Behaviors, Filters, or Object)

◆ Choose Window > Show Inspector and choose the appropriate tab.

◆ Use the appropriate function key:

Press F1 for Properties

Press F2 for Behaviors

Press F3 for Filters

Press F4 for Object (context sensitive)

✔ Tip

■ It isn't necessary to first reveal the Inspector and then reveal the tab. To more quickly open a specific tab in the Inspector, you can use the keyboard shortcuts listed above. For example, if you are currently in the File Browser (Command-1) and you want to go to the Properties tab of the Inspector, simply press F1.

What Are Parameters?

Parameters are the specific attributes of an object that can be changed. For instance, you can adjust the Scale, Position, and Rotation parameters of any object in the Canvas.

Effects have parameters, too. For example, if you have applied the Tint filter to an object, you can change the Color parameter to adjust the color of the tint.

In fact, virtually any element in Motion, whether it is an object (like a video clip), an effect (like a behavior or a filter), or a particle system, has parameters with values that you can set to a specific value or set to change values over time.

WORKING WITH THE UTILITY WINDOW

Exploring the Canvas

The Canvas is the work area where you build your project. It includes a Toolbar along the top where you can adjust how you view the Canvas and objects placed in it; you can choose tools to add shapes, masks, text, behaviors, and filters; you can make particles; and you can choose tabs to reveal in the Utility window. Along the bottom is a mini-Timeline that allows you to make time-based adjustments to a selected object or effect. In addition, the Canvas window contains two hidden panes (**Figure 2.8**): the Project pane and the Timing pane.

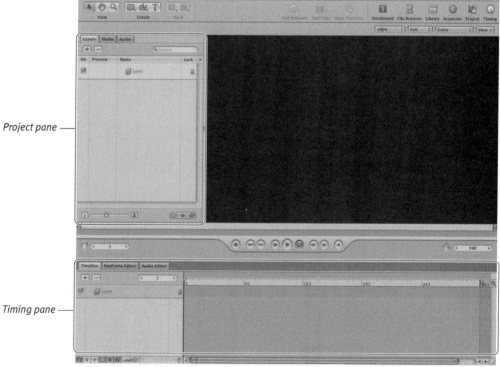

Project pane

Timing pane

Figure 2.8 The Canvas contains two hidden panes: the Project pane and the Timing pane.

The Project pane

The Project pane provides access to different views of your project through three tabs: Layers, Media, and Audio. The Layers tab shows a hierarchical view of all objects, masks, and effects used in the Canvas. The Media tab identifies the properties of each file imported into your project. And the Audio tab shows the properties of audio files used in your project.

To make the Project pane visible:

Do one of the following:

◆ Drag the divider bar on the left edge of the Canvas.

◆ Click the Project icon in the Toolbar.

◆ Press F5.

The Timing pane

The Timing pane also contains three tabs, each of which provide a different time-based view of your project elements. The Timeline shows all objects and effects in the Canvas, similar to the Layers tab in the Project pane, but it also includes how these elements are laid out over time. The Keyframe Editor allows you to view and make changes to keyframes that have been applied to objects and effects. And the Audio Editor allows you to make adjustments to audio levels and panning.

To make the Timing pane visible:

Do one of the following:

◆ Drag the divider bar on the bottom edge of the Canvas.

◆ Click the Timing icon in the Toolbar.

◆ Press F6.

EXPLORING THE CANVAS

Examining the Project Pane Tabs

The Project pane contains three tabs: Layers, Media, and Audio. Here's what you need to know about each of these tabs and some shortcuts for revealing them.

The Layers tab

The first tab in the Project pane is the Layers tab (**Figure 2.9**). It is here that you can view the stacking order of all the objects, masks, and effects in your project.

To reveal the Layers tab:

Do one of the following:

◆ Choose Window > Layers.

◆ Press F5 to open the Project pane and then click the Layers tab if it is not already the front tab.

◆ Press Command-4 (if the Project pane is closed, Command-4 opens the Project pane and reveals the Layers tab).

Figure 2.9 The Layers tab shows a hierarchical view of all objects, masks, and effects used in the Canvas.

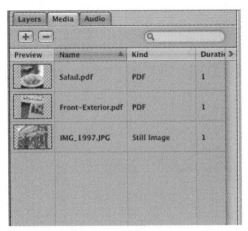

Figure 2.10 The Media tab identifies the properties of each file that you import into your project.

Figure 2.11 The Audio tab shows the properties of audio files used in your project.

The Media tab

The second tab in the Project pane is the Media tab (**Figure 2.10**). It contains a list of all media that you have brought into your project, whether or not that media is currently in the Canvas. You use the Media tab to review the more technical attributes of your underlying media files, such as the media type, file size, and frame rate.

To reveal the Media tab:

Do one of the following:

◆ Choose Window > Media.

◆ Press F5 to open the Project pane and then click the Media tab if it is not already the front tab.

◆ Press Command-5 (if the Project pane is closed, Command-5 opens the Project pane and reveals the Media tab).

The Audio tab

The third and final tab in the Project pane is the Audio tab (**Figure 2.11**). It contains a list of all media files you have brought into your project that have an audio component. You use the Audio tab to adjust the audio level and panning of an object or of the overall audio mix.

To reveal the Audio tab:

Do one of the following:

◆ Choose Window > Audio.

◆ Press F5 to open the Project pane and then click the Audio tab if it is not already the front tab.

◆ Press Command-6 (if the Project pane is closed, Command-6 opens the Project pane and reveals the Audio tab).

Examining the Timing Pane Tabs

The Timing pane, like the Project pane, contains three tabs. The tabs in the Timing pane are the Timeline, the Keyframe Editor, and the Audio Editor. Here's what you need to know about each of these.

The Timeline

The Timeline is located in the first tab of the Timing pane (**Figure 2.12**). The Timeline provides a graphical view of how all your objects, masks, behaviors, and filters in the Canvas are arranged over time.

To reveal the Timeline:

Do one of the following:

◆ Choose Window > Timeline.

◆ Press F6 to open the Timing pane and then click the Timeline tab if it is not already the front tab.

◆ Press Command-7 (if the Timing pane is closed, Command-7 opens the Timing pane and reveals the Timeline).

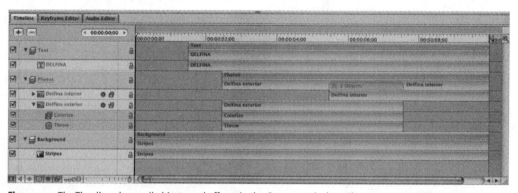

Figure 2.12 The Timeline shows all objects and effects in the Canvas and where they occur over time.

Keyframe Editor

The Keyframe Editor is located in the second tab of the Timing pane (**Figure 2.13**). It contains a graphical representation in the form of curves connecting the keyframes that you have added to any objects or effects. You can choose which parameters to view, then add, delete, and adjust keyframe values and positions for each parameter.

To reveal the Keyframe Editor:

Do one of the following:

◆ Choose Window > Keyframe Editor.

◆ Press F6 to open the Timing pane and then click the Keyframe Editor tab if it is not already the front tab.

◆ Press Command-8 (if the Timing pane is closed, Command-8 opens the Timing pane and reveals the Keyframe Editor).

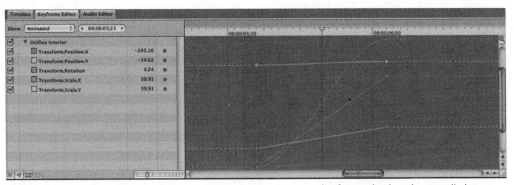

Figure 2.13 The Keyframe Editor allows you to view and make changes to keyframes that have been applied to objects and effects.

Audio Editor

The Audio Editor is located in the third and final tab of the Timing pane (**Figure 2.14**). It allows you to view the audio waveform for each object containing audio, to make adjustments to audio levels and panning, and to keyframe those adjustments over time.

To reveal the Audio Editor:

Do one of the following:

◆ Choose Window > Audio Editor.

◆ Press F6 to open the Timing pane and then click the Audio Editor tab if it is not already the front tab.

◆ Press Command-9 (if the Timing pane is closed, Command-9 opens the Timing pane and reveals the Audio Editor).

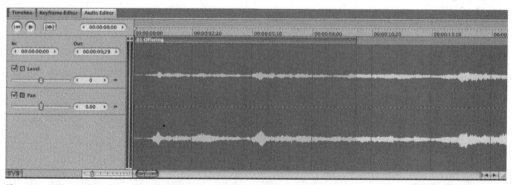

Figure 2.14 The Audio Editor allows you to make adjustments to audio levels and panning.

Navigating the Interface with Keyboard Shortcuts

Motion provides several ways to display a specific tab in a window or pane, such as the Properties tab in the Inspector (which is itself a tab in the Utility window) or the Keyframe Editor in the Timing pane. The keyboard shortcuts to access each of these tabs are arranged in a logical order and can provide a quick way to jump from tab to tab.

With the Project pane and Timing pane both open (press F5 and F6 respectively) and the File Browser on top in the Utility window, notice that there are a total of nine tabs visible: three in the Utility window, three in the Project pane, and three in the Timing pane (**Figure 2.15**). Reading from left to right, the key combination of the Command key and numbers 1 through 9 reveal each tab:

- Press Command-1 for the File Browser.
- Press Command-2 for the Library.
- Press Command-3 for the Inspector.
- Press Command-4 for Layers tab.
- Press Command-5 for the Media tab.
- Press Command-6 for the Audio tab.
- Press Command-7 for the Timeline.
- Press Command-8 for the Keyframe Editor.
- Press Command-9 for the Audio Editor.

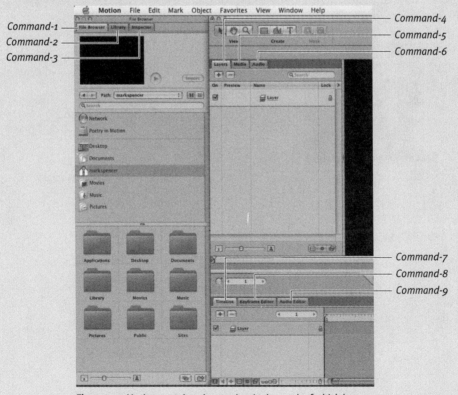

Figure 2.15 Motion contains nine top-level tabs, each of which has a keyboard shortcut.

Navigating the Interface with Keyboard Shortcuts

The Function keys (F1 through F6) have a similar flow, with the first four keys mapped to the four tabs in the Inspector and the last two opening and closing the panes in the Canvas (**Figure 2.16**):

◆ Press F1 for the Properties tab (in the Inspector tab).

◆ Press F2 for the Behaviors tab (in the Inspector tab).

◆ Press F3 for the Filters tab (in the Inspector tab).

◆ Press F4 for the Object tab (in the Inspector tab; the name on the tab changes depending on what type of element is selected).

◆ Press F5 to open and close the Project pane.

◆ Press F6 to open and close the Timing pane.

In addition, F7 and F8 provide special interface views. F7 reveals the context-sensitive Dashboard and F8 creates a full-screen preview (see "Working with the Canvas" in Chapter 3).

With a little practice you may find these keyboard shortcuts the quickest, easiest way to get where you want to go.

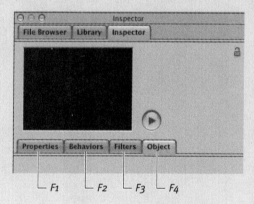

Figure 2.16 The Inspector contains four sub-tabs, all of which also have keyboard shortcuts.

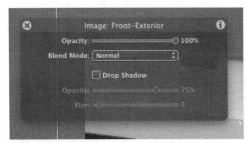

Figure 2.17 The Dashboard is a floating palette that contains a list of the key parameters of the currently selected object or effect.

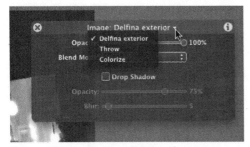

Figure 2.18 If an object has effects and/or masks applied, you can choose which control set appears from the drop-down list. Or, press D to cycle through them.

Introducing the Dashboard

The Dashboard is one more very important and useful part of the interface we haven't discussed yet (**Figure 2.17**). It's a semi-transparent floating palette that contains a list of the key parameters of the currently selected object or effect, which makes it very easy to adjust parameters on the fly.

But where is it?

To reveal the Dashboard:

Do one of the following:

◆ Click the Dashboard icon in the Toolbar.

◆ Press F7.

◆ Press D.

✔ Tip

■ If the selected object has effects applied, the key parameters for each effect can be displayed in the Dashboard by clicking on the small downward-facing triangle at the top of the dashboard and selecting from the drop-down list (**Figure 2.18**). Or, you can press D repeatedly to cycle through each set of controls—and pressing Shift-D cycles through them in reverse order.

INTRODUCING THE DASHBOARD

Changing Window Arrangements

By default, Motion opens with the Utility pane on the left and the Canvas on the right, and the Project pane and Timing pane are both hidden. However, a different arrangement may be more useful depending on the type of work you are doing and the type of display you are using. For example, if you have an Apple Cinema Display, you can take advantage of all that yummy screen real estate by rearranging the windows.

Motion includes several preset window arrangements, called layouts, that fit the bill nicely.

To change the window arrangement:

Do one of the following:

♦ Choose Window > Layouts, then choose a layout from the submenu (**Figure 2.19**).

♦ Use the appropriate keyboard shortcut: choose Control-U for the Standard Layout, Control-Shift-U for the Alternate Layout, and Control-Option-U for the Cinema Layout (if available). Here are descriptions of these layouts:

Standard Layout (Control-U) arranges the File Browser, Library, and Inspector all to the left of the Canvas, in one Utility window.

Alternate Layout (Control-Shift-U) breaks off the Inspector tab into a separate window and places it above the File Browser and Library.

Cinema Layout (Control-Option-U) is only available if you are connected to a Cinema display. It places the Inspector tab to the right of the Canvas.

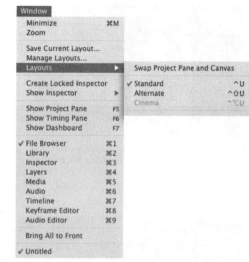

Figure 2.19 You can change the arrangement of windows by choosing a Layout from the submenu.

WORKING
WITH OBJECTS

3

To understand objects, think of them as incredibly varied, infinitely malleable building blocks. Whether digital photos, Apple QuickTime movies, scanned sketches, Adobe Illustrator vector art, layered Adobe Photoshop files, text, or simple shapes, objects are the source material for building your animated creation.

When working on a project, you or your client usually has a rough idea of what the final output should look like. This idea, whether it is a series of sketches (a *storyboard*), a formal written description (a *script*), or just a twinkle in someone's eye, serves as your guide as you select which objects are appropriate and how to manipulate them in space and time. *Compositing* is the process of choosing the properties of objects in space (how they look and where they are located). *Animation* is the process of making choices about how properties of objects change over *time*.

In this chapter, I explore how to browse and select objects using Motion's File Browser, how to import them into your project, and how to organize them in the Project pane and the Canvas.

Using the File Browser

The File Browser, which is the first tab in the Utility Window, is where you go to search through your media files, preview them, and select them for your project (**Figure 3.1**). It is divided into three separate functional areas: the Preview Area, the Sidebar, and the File Stack.

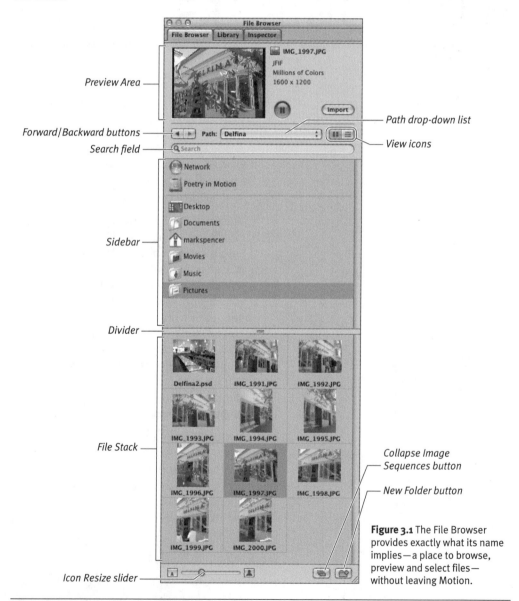

Figure 3.1 The File Browser provides exactly what its name implies—a place to browse, preview and select files—without leaving Motion.

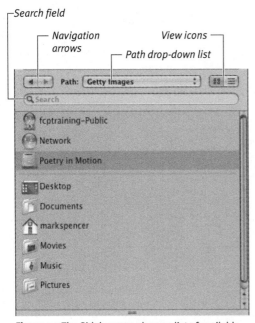

Search field

Navigation arrows

View icons

Path drop-down list

Figure 3.2 The Sidebar area shows a list of available drives, servers, and folders and provides navigation controls.

Supported Media Types

Motion supports QuickTime-compatible media types in the following categories:

- ◆ QuickTime movies
- ◆ Image sequences
- ◆ Still image files
- ◆ Layered Photoshop files
- ◆ PDF and PDF-compatible Illustrator files
- ◆ Audio files

Browsing media files

Motion is unique. It doesn't require you to first import all the files you want to use before you can start working with them. You have direct, immediate access to all media files on your computer (and any other connected drives or servers) through the File Browser.

The File Browser works much like the Finder in Mac OS X. You select drives and folders to drill down to the media files you want.

To browse for media files:

1. If it's not already the frontmost tab, click the File Browser tab in the Utility Window, or press Command-1.

   The Sidebar area contains a list of the drives, servers, and folders available on your computer and network (**Figure 3.2**). It also contains navigation controls. You use these to identify the full path of your selected media file, to step backward and forward through the path, to search for a specific file, and to change the view of the bottom section of the File Browser, the File Stack.

2. Click the appropriate drive, server, or folder. The contents appear in the File Stack.

3. In the File Stack area, double-click a folder to view its contents. Continue double-clicking to drill down into subfolders until you locate the media file you want.

✔ Tips

- ■ If you customize the Finder Sidebar by deleting or adding new folders, those changes aren't reflected in Motion's Sidebar.

- ■ Once you've selected a drive or folder in the Sidebar area, use the up and down arrows on your keyboard to select a different drive or folder.

To see the full path of the selected file or folder:

◆ Click the Path drop-down list in the Sidebar area.

To navigate in the current path:

◆ Click the arrow icons in the Sidebar area. Clicking the left arrow shows the next level up the path hierarchy; clicking the right arrow brings you back down.

To find specific file(s):

◆ Type the name or part of the name in the Search field.

All files that do not match the search criteria are no longer visible in the File Stack.

✔ Tips

■ Search works by showing just the current files in the File Stack that match the search term. In other words, it doesn't work like the Find command in the Finder, which collects all matches into a window; rather, it simply filters the current content of the File Stack.

■ Search doesn't filter out folders.

■ To clear the search, click the small "x" to the right of the search field. Doing this restores the File Stack area to the previous view.

■ Make sure you remember to clear your search! If you don't, it continues to filter out the contents in the File Stack as you select different drives and folders.

USING THE FILE BROWSER

Name	▲	Date	Size
029071.jpg		7/14/04	45 K
031045.jpg		7/14/04	128
112004.jpg		7/14/04	41 K
112081.jpg		7/14/04	77 K
112094.jpg		7/14/04	57 K
421033.jpg		7/14/04	132
421050.jpg		7/14/04	171
421060.jpg·		7/14/04	103
511030.jpg		7/14/04	89 K
511081.jpg		7/14/04	62 K
511090.jpg		7/14/04	154
893013f.mov		7/14/04	16.6
893020f.mov		7/14/04	21.1
893025f.mov		7/14/04	10.2
893026f.mov		7/14/04	21.9

Figure 3.3 In List view, you can sort files by any column.

To change the view in the File Stack area:

◆ Click the appropriate View icon.

The left button shows the files and folders in the File Stack in Icon view; the right button shows them in List view.

When the files are in Icon view, you can change their size by dragging the Resize slider at the bottom of the window.

When the files are in List view, information about the files is shown as a series of columns (**Figure 3.3**). You can sort your files by any of these columns, which can make it easier to locate a specific file.

✔ Tip

■ When browsing files in the File Stack area in List view, you can click the disclosure triangles to open a folder. Or, you can use the up and down arrows on your keyboard to navigate to a folder and then press the right arrow to open the folder. Pressing the left arrow closes it again. If you press the Return/Enter key, the contents of the selected folder open into the File Stack area.

To sort files in List view:

◆ Click the name at the top of the column by which you want to sort.

The head of the column darkens and the files are sorted by that column's data type (for example, name, date, size). Click again to sort in reverse order.

✔ Tip

■ You can change the amount of space available to display files in the File Stack area by dragging the divider located between the Sidebar and the File Stack areas.

USING THE FILE BROWSER

Organizing media files

As you browse through your files, you may find that you want to change how they are organized. For instance, you may want to collect photographs from several different locations in one folder. Normally you would switch to the Finder to do this, but Motion allows you to move files and even create new folders directly in the File Browser. Any changes you make are reflected in the Finder.

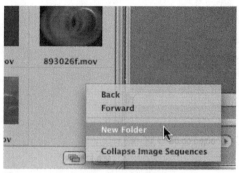

Figure 3.4 It's easy to create a new folder.

To move a file into a folder:

◆ In the File Stack, drag the file onto the desired folder.

✔ Tip

■ You cannot undo this action. If you change your mind, open the folder and drag the item back out.

To create a new folder:

Do one of the following:

◆ Click the New Folder icon at the bottom right corner of the File Browser.

◆ While in Icon view, control-click in the File Stack area and select New Folder (**Figure 3.4**).

Collapsing Animations

You may have an animation that was created in a graphics application and exported as a series of still images with sequential file names such as clouds001, clouds002, and so on. If you click the Collapse Image Sequences button at the bottom of the File Browser, any series of files with sequential filenames that are located together in a folder are represented as one icon instead of as individual icons for each file.

Collapsing the sequence of images allows you to select the entire animation by clicking just the single icon.

Note: Because digital cameras number file names sequentially, you may want to turn off the Collapse Image Sequences button when you are browsing for images from a digital camera.

Preview window ——— Import File button ——

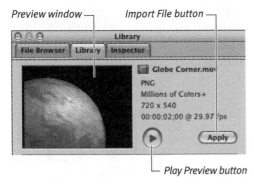

— Play Preview button

Figure 3.5 The Preview Area lets you see what your file looks like and provides details such as size, duration, and compression.

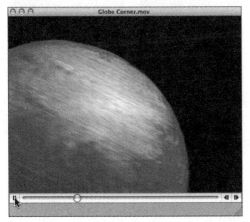

Figure 3.6 Double-clicking a file opens up the Viewer.

Previewing media files

The top section of the File Browser contains the Preview area where you can take a look at the content of your media files before you add them to your project.

To preview a file:

◆ Select the file in the File Stack area of the File Browser.

The file is displayed in the Preview Area (**Figure 3.5**). If your file is a graphic or photo, the image is displayed. If it is a movie or animation, the first frame is displayed.

To the right of the Preview Area is information about the file, such as its name, codec, bit-depth, size, duration, and frame rate, if applicable.

If the selected file is a movie, it automatically starts to play back in the Preview window. If the movie has audio, it plays as well. Press the pause button to stop playback.

✔ Tip

■ If you want to preview your media file at its full (native) size, just double-click it in the File Stack. It opens into its own Viewer window with playback controls along the bottom (**Figure 3.6**).

Importing media files

Importing files refers to the process of adding them to your project. You import files by using the Import button or by dragging them to the Canvas. When you add an object to the Canvas, it immediately appears in both the Project pane and the Timing pane.

In the Project pane, the object appears on the Layers tab contained in a new layer (**Figure 3.7**). It also appears in the Media tab, and if the object contains audio, it appears on the Audio tab.

Figure 3.7 Here's how an object appears in the Layers tab.

In the Timing pane, your object appears on the Timeline.

You can also drag files to the Layers tab and the Media tab in the Project pane, or to the Timeline in the Timing pane.

To import a media file:

1. Select a file in the File Browser.

2. *Do one of the following:*

   ▲ Click the Import button in the Preview Area of the File Browser.

   The file appears centered on the Canvas.

   ▲ Select the file in the File Stack area and drag it to the Canvas (**Figure 3.8**).

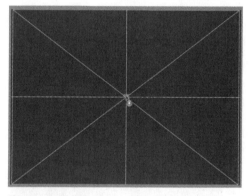

Figure 3.8 When dragging a file to the Canvas, alignment guides help you position it precisely.

As you drag the object toward the center of the Canvas, you'll see yellow horizontal and vertical lines, called *dynamic guides,* appear. If you want the object to be centered in the Canvas, drag until both lines appear, then let go. Otherwise, position the object where you want it.

✔ Tip

■ You can also import objects by using the File > Import menu, which takes you to the Finder. If you have created shortcuts in your Finder Sidebar that don't appear in Motion's Sidebar, this may be faster.

Line 'em Up!

A graphic designer's best friends, dynamic alignment guides do more than allow you to precisely center an object on the Canvas. The guides also make it easy to align objects relative to each other, thus creating precise layouts (**Figure 3.9**). As you drag an object, a guide turns on when you approach the center or the horizontal or vertical edge of another object, and the object you are dragging snaps to the guide as if it has a small magnetic field.

Sometimes, however, the guides become annoying—for instance, when you have several objects on the Canvas, and you don't want to align to them. In these cases, you can just turn the guides off by pressing Command-Shift–; or by going to View > Overlays > Dynamic Guides; or by using the View button at the top right of the Canvas window. Even better, you can tap the N key while dragging to turn off snapping and the object won't snap to any guides.

For additional alignment information, you can display rulers with tick marks along the horizontal and vertical axes of the Canvas (to turn them on, choose View > Show Rulers, press Shift-Command-R, or click the View button and select Rulers from the drop-down menu), and you can even turn on a Grid overlay (View > Overlays > Grid, Command-'; or again, the View button).

Figure 3.9 Alignment guides help you make precise layouts.

Using Network and Removable Drives

If you use media in your project that is located on a remote server or on a removable drive that you then disconnect, or you move files referenced by your project to another folder, then the next time you open your project, Motion won't be able to link to the files and your media will appear as a checkerboard pattern in the Canvas (**Figure 3.10**). Motion displays a dialog offering you the opportunity to locate the media; if the media is available, click the Search button to relink it to the project. If the media is not available, click Cancel. You can still work with the offline representation of the clip and reconnect later when the media is available by Control-clicking the object in the Media tab of the Project pane (**Figure 3.11**).

If you intend to use media from sources that may not always be connected to your Mac when you are working, it's best to first copy all the media you intend to use to a local drive before you import it into your project.

Figure 3.10 Offline media appears as a checkerboard pattern.

Figure 3.11 You can work with an offline representation of an element and then reconnect the media when it is available.

Adding Multiple Files to the Canvas

Rather than dragging objects to the Canvas one by lonely one, you can select multiple objects and bring them all in together.

To select multiple files:

1. Open the File Browser by clicking its tab or pressing Command-1.

2. *Do one of the following:*

   ▲ In List View, select one file, then hold down the Shift key and click another file to select it as well as all of the files in between.

   ▲ In the List view, click to the left of the file and drag up or down to select multiple contiguous files.

   ▲ In the List view, select one file, then hold down the Shift key and use the up or down arrows to select additional files.

   ▲ In the List or Icon view, select one file, then hold down the Command key and click each additional file.

✔ Tip

■ Once you have selected several files, you can deselect a file by clicking it again while holding down the Shift or Command key.

What Does Importing Really Mean?

Because Motion has a built-in File Browser, what's all this business about importing?

Objects in your File Browser don't actually become part of your project until you add them to the Canvas by dragging them in or by clicking the Import button. Once you do this, they appear in the Media tab of the Project pane. Even if you then decide to delete an object from the Canvas, it remains in the Media tab, because it has been imported. So if you delete an object from your Canvas and want it back, you don't need to go digging in the File Stack; just open the Media tab and grab it from there.

You can also use the Media tab to import files you know you will want in your project *before* adding them to the Canvas. Just drag the files directly to the Media tab. You can use this approach to browse for assets and then "park" your selects all in the Media tab. Once you have everything, drag from the Media tab to the Canvas to build the project.

To add multiple files to the Canvas simultaneously:

1. Select multiple files in one of the ways just mentioned.

2. *Do one of the following:*

   ▲ Drag any one of the selected files to the Canvas. The other files follow (**Figure 3.12**).

   ▲ Click any of the selected files and then click the Import button in the Preview Area of the File Browser. All selected files are added to the center of the Canvas.

✔ Tips

■ Instead of selecting multiple files first, you can choose File > Import and then select multiple files in the dialog box by holding down the Shift key to select contiguous files or the Command key to select noncontiguous files, just as you would in the Finder.

■ Just as with a single file, you can add multiple files to the Canvas by dragging them to the Layers tab in the Project pane or to the Timeline in the Timing pane.

■ The *stacking order* in which objects appear in the Canvas that were added at the same time depends on the order they were selected in the File Browser: the first selected object appears at the bottom of the stack, and subsequent layers appear on top. For more information on working with the stacking order of objects and layers, see "Working with Layers" later in this chapter.

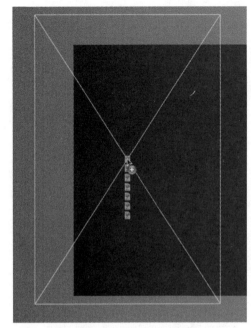

Figure 3.12 Dragging multiple files to the Canvas.

Importing Photoshop Files

If you import a multilayered Photoshop (.psd) file using the methods described earlier, Motion merges all the Photoshop layers together into one object. However, you can also choose to import the file with all the separate layers intact, or you can select just one specific layer to import.

To import Photoshop files:

1. Select the .psd file in the File Stack and drag it to the Canvas.

2. Pause while continuing to hold down the mouse button. A drop-down menu appears.

3. Drag the object down the drop-down menu and let go at the appropriate command:

   Import Merged Layers is the same as the default import behavior—all layers are merged into one object and placed in the currently selected Motion layer.

   Import All Layers creates an object for each Photoshop layer and places all the objects in a new Motion layer, which is nested inside the currently selected layer.

   Individual Layers imports just the Photoshop layer that you select from the list.

Working with the Canvas

As you add objects to your project, you may find that you'd like to zoom in closer, or perhaps just view the alpha channel of an object.

On the right side of the Toolbar are four pop-up menus that allow you to control how objects appear in the Canvas. You can zoom in and out on the Canvas, change the resolution to improve playback performance for complex projects, choose which color channels appear, and choose what types of overlays appear, such as grids, guidelines, and rulers.

To choose the zoom level:

◆ Select one of the options from the pop-up menu (**Figure 3.13**).

✔ Tips

■ The keyboard shortcut for Fit to Window is Shift-Z.

■ To zoom the Canvas to exactly 100 percent, press Option-Z.

■ You can also select the Zoom tool (press Z) and click in the Canvas to zoom in or Option-click to zoom out. Better yet, click and drag right or left to zoom in or out, respectively.

■ To reposition the Canvas in the window without zooming, select the Pan tool (press H) and drag the Canvas to where you want it. Rather than selecting the Hand tool, you can just press the space-bar and drag at any time.

To change the resolution:

◆ Choose a setting from the resolution pop-up menu.

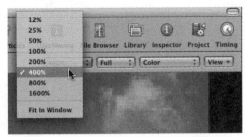

Figure 3.13 You can choose from a wide range of zoom levels.

Figure 3.14 Transparent removes the background color and displays a checkerboard pattern instead.

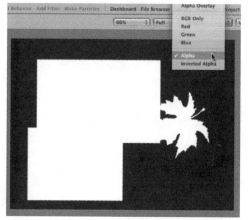

Figure 3.15 Alpha displays transparency information with white being fully opaque and black being fully transparent.

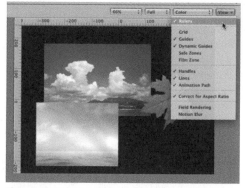

Figure 3.16 You can easily change the View options for the Canvas.

To change the channel view:

◆ Choose from the following options in the Channels pop-up menu:

Color is the default setting, and shows all objects in full color, with the background color as set in the Project Properties (see Appendix A).

Transparent removes the background color and shows a checkerboard pattern (**Figure 3.14**).

Alpha Overlay adds a red overlay to transparent areas of the Canvas to help identify areas of transparency.

RGB Only treats transparent areas as opaque.

Red, Green, or Blue displays the color information for the selected channel as grayscales values, with white indicating 100 percent of the color is present, black indicating 0 percent of the color is present, and shades of gray for varying levels of color.

Alpha displays transparency information only in grayscale values from white for fully opaque to black for fully transparent (**Figure 3.15**).

Inverted Alpha is the same as Alpha, but inverts the black and white values.

✔ Tip

■ Channel options are also available under the View menu (View > Channels), which shows the keyboard shortcuts.

To change the View options:

◆ Select the appropriate options from the View pop-up menu (**Figure 3.16**).

See "Canvas Viewing Options" in Chapter 4 for more information.

Working with Layers

Layers in Motion act as containers for objects. The first time you add an object to the Canvas, Motion creates a new layer and places the object in that layer. Each additional object gets added to the same layer, unless you first create a new layer and select it. If you add multiple objects at the same time, they are all added to the same layer.

The Layers tab in the Project pane is useful for working with the different objects and layers in your project.

The arrangement of which objects and layers appear on top in the Canvas and which appear behind, is called the *stacking order*. You can inspect and change the stacking order of both objects and layers in the Layers tab. In fact, you can even change the order of masks, filters, and behaviors applied to objects and layers.

You can import objects directly into a specific layer, change the stacking order of objects within a layer, and change the order of layers themselves by working in the Layers tab.

The Layers tab is also one place to go to select specific objects in order to adjust their properties (see Chapter 4).

Filters, behaviors, and masks that are applied to objects appear beneath their respective objects in the Project pane. However, you can also add them directly to a layer itself to affect all the objects contained in that layer. Furthermore, layers can be grouped, or *nested*, within other layers to create complex animations.

The Layers tab allows you to group objects and/or layers together; to solo certain objects or layers so that only they are visible; and to lock them so they can't be changed. You can also search the Layers tab to find just those objects or layers that you need.

About Objects and Layers

If you use other graphics applications such as Photoshop or Illustrator, the concept of layers is not new. However, layers in Motion work a little differently than what you may be used to.

In Motion, a layer acts as a *container* for objects and the masks, filters, and behaviors that are applied to those objects. You can have as many objects in the same layer as you wish.

The twist in Motion is that layers are actually objects themselves! This means that you can change their properties such as Position, Scale and Rotation. You can even apply masks, filters, and behaviors directly to a layer. Any changes made to a layer affect every object contained in the layer. Furthermore, you can place layers *inside* other layers using the Object > Group command (Shift-Command-G) or simply by dragging one layer onto another.

This capability of nesting objects within layers and layers within other layers is a very powerful way to control how your animation and effects impact groups of objects.

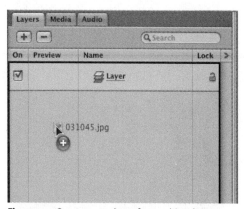

Figure 3.17 Create a new layer for an object by dragging it to the blank area.

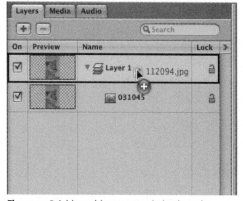

Figure 3.18 Add an object to an existing layer by dragging it onto the layer name.

To add objects to the Layers tab:

1. Open the Layers tab by pressing Command-4 (Pressing F5 opens the Project pane but does not change the front tab).

2. Select an object in the File Browser and drag it to the Layers tab.

3. *Do one of the following:*

   ▲ To create a new layer for the object, drag the object to the blank bottom area (**Figure 3.17**).

   ▲ To add the object to an existing layer, drag it onto the layer name (**Figure 3.18**).

   When you've finished, the object appears centered in the Canvas.

✔ Tip

■ Dragging an object directly to the Canvas or using the Import button in the Preview Area of the File Browser also adds the object to the Layers tab (and the Timing pane as well), but dragging directly into the Layers tab gives you more control over placement by allowing you to select which layer you place the object into and where you place it in relation to other objects in the layer.

Organizing objects and layers

The order of the objects and layers in the Layers tab determines which objects are in front in the Canvas and which are behind. Each time you add a new object to the Canvas by dragging or using the Import button, it is added in front of all previous objects and layers.

The first step in staying organized is to name your layers as you build your composition. Then, as you add objects, you may want to make changes to the stacking order of the objects in the Canvas. You may also want to change which objects are grouped together on the same layer because you know you want to apply the same transformation, behavior, effect, or animation keyframes to all of them at the same time.

To change the name of a layer:

◆ In the Layers tab, double-click the layer name to highlight it and type a new name.

✔ Tip

■ When you create new layers, Motion names them "Layer" followed by a number based on the number of layers you already have. When you double-click the layer name to rename it, the number is not highlighted and remains as part of the new name unless you highlight it manually.

To change the stacking order of objects within a layer:

1. Open the Layers tab of the Project pane and select the object.

2. Drag the object up or down.

   A position indicator shows the new position of the object before you release the mouse (**Figure 3.19**).

Figure 3.19 When you change the stacking order of an object by dragging it, a position indicator shows the new position.

Figure 3.20 Drag an object onto the target layer to add it on top.

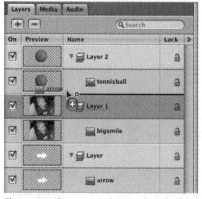

Figure 3.21 If you see a plus symbol, then you know the element you are dragging will be placed below the upper layer.

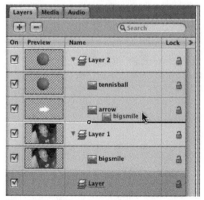

Figure 3.22 If there's no plus symbol, then the element will be placed inside the upper layer.

To move an object to a different layer:

1. Click an object name to select it.

2. Drag the object onto the target layer name (**Figure 3.20**) to add the object to the top of the layer.

   You can also drag the object between other objects on a new layer to place it between different objects.

To change the stacking order of layers:

1. Click the layer you want to move to select it.

2. Drag the layer up or down. An indicator shows the new location before you release the mouse.

   When you drag in the Layers tab, it can be difficult to tell whether you are dragging an item *inside* another layer or *beneath* it. The position indicator provides the clue, but it's subtle: when it's slightly further to the left and includes a plus symbol, the element you are dragging is placed below the upper layer (if it is an object, it is placed into a new layer); when it's slightly further to the right, it is placed inside the upper layer (**Figure 3.21** and **3.22**).

Using the Object menu

As an alternative to dragging objects and layers in the Layers tab, you can use the commands available in the Object menu. This method can be faster and easier when you want to move an object to the front or back of the layer stack.

To change the stacking order of objects and layers using the Object menu:

1. Select the objects(s) or layer(s).

2. Choose from among the following commands in the Object menu:

   Bring to Front moves the selected object to the front of all other objects on the same layer (**Figure 3.23**). If a layer is selected, this command brings the layer with all the objects contained in it to the front of all other layers.

   Send to Back moves the selected object behind all other objects on the same layer (**Figure 3.24**). If a layer is selected, this command moves the layer with all the objects contained in it to the back of all other layers.

   Bring Forward moves the selected object one level closer to the front of the Canvas by moving it up one row within the layer that contains it. If a layer is selected, Bring Forward moves the layer up above the layer immediately above it, taking all objects in the layer along. If the object is already on the top row of the layer that contains it, Bring Forward has no effect. Similarly, if the selected layer is at the top of all layers in the Layers tab, applying Bring Forward to the layer has no effect.

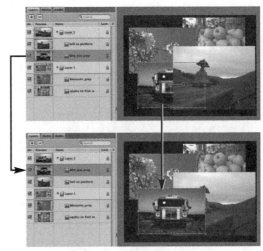

Figure 3.23 Bring to Front moves a selected object in front of all other objects on the same layer.

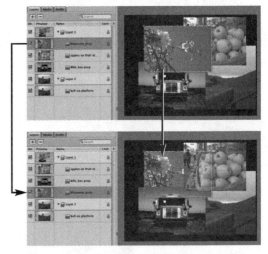

Figure 3.24 Send to Back moves a selected object behind all other objects on the same layer.

WORKING WITH LAYERS

Send Backward moves the selected object further away from the front of the Canvas by moving it down one row in the layer that contains it. If a layer is selected, Send Backward moves the entire layer, with all the objects contained in it, below the layer currently below it. If the selected object is already on the bottom row of a layer, then Send Backward has no effect. Similarly, if the selected layer is already at the bottom of all the layers in the Layers tab, Send Backward has no effect.

✔ Tips

■ You can use the Object menu to move multiple objects or layers at the same time, even if they are not contiguous. Select the objects or layers by Command-clicking them; then choose the appropriate command from the Object menu. Each object or layer moves relative to its current position.

■ Bring Forward and Send Backward do not move an object out of its current layer. In order to move an object to a new layer, drag it there.

WORKING WITH LAYERS

Grouping objects and layers

Grouping is the process of collecting objects and nesting them together into their own layer. You can also group layers into new layers. Because masks, filters, and effects applied to a layer affect all the objects and layers within that layer, grouping (aka nesting) is a very powerful way to control the animation and appearance of your project.

To group objects and layers:

1. Select the objects and/or layers you want grouped into their own layer by clicking one object and then Command-clicking on the other objects. You can select objects and layers at the same time.

2. *Do one of the following:*

   ▲ Control-click and choose Group from the drop-down menu.

   ▲ Choose Object > Group.

   ▲ Press Shift-Command-G.

Hiding and Revealing Objects

As you add more and more objects to your project, the Canvas and the Layers tab can start to get very full. You can choose which objects are visible in the Canvas, and you can collapse layers in the Layers tab when you need to focus your work on specific layers and objects.

To hide objects or layers in the Canvas:

1. Select the object(s) or layer(s) in the Layers tab.

2. *Do one of the following:*

▲ In the Layers tab, click the Active check mark in the On column next to the object you want to hide.

▲ Control-click the layer and choose Active from the drop-down menu.

▲ Choose Object > Active.

▲ Press Control-T.

✔ Tips

■ If some, but not all, of the objects in a layer are made inactive, a dash appears in the check box for the layer.

■ To reveal a hidden layer, simply repeat the action: click the check box, choose Object > Active, or press Control-T.

■ You can also turn off the visibility of any filters, effects, and masks applied to objects using the same procedure.

Soloing Objects

Sometimes you want to drastically reduce the clutter in the Canvas and focus on just one object. Motion gives you a shortcut for hiding all objects except the one(s) you specify.

To solo an object:

1. Select the object(s).

2. *Do one of the following:*

   ▲ Choose Object > Solo.

   ▲ Press Control-S.

   ▲ Option-click the check box in the On column of the Layers tab (**Figure 3.25**).

   To unsolo the selected object(s), repeat the same procedure.

✔ Tips

■ You can solo multiple objects. Either select them all first and choose Object > Solo (or Control-S) or Option-click on each Active check box.

■ When unsoloing an object, you have a choice in the Object > Unsolo menu to unsolo just the video, just the audio, or both.

Figure 3.25 Soloing an object lets you focus on just one element at a time.

Locking Objects

Locking an object protects against making any accidental changes once you are happy with the adjustments you've made, including making transformations (Chapter 4) and adding behaviors (Chapter 6), filters (Chapter 9), keyframes (Chapter 7), and masks (Chapter 12).

To lock an object:

1. Select the object(s).

2. *Do one of the following:*

   ▲ Select Object > Lock.

   ▲ Press Control-L.

   ▲ Click the lock icon at the far right of the layer in the Layer tab.

   To unlock the selected object(s), repeat the same procedure.

✔ Tip

■ If you lock a layer, all the objects and layers nested inside the layer become locked.

Searching Layers and Objects

When you have a large number of objects and layers in your composition, it can be difficult to find a specific object or layer. The Search field allows you to quickly zero in on what you are looking for. The Search field works like the same field in the File Browser.

To find a layer or object in the Layers tab:

◆ Type the name of the object or layer in the Search field.

As you type, Motion filters the Layers tab, only showing objects and/or layers that match; everything else is hidden (**Figure 3.26**).

✔ Tips

■ The layers that contain matching objects are still displayed.

■ Hidden objects are not disabled in the Canvas, meaning they are still visible.

■ If you don't clear the search field, the Layers tab continues to be filtered by the the search field contents. Clear it by clicking the "x" on the right side of the field.

Figure 3.26 The search field filters the Layers tab, showing only objects and layers that match its contents.

WORKING WITH LAYERS

Working with the Media Tab

The Media tab is another useful tool for organizing the media files in your project. At first glance, it seems similar to the Layers tab, but it works quite differently.

Every time you import a clip or drag it to the Canvas, Layers tab, or Timeline, it appears in the Media tab. The Media tab continues to show a listing of all media files that you have imported into your project, whether or not those files are currently in the Canvas. It provides a great deal of technical information about each of your media files. However, any effects, filters, or masks you have applied to your media files are not reflected in the Media tab; nor are any objects created directly in Motion, like generators or shapes. You can adjust some of the properties listed in the Media tab by using the Inspector.

Figure 3.27 shows some of the 14 columns of information available in the Media tab.

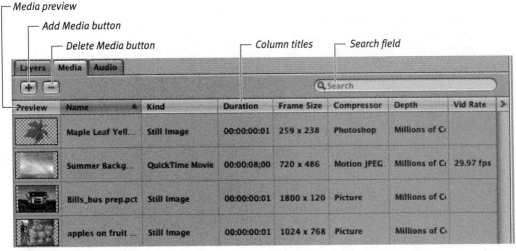

Figure 3.27 The Media tab is another place you can go to organize the media files in your project.

To reveal the Media tab:

Do one of the following:

◆ Choose Window > Media.

◆ Press Command-5.

◆ If the Project pane is already open (pressing F5 opens it), click the Media tab.

To add files to the Media tab:

1. Open the Media tab (Command-5).

2. *Do one of the following:*

   ▲ Click the plus sign (+) at the top left of the Media tab and navigate to the file.

   ▲ Select the media file from the File Browser and drag it to the lower blank section of the Media tab (**Figure 3.28**).

   Note that files added directly to the Media tab do *not* appear in the Canvas. And, if you remove media files that *are* in the Canvas, they remain available in the Media tab.

✔ Tip

■ You can use the process of adding files to the Media tab to build a collection of candidate files that you may want to use in your project. You won't clutter up the Canvas with files you may not want to use, and if you change your mind, you can grab them right away from the Media tab, rather than digging back through folders in the File Browser.

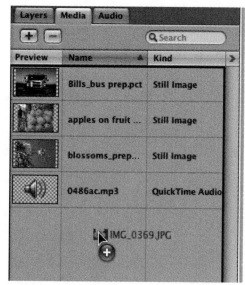

Figure 3.28 Add files directly to the Media tab by dragging them to the blank area.

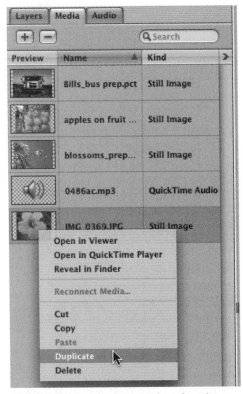

Figure 3.29 You can duplicate an object from the shortcut menu.

Figure 3.30 You can also duplicate an object by holding down the Option key and dragging the object.

Duplicating Objects

Often you may want to have multiple instances of the same object in your project, perhaps at different positions, using different sizes, and with different effects applied. In Motion, you can reimport the same object repeatedly from the File Browser, or you can duplicate a file that is already imported into your project. By duplicating there is still only one instance of the object in the Media tab and any changes made to its attributes in the Media tab of the Inspector apply to all copies of the object in the project. You can duplicate objects from the Layers tab, the Canvas, or the Timeline.

To duplicate an object:

1. Select the object.

2. *Do one of the following:*

   ▲ In the Media tab, select the object and drag it into the Canvas.

   ▲ In the Layers tab, Canvas, or Timeline, Control-click the object and select Duplicate from the shortcut menu (**Figure 3.29**).

   ▲ In the Canvas, hold down the Option key and drag the selected object (**Figure 3.30**).

3. Choose Edit > Duplicate.

4. Press Command-D.

✔ **Tips**

■ If your Project pane is closed and you are busy working in the Canvas, you can duplicate an object directly in the Canvas by Control-clicking it and choosing Duplicate from the shortcut menu. However, if you have many objects stacked on top of each other, it may be difficult to select the one you want—in that case, Control-clicking the object in the Layers tab in the Project pane is the way to go.

■ When you duplicate an object, the duplicate inherits all of the current parameter settings of the original, as well as all the applied behaviors, filters, and masks. So if you know you want to make five copies of an object that are all scaled, rotated, and blurred by the same amount, make all your transformations (Chapter 4) and add all your effects (Chapters 6, 7, 9, and 12) first, then duplicate. What a timesaver!

Duplicating vs. Reimporting: Cut Down on Your Trips to the File Browser

Did you ever eat at a restaurant with a salad bar, fill up your plate, sit down, and realize you wanted more of that yummy garlic bread? What if you could just duplicate the piece you had so you wouldn't have to make another trip?

Well, that's exactly what you can do with Motion, and although it may not do much for your diet, it does help keep your Media tab nice and trim.

Every time you import an object from the File Browser, Motion creates a new item in the Media tab for that object—even if you import the same object! To avoid this behavior, use the Duplicate command in the Layers tab, Canvas, or Timeline. This way, all copies of the object in your project are referred to by the same single item in the Media tab.

You can still change the parameters of each duplicate individually—like their Position, Scale, and Rotation—and apply filters and effects to them individually as well, but if you want to change the properties of the underlying media, like the frame rate or the alpha channel interpretation, you'll have just one "master" element in the Media tab to adjust. Sweet!

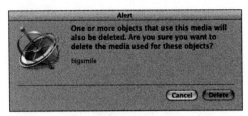

Figure 3.31 Deleting objects from the Media tab removes all instances of them from the Canvas.

Deleting Objects

When you want to remove objects from your project, you have two choices: you can remove a specific instance of the object by selecting it, or you can remove all instances that were created from the same imported object at once.

To delete one or more objects:

1. Select the object(s).

2. *Do one of the following:*
   ▲ Choose Edit > Delete.
   ▲ Control-click the object and select Delete from the drop-down menu.
   ▲ Press the Delete key.
   The selected objects are deleted, but they remain imported on the Media tab.

✔ Tip

■ Deleting a layer will delete all the objects it contains.

To delete all objects created from one source in the Media tab:

1. Select the object in the Media tab.

2. *Do one of the following:*
   ▲ Choose Edit > Delete.
   ▲ Control-click the object and select Delete from the drop-down menu.
   ▲ Press the Delete key.

3. Motion brings up a dialog warning you that all the objects using the selected media will be deleted (**Figure 3.31**). Click Delete.

Replacing Media

Creating motion graphics is a process of constant revision and refinement. And with indecisive clients, it means constant reinvention! Motion makes it easy to swap out one media file for another, without affecting any of the transformations, masks, keyframes, or effects that have been applied to it. So you can change your mind about the underlying media file even after you've transformed, filtered, and animated it. Very cool!

To replace a media object:

1. Open the Layers tab in the Project pane by pressing F5 or Command-4 (F5 just opens and closes the Project pane while Command-4 both opens the Project pane *and* brings the Layers tab to the front).

2. In the File Browser (Command-1), drag the new media file over to the Layers tab and drop it on the thumbnail of the object you wish to replace (**Figure 3.32**).

✔ Tips

- You can only replace media files with other media files; you can't replace Motion-created objects like generators, text, and shapes.

- Replacing is a great tool when you don't have the final artwork, but you want to get to work on your project. You can use a temporary file as a *proxy* in the project; apply all your transformations, filters, and animations; and replace the temporary file with the final media when it's ready.

- You can also replace media files in the Media tab. Doing so replaces every instance of the object that was created from that instance in the Media tab.

Figure 3.32 Replace a file by dragging the new file onto the thumbnail of the file to be replaced.

To replace media in the Media tab:

1. Open the Media tab in the Project pane and select the media object.

2. Open the Inspector and click the context-sensitive fourth tab, which is now called Media (the keyboard shortcut is F4).

3. Click the Replace Media File button.

4. Select a new file in the dialog box.

✔ Tip

■ If you have duplicated objects in the Canvas so that they refer to the same imported object in the Media tab, then replacing a media object in the Media tab is an incredibly efficient way to replace every instance of that object at once and retain all of the individual parameter changes and effects applied to each object.

REPLACING MEDIA

CHANGING
OBJECT PROPERTIES

The previous chapter discussed browsing media files, which are a type of *object,* and importing them into your project. Once you have imported objects, the next step is to *compose* them by adjusting certain properties common to all objects called *parameters.*

You set a parameter to a specific value at a specific point in time. For example, you may want to change the location of an object in the Canvas (the *Position* parameter), the size of an object (the *Scale* parameter), or the orientation of an object (the *Rotation* parameter). You can change the value of each parameter over time by setting *keyframes* (see Chapter 7), which is one way of creating animation.

In this chapter, you will learn how to adjust the properties of any object or layer (remember, a layer is an object, too!). These adjustments include a group of parameters called *transformations* (like Position, Scale, and Rotation); controls for how objects that overlap interact with each other, called *blend modes*; and settings for applying and adjusting a drop shadow. You can control most of these properties directly in the Canvas, but for more precise control, you use the Properties tab of the Inspector in the Utility pane.

Selecting Objects

To change the properties of an object, you first need to select it. As you might expect, there are several ways to do this.

To select an object:

Do one of the following:

◆ Click the object in the Canvas.

◆ Click the object in the Layers tab.

◆ Click the object in the Timeline (for more information on working with the Timeline, see Chapter 5).

Selecting an object in one of these areas selects it in all of them. When the object is selected, a *bounding box* appears around the object in the Canvas, the object row becomes highlighted in the Layers tab and in the Timeline, and the object bar in the Timeline darkens. (**Figure 4.1**).

✔ Tips

■ The object you want to select may be obscured behind another object in the Canvas, making it difficult or impossible to select by clicking it. In this case, it's easier to select the object using the Layers tab.

■ While you're in the Layers tab, you can temporarily hide the object(s) in front of the object you want to work on by clicking the Active check box under the On column for each object you want to hide, or you can Option-click the selected object's Active check box to "solo" the object and make all other objects inactive and therefore hidden. Option-clicking the same check box again makes the rest of the objects visible again (active). Note that you can still manipulate inactive objects by changing their Position, Scale, Rotation, and other properties.

Bounding box

Highlight indicates object is selected.

Figure 4.1 When you select an object in the Canvas, a bounding box appears around it. Selecting an object in the Canvas, Layers tab, or Timeline selects it in all three places.

Don't Forget to Play!

Remember that you can do pretty much anything you want in Motion *while the project is playing*—this unique capability opens up your creativity because you can see your project unfold in real time as you build it. However, if the object you want to select and manipulate is moving because you have previously animated it, it could be a little difficult to grab! In those cases, pause playback to make your adjustments.

Figure 4.2 If you select multiple objects, then bounding boxes will appear for each one.

To select multiple objects:

Do one of the following:

◆ In the Canvas, click one object to select it; then, hold down the Shift key and click additional objects.

◆ In the Canvas, click in an empty area and drag a bounding box around the objects you want to select.

◆ In the Layers tab, select one object by clicking it, then either Shift-click another object to select all objects in between, or Command-click additional objects one at a time.

When you select multiple objects using any of these methods, bounding boxes appear in the Canvas around every selected object (**Figure 4.2**).

✔ Tips

■ Drawing a bounding box in the Canvas is a good way to quickly select multiple objects that are all in the same area.

■ To select two groups of objects, draw a bounding box around one group, then hold down the Shift key and draw a bounding box around the second group.

■ To select all objects in the Canvas (including all layers that contain objects), choose Edit > Select All or press Command-A. To deselect all, choose Edit > Deselect All, press Shift-Command-A, or just click in a blank area of the Canvas.

■ To remove an object from a selection, Shift-click it in the Canvas or Command-click it in the Layers tab.

■ You can also select objects by using the Timeline tab in the Timing pane. The Timeline is discussed in Chapter 5.

SELECTING OBJECTS

Selecting Layers

Because layers are also objects, they have the same set of properties as objects, such as Position, Rotation, and Scale. Changing the parameters of a layer affects all the objects contained in the layer, but not necessarily in the same manner as selecting all the objects directly (see "Transforming Layers," later in this chapter).

To select a layer:

◆ In the Layers tab, click the layer row.

When you select a layer, a single bounding box appears in the Canvas around the edges of the entire layer (**Figure 4.3**).

To select multiple layers:

◆ In the Layers tab, click one layer row, then Command-click additional layer rows.

✔ Tip

■ If you select a layer row and then Shift-click another layer, you select all the objects in between the layers as well.

Figure 4.3 When you select a layer, a bounding box appears around the edges of the entire layer.

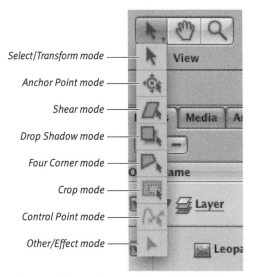

Select/Transform mode

Anchor Point mode

Shear mode

Drop Shadow mode

Four Corner mode

Crop mode

Control Point mode

Other/Effect mode

Figure 4.4 The transform modes are all available in the toolbar at the top of the Canvas.

Figure 4.5 The bounding box gives you visual clues as to which transform mode is currently active. Here, the Anchor Point mode is selected.

Transforming Objects in the Canvas

Transforming objects refers to the process of making changes to the values of specific parameters. The parameters of every object that can be transformed are Position, Rotation, Scale, Shear, Anchor Point, Four Corner, and Crop. These parameters can be changed in two different locations in Motion: in the Properties tab of the Inspector (located in the Utility pane) or directly in the Canvas. Because the Canvas is more direct and intuitive, let's discuss transformations there first.

As we have seen earlier, when you select an object to transform, the bounding box that appears around the object in the Canvas has several *control points*. You use the control points in combination with a *transform mode* to change the objects' parameters. The different transform modes are available in the Toolbar at the top left of the Canvas (**Figure 4.4**). The appearance of the bounding box changes depending on the current transform mode (**Figure 4.5**).

By default, the Select/Transform mode is active; this mode allows you to change the position, scale, and rotation of an object.

To choose a transform mode:

Do one of the following:

◆ Click and hold the Select/Transform icon in the Toolbar and choose a transform mode from the drop-down list.

◆ Press the Tab key to cycle through the different transform modes. The icon in the Toolbar updates to reflect the currently active mode.

◆ Control-click any object in the Canvas and choose a transform mode from the shortcut menu.

Changing the Position of an Object

One way to adjust the composition of your objects is to change where each is located in the frame. When you work in the Canvas, it's easy to quickly reposition objects. *Dynamic alignment guides* help by snapping an object into alignment with the center of the Canvas or with the edges of other objects. And the Object commands give you control over aligning multiple objects simultaneously.

To change the position of an object in the Canvas:

1. Select an object.

2. *Do one of the following:*

▲ Click anywhere inside the bounding box of the object and drag to the desired location.

▲ Hold down the Command key and press the arrow keys on your keyboard to move the object up, down, left, or right one pixel at a time.

Figure 4.6 If you select an object that is located outside the visible frame of the Canvas, its bounding box will still show up.

Figure 4.7 Dynamic guides can help you precisely position objects in relation to each other.

✔ Tips

- You can reposition an object with any transform mode active except for Drop Shadow.

- Hold down the Shift key after you click an object and then drag to constrain the movement to the vertical or horizontal axis.

- Press Command-Shift and whatever arrow key you choose to move the object 10 pixels in the specified direction.

- You can move an object completely out of the visible area (the *frame*) of the Canvas. When you do, the object is no longer visible, but you can still see its bounding box when you select it (**Figure 4.6**).

  Positioning objects outside the frame can be useful when you want them to fly in or fly out of the frame. To make more of the area outside the frame visible, use the Zoom Level menu at the top right of the Canvas (for more information on the various viewing options for the Canvas, see Appendix B).

- Use the dynamic alignment guides to more precisely position objects in relation to each other (**Figure 4.7**). These guides allow you to align the top, bottom, sides, or center points of objects. You can change their behavior in Motion's Preferences dialog (see Appendix B). To change position with precise numerical entries, use the Properties tab (see "Making Transformations in the Properties Tab" later in this chapter).

Using object alignment commands

Several commands in the Object > Alignment submenu control the layout of multiple objects. These commands let you quickly create a precise layout for many objects, which would take quite a bit of time to do manually.

To use the object alignment commands:

1. Select all the objects to align.

2. Go to the Object menu and choose the appropriate command:

   Align Left Edges moves all the objects so that the left edges of their bounding boxes are on the same vertical line as the left-most object.

   Align Right Edges moves all the objects so that the right edges of their bounding boxes are on the same vertical line as the right-most object.

   Align Top Edges moves all the objects so that the tops of their bounding boxes are on the same horizontal line as the highest object.

   Align Bottom Edges moves all the objects so that the bottoms of their bounding boxes are on the same horizontal line as the lowest object.

   Align Horizontal Centers moves every object only horizontally so that their center points are along the vertical center of the Canvas (**Figure 4.8**).

   Align Vertical Centers moves every object only vertically so that their center points are along the horizontal center of the Canvas (**Figure 4.9**).

Figure 4.8 Align Horizontal Centers moves every object only horizontally so that their center points are along the vertical center of the Canvas.

Figure 4.9 Align Vertical Centers moves every object only vertically so that their center points are along the horizontal center of the Canvas.

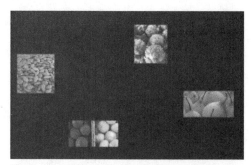

Figure 4.10 Distribute Vertical Centers moves objects vertically so that they are spread evenly, based on center points, between the highest and lowest objects.

Distribute Lefts moves the objects only horizontally so that they are spread evenly, based on left edges, between the furthest left and furthest right objects, which remain stationary.

Distribute Rights moves the objects only horizontally so that they are spread evenly, based on right edges, between the furthest left and furthest right objects, which remain stationary.

Distribute Tops moves the objects only vertically so that they are spread evenly, based on top edges, between the highest and lowest objects, which remain stationary.

Distribute Bottoms moves the objects only vertically so that they are spread evenly, based on bottom edges, between the highest and lowest objects, which remain stationary.

Distribute Horizontal Centers moves the objects only horizontally so that they are spread evenly, based on center points, between the furthest left and furthest right objects, which remain stationary.

Distribute Vertical Centers moves the objects only vertically so that they are spread evenly, based on center points, between the highest and lowest objects, which remain stationary (**Figure 4.10**).

Canvas View options

Motion includes a host of onscreen tools
to assist you as you composite your objects.
Dynamic guides allow you to drag objects
with precise alignment to the Canvas center
or to other objects. A grid and rulers give you
additional control over alignment of objects.
In addition, you can create, lock, and hide
your own guides and use safe areas to help
make sure your viewers see all your hard work.

You can find these options and more on the
View pop-up menu at the far right side of
the Status bar in the Canvas.

Figure 4.11 The View
menu gives you a
variety of handy tools
for compositing your
images.

To change the Canvas View options:

Do one of the following:

◆ Click the View pop-up menu in the
Status bar area of the Canvas.

◆ Select the appropriate option under the
View menu in the menu bar (**Figure 4.11**).

Safe!

If your project is destined for television, you'll
want to turn on the Safe Zones (located in
the View pop-up menu) to check your work.
That's because TVs don't display the full available image, or *raster,* that you see in the Canvas.

When you turn on Safe Zones, two concentric
rectangles appear on the Canvas (**Figure
4.12**). The outer rectangle is called the
Action Safe area—make sure any critical
action stays within this box. The inner
rectangle is the *Title Safe* area. To ensure
legibility and to avoid crowding the edge,
keep all text elements within this box.

Figure 4.12 Safe Zones let you double check how your
project will look on a television. Critical action should
stay within the outer rectangle, whereas text should
stay within the inner rectangle.

You can also choose the Film Zone option
from the View menu. If you are creating a
project that will be viewed in two different aspect ratios, such as 4:3 for standard definition
TV and 16:9 for high definition TV, these guides will help you find the best compromise for
your composition. The specific aspect ratio for the Film Zone is adjustable in Motion's
Preferences dialog (Motion > Preferences, or Command-,).

Figure 4.13 Grids give you even more control over the alignment of objects.

To create an alignment grid:

Do one of the following:

◆ Select Grid from the Canvas View pop-up menu (**Figure 4.13**).

◆ Choose View > Overlays > Grid.

◆ Press Command-' (apostrophe).
 Repeat the same command to turn the grid back off. You can adjust the grid spacing and color in the Canvas preferences—select Motion > Preferences or Command-, (comma).

✔ Tip

■ Objects snap to the grid as you drag them across the Canvas. If you want to turn off this snapping behavior to place an object close to, but not on, a grid line, disable snapping by pressing the N key. You can even press N while you are dragging an object to toggle snapping on and off (just like Final Cut Pro).

To show rulers:

Do one of the following:

◆ Select Rulers from the View pop-up menu.

◆ Choose View > Show Rulers.

◆ Press Shift-Command-R.

To add a guide:

Do one of the following:

◆ Turn on Rulers, then click a ruler area and drag into the Canvas.

◆ Choose View > Guides > Add Vertical Guide or Add Horizontal Guide.

To lock guides:

Do one of the following:

◆ Choose View > Guides > Lock Guides.

◆ Press Option-Command-; (semicolon).

✔ Tip

■ Unlike other commands, pressing Option-Command-; again does not unlock guides once they are locked. You need to select View > Guides > Unlock Guides.

To hide guides:

Do one of the following:

◆ Select Guides in the View pop-up menu in the Canvas.

◆ Press Command-; (semicolon).
  Pressing Command-; again toggles guide visibility back on.

To delete guides:

Do one of the following:

◆ Drag the guide off the Canvas area.
  It disappears in a puff of smoke.

◆ Choose View > Guides > Clear Guides.

Showing Overlays

Guides, Dynamic Guides, the Grid and Safe Zones are all *overlays*. They can be turned on and off individually as described above or by using the View > Overlays flyout menu. Or, you can turn all currently active overlays off and on with one command.

To show or hide all overlays:

Do one of the following:

◆ Choose View > Show Overlays.

◆ Press Command-/.

Figure 4.14 To rotate an object in the Canvas, simply drag the rotation handle of the bounding box.

Rotating Objects

Every object has an *anchor point*, which is usually located by default at the center of the object, as determined by its bounding box (text objects, covered in Chapter 13, have their anchor point located at the bottom left corner of the first letter). The Rotation parameter lets you rotate an object around this anchor point. The bounding box has a special handle just for rotation, which is attached to the anchor point. You can rotate freely or in 45-degree increments for precise values, and you can complete as many revolutions as you wish. Motion stores the number of revolutions along with the angle value in the Properties tab for animation purposes (see Chapter 7).

To rotate an object in the Canvas:

1. If you need to, choose the default Select/Transform mode.

   The keyboard shortcut is Shift-S.

2. Click and drag the rotation handle of the bounding box (**Figure 4.14**).

   Hold down the Shift key while dragging to constrain the movement to 45-degree increments.

✔ Tip

■ If you want to create a static composition, you usually wouldn't rotate an object more than 180 degrees in either direction. If your purpose in rotating is solely to wind up the object for an animation, it may be easier to use the Properties tab to enter a value. See Chapter 7.

ROTATING OBJECTS

Scaling Objects

When you import an object into Motion, it's displayed at its native dimensions based on the number of horizontal and vertical pixels it contains. You can use the Scale parameter to increase or decrease the overall size of the object, or to stretch or squeeze the object by changing its *aspect ratio* (the relationship between the object's height and width). You can also choose *how* the object scales—around a corner point, a side, or its anchor point.

Figure 4.15 To resize an object in the Canvas just drag one of the corner handles of the bounding box.

To change the size of an object in the Canvas:

1. If necessary, choose the default Select/Transform mode.

   The keyboard shortcut is Shift-S.

2. *Do one of the following:*

   ▲ Click and drag one of the corner handles of the bounding box (**Figure 4.15**).

   The horizontal and vertical changes aren't locked to each other, so you can change the aspect ratio of the object as you drag. If you want to lock the aspect ratio so that it doesn't change, hold down the Shift key as you drag.

   ▲ Click and drag one of the side handles of the bounding box.

   Dragging a side handle resizes the object in just one dimension— horizontally or vertically—depending on which handle you grab.

Figure 4.16 Scaling below 0 percent flips the object.

✔ Tips

■ By default objects scale with the handle opposite to the one you drag "pinned" to the Canvas, meaning that it scales around that opposing handle. To have your object scale around its anchor point rather than by the opposing handle, press Option while you drag. To have it scale proportionally and around its anchor point, hold Shift-Option as you drag.

■ Try to avoid scaling objects over 100 percent because the image can degrade, or *pixelate*. Use the Info box that appears when you drag as a guide. If the object isn't large enough for your needs, see if you can re-create it or export it at a larger size (see the sidebar "Pixels and Resolution").

■ Scaling below 0 percent flips the image so that it becomes a mirror image of itself (**Figure 4.16**).

■ Vector-based objects such as ones created in Adobe Illustrator can be scaled over 100 percent with no loss in quality, but only if you first uncheck the Fixed Resolution check box in the Media tab of the Inspector. Select the object and press Shift-F to reveal the tab.

Pixels and Resolution

If you have a print background (or even if you print digital photos at home), you may be thinking about *resolution* when you're importing graphics. For example, how many pixels per inch (ppi) or dots per inch (dpi) should you use?

Well, in video, there is no such thing as ppi or dpi, which simplifies things a bit. For instance, DV-NTSC video is 720 pixels wide by 480 pixels tall—no more, no less. So if you import a photograph that is less than 720 pixels wide or 480 pixels tall, it won't fill up the screen unless you scale it over 100 percent, which, as I mentioned earlier, can create an unacceptable quality loss. And if you want to scale up a photo so you can zoom in on it or pan across it, you need even more pixels to start with.

Using Shear

Shearing refers to slanting an object either horizontally or vertically. You accomplish this by using the Shear tool and dragging the control handles.

To shear an object in the Canvas:

1. Choose the Shear mode by selecting it from the pop-up menu in the Toolbar, by pressing the Tab key until it appears, or by Control-clicking the object in the Canvas and selecting Shear from the drop-down menu.

2. Click and drag one of the object's control handles (**Figure 4.17**).

   Use the top and bottom handles to shear horizontally and the side handles to shear vertically.

Figure 4.17 Shear, or slant, objects by dragging a control handle.

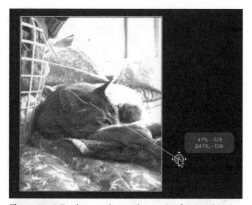

Figure 4.18 To change the anchor point for an object, simply drag it to a new location.

Changing the Anchor Point

Every object has an anchor point, which is located at the center of the object by default (the center as defined by the rectangular bounding box that surrounds the object).

At first, it may not seem very interesting—you drag the anchor point to a new location, and nothing seems to happen. But the anchor point is a powerful animation tool. If you think of the object as a two-dimensional picture and the Canvas as a corkboard, the anchor point is the pushpin that holds the picture to the corkboard. If you rotate the object, it rotates around the anchor point. If you change the size of the object, it scales around the anchor point.

You can make changes to the anchor point using another mode in the Toolbar called the *Anchor Point* mode.

To change an object's anchor point:

1. Choose the Anchor Point mode by selecting it from the pop-up menu in the Toolbar, pressing the Tab key until it appears, or Control-clicking in an empty area of the Canvas to bring up a shortcut menu.

2. Click directly on the anchor point (the circle in the center of the object) and drag it to a new location (**Figure 4.18**).

   As you drag, a line appears connecting the previous and new locations. Additionally, an Info box appears, showing you the old and new coordinates as well as the change, or *delta*, between the two.

✔ Tips

- You can drag an object's anchor point completely outside of its bounding box. If you place the anchor point on the center of a second object that is stationary, the first object appears to rotate around the second object when animated (**Figure 4.19**).

- When you drag the anchor point, it snaps to the center or bounding box edges of objects.

- By placing the anchor point at the bottom edge of an object and increasing the object's vertical Scale parameter, you can make the object grow up out of its base rather than expanding from the center. Remember to hold down the Option key to scale around the anchor point.

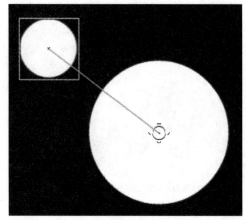

Figure 4.19 You can move an object's anchor point to the center of another object in order to make it rotate around the second object.

Switching Transform Modes

When you are deep into compositing objects in the Canvas, adjusting their positions, rotating, scaling, cropping, and perhaps shearing them, you may not want to make a lot of trips up to the Toolbar to change transform modes.

I find the best way to stay focused on the Canvas is to Control-click the object to select the appropriate mode, make the transformation, and then immediately press Shift-S to get back to the default Select/Transform tool.

Pressing the Tab key rotates you through the different tools, but I prefer Control-clicking. Or even better, get a two-button mouse and right click!

Figure 4.20 Four Corner, or corner-pinning lets you move each corner of an object's bounding box independently of the others.

Working with the Four Corner Parameter

Corner pinning is similar to shearing, but it is more flexible, because you can move each corner of an object's bounding box independently, stretching and squeezing it as if it were a rubber sheet.

With corner pinning, you can create a sense of perspective with your object, as if it were located in a 3D space. You can also attach an object to another by pinning their corners together.

Motion calls this mode Four Corner, and once again, you access it by choosing a transform mode from the Toolbar.

To corner pin an object in the Canvas:

1. Select the Four Corner mode by selecting it from the pop-up menu in the Toolbar, pressing the Tab key until it appears, or Control-clicking in an empty area of the Canvas to bring up the shortcut menu.

2. Click the control handles at the corners of the objects' bounding box and drag them each to the desired locations (**Figure 4.20**).

✔ Tip

■ If you've corner pinned an object and you want to return it to its original dimensions but it's too late to use Undo (File > Undo or Command-Z), the quickest way is to either turn off or reset the parameter in the Properties tab of the Inspector. In fact, you can use this procedure to reset any parameter. See "Making Transformations in the Properties Tab" later in this chapter.

WORKING WITH THE FOUR CORNER PARAMETER

Cropping an Object

Cropping allows you to cut off the top, bottom, left, or right edges of an object. You can use cropping to improve the composition of a photo, isolate a particular element in an object, or remove unwanted artifacts from the edges of scaled-down video.

To crop an object:

1. Select the Crop mode by selecting it from the pop-up menu in the Toolbar, pressing the Tab key until it appears, or Control-clicking the object in the Canvas to bring up the shortcut menu.

2. Drag the appropriate bounding box control handle:

   ▲ The handles in the middle of each side move just that side (**Figure 4.21**).

   ▲ The corner handles move both adjacent sides (**Figure 4.22**).

✔ Tips

■ To keep the aspect ratio of the cropped edges fixed, hold down the Shift key while dragging a corner handle.

■ Once you have corner pinned an object, you can no longer crop it in the Canvas. You can, however, change the Crop parameters in the Properties tab of the Inspector (see "Making Transformations in the Properties Tab" later in this chapter).

Figure 4.21 To crop one side, move the middle handle of the side you want to crop. Here it is the right side.

Figure 4.22 Drag a corner handle to move both sides at once.

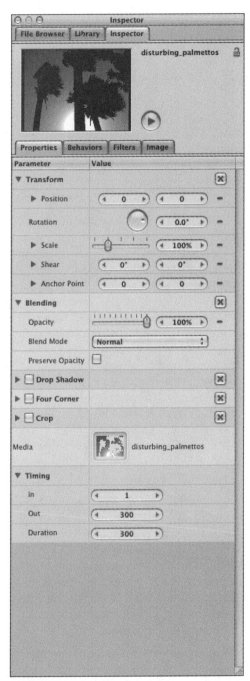

Figure 4.23 The Properties tab gives you precise control over parameter values.

Making Transformations in the Properties Tab

Although using the Canvas is often the fastest, most intuitive and interactive way to make transformations to your objects, Motion offers a separate interface that you can use when you need precise control over parameter values.

This interface is located in the Properties tab, which is the first of the four tabs you can access in the Inspector tab of the Utility pane (**Figure 4.23**). Any change you make to a parameter in the Canvas is stored in the Properties tab, and changes you make directly in the Properties tab are immediately reflected in the Canvas.

The Properties tab also makes it easy to quickly reset parameters to their default values and toggle the visibility of certain parameters on and off. And this tab provides access to a couple of additional parameters that you can't adjust in the Canvas.

To adjust an object's parameters in the Properties tab:

1. Select the object by clicking it in the Canvas, the Layers tab, or the Timeline.

2. Reveal the Properties tab in the Inspector tab of the Utility pane by doing one of the following:

   ▲ Click the Inspector tab, then click the Properties tab if it isn't already the foremost tab.

   ▲ Press F1.

3. Adjust the appropriate parameter.

✔ Tips

■ Each group of parameters has a disclosure triangle next to it that allows you to hide or reveal that set of parameters. Some individual parameter have disclosure triangles, such as Scale, so that you can set keyframes for the x and y coordinates independently. See Chapter 7 for more on working with keyframes.

■ Drop Shadow, Four Corner, and Crop each have a check box next to the category name. When checked, changes to the parameters in that category are reflected in the Canvas; when unchecked, any changes are hidden.

To reset a parameter in the Properties tab:

1. Select the object.

2. In the Properties tab, click the "x" for the appropriate parameter(s).

   Clicking the "x" in the Transform category resets all the transform parameters at once (Position, Rotation, Scale, Shear, and Anchor Point). To change an individual transform parameter, type in the default values.

Canvas vs. Properties Tab

Because there are two ways to change parameter values, which one should you use? Why, both of course! Any changes you make in one are immediately reflected in the other, so there's no functional difference between them, but when it comes to workflow, they are suited to different tasks.

For fast, rough compositing, work directly in the Canvas. You can quickly and easily position, scale, and rotate objects without even changing the tool mode. Dynamic guides can be lifesavers here, but once you get a lot of objects on the Canvas, you may want to turn them off. And don't forget the object alignment commands under the Object menu to create precise alignment and distribution among multiple objects. To shear, corner pin, or change the location of the anchor point , you'll need to change the tool mode. And remember, it's faster to Control-click in the Canvas or press the Tab key to switch modes than it is to use the Mode pop-up menu in the Toolbar.

Once you have roughed in your layout, you can jump to the Properties tab to clean things up by making precise value entries. Also, you may find it easier to manipulate the parameters of some objects in the Properties tab, such as graphics files that fill Canvas so that you can't access the bounding box without changing the Canvas view.

In addition to entering specific parameter values, use the Properties tab to instantly reset parameter values and to toggle the visibility of certain parameters like Drop Shadow, Four Corner, and Crop.

Working with Parameter Controls

Each parameter in the Properties tab has a set of controls you can use to enter and adjust values. The transform parameters (Position, Rotation, Scale, Shear and Anchor Point) all have at least one *value field*. Other parameters have *dials*, like Rotation, and *sliders*, like Scale.

Although making changes with dials and sliders is straightforward (spin the dial and drag the slider), you can manipulate value fields in several different ways.

To change the value in a value field:

Do one of the following:

◆ Click in the field to highlight the current value and type a new value.

◆ Click and drag left or right in the field to scrub a new value.

Dragging to the right increases the value; dragging to the left decreases the value.

◆ Click the arrows to the left or right to change the value in one-unit increments.

✔ Tips

■ To make large value changes, hold down the Shift key while dragging in the value field or clicking the arrows. Values change ten times faster than by simply dragging.

■ To make very small changes, hold down the option key while dragging or clicking. Values change at one-hundredth the rate of simply dragging.

To adjust the Position parameter in the Properties tab:

◆ Enter a new value using any of the methods just described.

✔ Tips

■ Position values are measured in *pixels*. Motion is capable of *sub-pixel positioning*, meaning you can enter up to two decimal places of precision.

■ Position is a *two-dimensional* parameter. This means that the first value field changes the horizontal, or *x* value of an object's center point, whereas the second field controls the vertical, or *y* value.

■ Motion sets the center of the Canvas to (0,0). Moving to the left creates negative *x* values and moving down creates negative *y* values (**Figure 4.24**).

■ Dragging in the value field is a great way to quickly make large changes in parameter values. Because the changes are updated immediately in the Canvas, you can interactively drag as you watch the object move. This method is great if you want to move an object all the way off the screen in a horizontal or vertical direction without needing to see the area outside the Canvas.

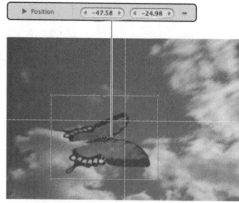

Figure 4.24 Moving an object left and down from center creates negative values.

Figure 4.25 To adjust the Rotation parameter, simply twist the dial and watch as the object moves to reflect the new settings.

To adjust the Rotation parameter in the Properties tab:

Do one of the following:

◆ Enter a new value in the value field.

◆ Click and drag the dial (**Figure 4.25**).

✔ Tips

■ Rotation values are measure in *degrees*, with 360 degrees for each full revolution.

■ It seems counterintuitive, but positive values rotate counterclockwise and negative values rotate clockwise.

■ You can rotate an object multiple times by using values greater than 360 (or –360) degrees. This can be useful when keyframing an object to rotate for several cycles. See Chapter 7 for more information.

To adjust the Scale parameter in the Properties tab:

◆ Enter a value in the value field or drag the slider.

✔ Tips

■ Scale values are measured in *percentage* of the original value.

■ Avoid scaling objects over 100 percent because image quality can start to degrade (see "Pixels and Resolution" earlier in this chapter).

■ Scaling below 0 percent results in negative values and causes the image to flip, creating a mirror image of itself.

■ To scale an object without constraining its aspect ratio, click the disclosure triangle to reveal individual value fields for horizontal and vertical scaling. A dot appears on the combined slider to indicate that the x and y values have been adjusted independently.

WORKING WITH PARAMETER CONTROLS

To adjust the Shear parameter in the Properties tab:

◆ Enter a new value in the value field.

✔ Tips

■ Shear values are measured in *degrees*, based on the difference between the new bounding box corner angle and the original 90-degree value.

To adjust the Anchor Point parameter in the Properties tab:

◆ Enter a value in the value field.

✔ Tip

■ Anchor point values are measured in *pixels*, based on the difference between them and the original value of (0,0).

Anchor Point and Position

You might have noticed that when you change the location of the anchor point in the Canvas, only the anchor point moves, but when you use the Properties tab of the Inspector to do the same thing, the object moves in the opposite direction! What's going on here?

Think of it this way: position is determined by the relationship of the anchor point location to the center of the *layer* on which the object lies. Yet the location of the anchor point is determined by its relationship to the center of the *object*, not the layer.

So when you change the anchor point without changing position, the object moves in the opposite direction so that *the relationship of the anchor point to the layer does not change.* I know; it's difficult to visualize.

When you move the anchor point directly in the Canvas, Motion is actually dynamically adjusting the position values at the same time to compensate for your adjustment. Try it with the Properties tab visible and see for yourself.

Disclosure triangle

Visibility check box

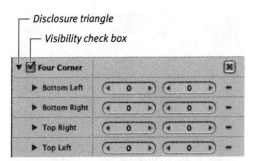

Figure 4.26 Reveal the Four Corner properties by clicking the disclosure triangle.

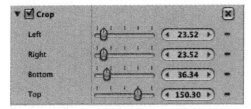

Figure 4.27 Crop properties can be revealed by clicking the disclosure triangle.

To adjust the Four Corner parameter in the Properties tab:

1. Click the disclosure triangle to reveal the Four Corner parameters (**Figure 4.26**).

2. Click the check box to the left of Four Corner to make your changes visible in the Canvas.

3. Make changes in the value fields for the x,y coordinates for each corner of the bounding box.

✔ Tips

- It's usually much easier to set the Four Corner parameters by dragging the bounding box in the Canvas (after switching to the Four Corner mode).

- The visibility check box is very useful for quickly turning off your changes. The values remain stored with the parameter, so you can turn them back on anytime by clicking the check box again.

To adjust the Crop parameter in the Properties tab:

1. Click the disclosure triangle to reveal the Crop properties (**Figure 4.27**).

2. Click the check box to the left of Crop to make your changes visible in the Canvas.

3. Make changes in the four value fields for the number of pixels you want cropped from each side of the selected object.

✔ Tip

- If you scale down video so that the edges are visible in the Canvas, it's a good idea to crop one or two pixels from each edge to eliminate any artifacts.

WORKING WITH PARAMETER CONTROLS

Transforming Multiple Objects

Because every object has the same set of transformation parameters, such as Position, Rotation, Scale, and Shear (except shapes and masks, discussed in Chapter 12), it's easy to apply the same changes to multiple objects simultaneously. First, select all the objects you want to affect, then adjust the appropriate parameter values either in the Canvas or in the Properties tab. Transformations are made around the anchor point of each object as if you transformed them individually.

Figure 4.28 You can perform the same transformation on multiple objects at once.

To transform multiple objects:

1. Select the objects (see "Selecting Objects" earlier in this chapter).

2. Perform the transformation on the desired parameter in either the Canvas or the Properties tab (**Figure 4.28**).

Figure 4.29 You can perform a transformation on all objects in a layer. Note that there is a single anchor point for the entire layer—all objects transform around it.

Transforming Layers

The layers that you access in the Layers tab of the Project pane or in the Timeline are containers for objects. But they are also object themselves. This fact means that you can select a layer and change its Position, Rotation, Scale, and other parameters just like you can with any other object. The transformations are applied to all objects contained in the layer. The difference is that *when you select a layer, there is only one bounding box and one anchor point*, so all objects transform around that anchor point (**Figure 4.29**).

To apply transformations to a layer:

1. Select the layer (see "Selecting Layers" earlier in this chapter).

2. *Do one of the following:*

   ▲ Use the Toolbar and the bounding box to make transformations in the Canvas.

   ▲ Enter values for the desired parameters in the Properties tab in the Inspector.

✔ Tip

■ If you want all the objects in a layer to scale, rotate, or shear around their own anchor points rather than the anchor point of the layer, then select all the objects directly and transform them, rather than selecting the layer.

Blending Objects

Normally when objects overlap each other in the Canvas, the top object completely obscures the object(s) below it (**Figure 4.30**). *Blending* objects is the process of changing how the pixels of objects that are stacked on top of each other interact. By changing the *opacity* or the *blend mode* of an object, you can dramatically alter the look of your composition (**Figure 4.31**).

Figure 4.30 When objects overlap in the Canvas, the top object obscures those beneath it. Here the text obscures the cloth, and the cloth obscures the clouds.

Figure 4.31 If you apply a blend mode, overlapping objects can take on a completely new look.

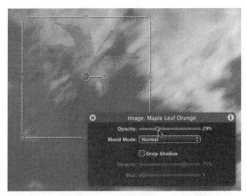

Figure 4.32 To change an objects' opacity in the Dashboard, just drag the Opacity slider.

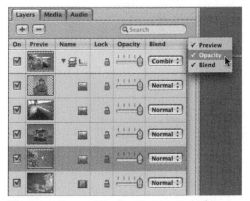

Figure 4.33 To reveal the Opacity property in the Layers tab, click the small arrow in the top right.

Blending with opacity

Opacity refers to how opaque or transparent the pixels in an object are: 100-percent opacity is fully opaque (visible) and 0-percent opacity is fully transparent (invisible). Values between 0 percent and 100 percent are partially visible. You can adjust opacity on the Properties tab or in the Dashboard.

To change an objects' opacity:

1. Select the object(s).

2. *Do one of the following:*

   ▲ In the Properties tab (press F1 to reveal it), drag the Opacity slider or enter a value in the value field.

   ▲ In the Dashboard (press D to reveal it), drag the Opacity slider (**Figure 4.32**).

   ▲ In the Layers tab of the Project pane (press F5 to reveal it), first reveal the Opacity sliders by clicking the small arrow in the top right (**Figure 4.33**), select Opacity, and then drag the slider in the object row.

✔ Tips

■ Because layers are also objects, you can adjust the opacity of a layer. All objects in the layer inherit the new opacity setting. Note that the opacity level for individual objects remains at 100 percent.

■ Decreasing opacity can improve the effect of a blend mode (discussed momentarily) by decreasing the intensity of the result.

BLENDING OBJECTS

Using blend modes

Although lowering the opacity of an object allows objects below it to show through, *blend modes* perform different mathematical operations that impact how pixels on a selected object interact with pixels on objects below it. How the pixels interact depends on the color and brightness of each pixel. Results can be surprising, so it's useful to experiment. You can apply blend modes to objects, layers, or both at the same time. With Motion's real-time capabilities, you can immediately view the impact of blend modes on video and animations without rendering.

To apply a blend mode to an object:

1. Select an object that has at least one object beneath it.

2. *Do one of the following:*

   ▲ In the Properties tab (press F1 to reveal it), choose a blend mode from the pop-up menu.

   ▲ In the Dashboard (press D or F7 to reveal it), choose a blend mode from the pop-up menu.

   ▲ Go to Object > Blend Mode and choose an option from the submenu.

   ▲ In the Layers tab of the Project pane (press Command-4 to reveal it), use the Blend Mode pop-up menu located on the object row (**Figure 4.34**).

   If the menu isn't available, make it visible by selecting Blend from the pop-up list at the top right of the Layers tab (**Figure 4.35**).

   ▲ Control-click the object in the Canvas and select a blend mode from the drop-down list.

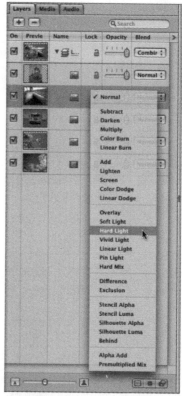

Figure 4.34 The Blend Mode pop-up menu in the Layers tab displays a variety of options.

Figure 4.35 Choose Blend from the pop-up list at the top of the Layers tab to reveal the blend property.

✔ Tips

- Applying a blend mode to an object affects all the overlapping layers below it but not any of the layers above.

- Blend modes have no impact on the background color of the Canvas defined in Edit > Project Properties.

- Depending on the blend mode, the stacking order of the objects may or may not change the result.

- If you apply blend modes to multiple overlapping objects, Motion first determines the result of blending the bottommost two objects. It then combines that result with the blend mode of the next-higher object and keeps progressing up the object stack until it reaches the top.

- By default, the layer on which an object is located does not impact the results of the blend mode. Two objects could be on the same layer or different layers—as long as one object is below the other, applying a blend mode directly to objects yields the same result either way. This behavior changes if the Layer blend mode is changed from the default Combine (see "Blend modes and layers," on the next page).

- Using the Opacity parameter in conjunction with blend modes gives you great creative flexibility in controlling the intensity of the blend.

Blend modes and layers

Because layers are also objects, you can apply blend modes directly to them. One additional blend mode is available for layers—the default mode called *Combine*.

When a layer has the Combine blend mode applied, every object in the layer that has a blend mode applied is combined with objects in all lower layers (**Figure 4.36**).

If the layer blend mode is set to Normal, objects in the layer blend with each other as you apply blend modes, but they do not blend with any lower layers.

To apply a blend mode to a layer:

1. Select the layer.

2. *Do one of the following:*

   ▲ Use the Blend drop-down menu in the Layers tab.

   ▲ Control-click the layer in the Canvas and select the blend mode from the Blend Mode submenu. Note that if the layer isn't already selected, you need to first select it by clicking the layer row in the Layer tab.

   ▲ Select a blend mode from the Properties tab of the Inspector.

   ▲ Choose Object > Blend Mode and select a blend mode.

   ▲ In the Dashboard, select a blend mode from the drop-down list.

Figure 4.36 Combine allows blend modes to pass through to lower layers. Notice how the clouds in the lower layer blend through the rectangle in the upper layer.

What's an Alpha Channel and Can I Get It on Cable?

Certain graphics formats, like pict, tiff, and psd, as well as video formats like Animation or Motion JPEG, have the capability of storing four *channels* of information about the contents of the image. Each channel is a grayscale representation of the image.

The first three channels are the RGB (red, green, blue) channels that store information on how much of each primary color is contained in each pixel of the image. The fourth channel stores information on the level of *opacity*, or transparency, of each pixel. For instance, a graphic file of some text with a drop shadow on an empty background would have an alpha channel with the text pixels all white (100-percent opaque), the drop shadow pixels mostly white but fading to gray and then black at the very edges, and the rest of the pixels all black (100-percent transparent) (**Figure 4.37**).

Figure 4.37 An alpha channel stores information on the opacity of each pixel. Here the text, drop shadow, and background pixels all have different levels of opacity.

Certain blend modes use the alpha channel of one object to determine the areas of transparency of another object. For example, you can use the transparency of a text object on a video object to place the video inside the text (**Figure 4.38**). See Chapter 12 for more information.

Figure 4.38 This video in text effect takes advantage of an alpha channel to determine the areas that should be transparent.

Alpha channel blend modes

A subset of the blend modes uses the *alpha channel* information of an object to determine how objects blend together.

Preserving opacity

The Preserve Opacity check box in the middle of the Properties tab tells a selected object to only be visible in areas determined by the object(s) beneath it (**Figure 4.39**). It essentially uses the lower object(s) as a *mask* on the selected objects. For more on masks, see Chapter 12.

To enable Preserve Opacity:

1. Select an object or objects.

2. In the Properties tab, click the Preserve Opacity check box.

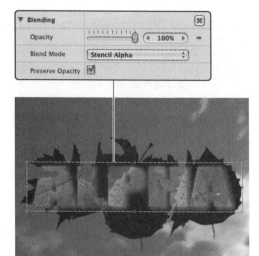

Figure 4.39 Preserve Opacity turned on for the text layer makes the leaves below the text act as a mask.

Figure 4.40 The ever-popular drop shadow helps text stand out from background images.

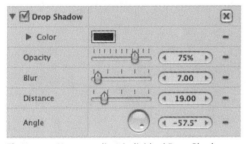

Figure 4.41 You can adjust individual Drop Shadow parameters in the Properties tab.

Applying a Drop Shadow

Ah, the ubiquitous and always fashionable drop shadow, which is great for making text or other graphics elements stand out from the background (**Figure 4.40**). In Motion, you can control the color, distance, blur, opacity, and angle of a drop shadow applied to an object in the Properties tab. You can control a subset of these parameters with the Dashboard or directly in the Canvas.

To apply a drop shadow to an object:

1. Select the object.

2. *Do one of the following:*

   ▲ On the Properties tab, click the enable check box, then click the disclosure triangle to reveal the Drop Shadow properties. Adjust each parameter you desire (**Figure 4.41**).

   ▲ In the Dashboard, click the enable check box. Then adjust the opacity and blur directly in the Dashboard.

   ▲ In the Canvas, either select the Adjust Drop Shadow mode from the Toolbar or Control-click the object and select Drop Shadow from the drop-down list. You can then adjust the distance and angle of the drop shadow by clicking it and dragging or adjust the blur by clicking and dragging the control handles.

Using Timing

The last property on the Properties tab is called Timing (**Figure 4.42**). It allows you to set a starting point, ending point, and/or a duration for the selected object. You can also perform these operations in the mini-Timeline and in the Timing pane. For more information on working with timing of objects, see Chapter 5.

Figure 4.42 Timing properties let you set start points, end points, and durations for a selected object.

COMPOSITING AND EDITING IN THE TIMELINE

This chapter introduces a powerful tool for working with objects in your composition over time—the aptly named Timeline. First, I cover how to change the appearance of the Timeline, how to navigate in time, and how to add objects to the Timeline (as opposed to adding them to the Layers tab in the Project pane or to the Canvas). Then, I explore how to manage objects once they are in the Timeline, how to perform editing operations, and how to work with Motion's very slick and convenient mini-Timeline. By building familiarity and comfort with the Timeline, you can work with greater speed and ease. Like driving a car, once you know how to shift, you can focus on the road.

Introducing the Timeline

The Timeline (**Figure 5.1**) provides a view of how objects and effects are arranged over the duration of your composition. On the left side is the Layer list, which is almost identical to the Layers tab. Here, you can view and change the order of your layers; view what behaviors, masks, and filters are applied; group layers; and do almost anything you can do in the Layers tab. See Chapter 3 for more information on the Layers tab.

The right side of the Timeline contains the Track area. This area is where you can precisely determine the timing of every object in the composition, synchronize objects and effects, and even perform editing operations that you would normally perform in non-linear editor like Final Cut Pro HD.

The Timeline is the first tab in the Timing pane, and can be opened in several ways.

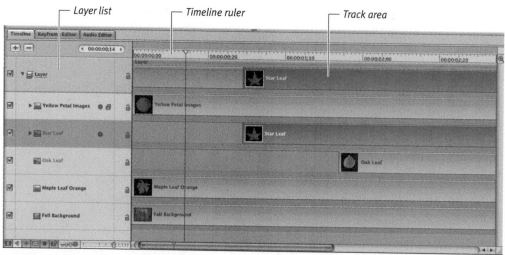

Figure 5.1 An essential tool in Motion, the Timeline provides a view of how objects and effects are arranged over time.

Layers Tab or Layers List?

Given that the Layers tab in the Project pane (which you can open by pressing F5) is almost identical to the Layers list in the Timeline tab of the Timing pane (which you can open by pressing F6), which should you use as you build and tweak your project?

The Layers tab (F5) is most useful when you want to quickly identify what objects and effects are in your project, when you want to solo, duplicate, delete, reorder, or replace objects, or when you want to add effects such as filters, behaviors, and masks to objects.

Use the Layers list in the Timeline if you are already using the Track area to work on the timing of individual objects and effects—basically, it saves you the step (and the screen real estate) of opening up the Layers tab.

So if you are already working in the Timeline, use it to perform all those layer-related tasks; otherwise keep the Timeline closed and use the Layers tab.

To reveal the Timeline:

Do one of the following:

- ◆ Click the Timing icon in the Toolbar.

- ◆ Press F6.

- ◆ Drag up on the drag handle located directly below the Play button, located at the bottom center of the Canvas.

- ◆ Press Command-7.

✔ Tips

- ■ Note that the first three methods just open the Timing pane—if you made a different tab in the Timing pane active previously, such as the Keyframe Editor, then that tab is in front and you need to click the Timeline tab to bring it forward. By pressing Command-7, you are both opening the Timing pane and bringing the Timeline tab to the front.

- ■ Pressing F6 or Command-7 again closes the Timing pane.

INTRODUCING THE TIMELINE

Identifying Objects in the Timeline

You can identify what type of object you are working with (such as a video clip, filter, behavior, mask, or layer) in either the Layer list on the left of the Timeline or in the Track area on the right. The Layer list is almost identical to the Layers tab; the only exception is that you cannot display previews, opacity, or blend modes (although you can Control-click to set the blend mode). Objects in the Track area are identified by both the icon in the track and the color of the bar.

Layer Objects are identified with a thin blue bar. The layer name and the name of the object also appear on a thicker bar just below the thin bar. If there are multiple objects in a layer, in the thicker bar you'll see three short vertical lines and a number representing the number of objects the layer contains at each point in time, rather than the names of individual objects (**Figure 5.2**).

Image Objects, such as graphics, video, text, and shapes, are also identified with a blue bar on each object row.

Masks are identified with a gray bar. Masks are discussed in Chapter 12.

Behaviors and Filters are identified with a thin purple bar and they show up under the object to which they have been applied (**Figure 5.3**). Behaviors are discussed in Chapter 6 and filters are covered in Chapter 9.

Keyframes are identified with diamonds on a thin gray bar under the object that has been keyframed (**Figure 5.4**). Keyframing is discussed in Chapter 7.

Audio is identified with a green bar that contains a representation of the audio waveform. Working with audio is discussed in Chapter 14.

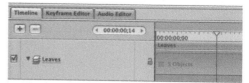

Figure 5.2 Layers can contain multiple objects. Here, the Leaves layer contains five objects.

Figure 5.3 Behaviors and filters, such as Colorize and Throw here, are identified with thin purple bars and appear under the object to which they have been applied.

Figure 5.4 Keyframes are easily identified by diamonds placed on a thin gray bar under the object that has been keyframed.

Figure 5.5 The name of the selected object appears in the Layer object.

Selecting Objects in the Timeline

You can select objects in the Layers tab, the Canvas, or the Timeline. Selecting in one area selects the objects in all areas.

To select an object in the Timeline:

◆ Open the Timeline and click the object in either the Layer list or the Track area.

Selected objects turn a darker shade of the same color. Note that both the object and the layer in which it is contained turn a darker color in the Timeline (as opposed to what happens in the Layers tab), and the name of the selected object appears in the Track area for that layer (**Figure 5.5**). This feature makes it possible to edit individual objects directly on the Layer track without even opening the layer to reveal the individual objects and effects.

Changing the Timeline's Appearance

The Timeline is very flexible. It allows you to choose which objects to view, to zoom in and out, and to adjust the height of tracks and how they are displayed. By making these adjustments, you can streamline the Timeline and focus your attention on specific areas.

View options

At the lower left of the Timeline are a series of buttons that determine which types of objects are displayed or hidden (**Figure 5.6**). To show or hide the object, click the appropriate button to toggle its state between Show and Hide. Hiding filters, behaviors, masks, and keyframes that you aren't working with condenses the Track area so that you can see more tracks without scrolling.

Note that these controls only hide the objects in the Timeline—showing or hiding them in the Timeline does not affect their visibility in the Canvas, which is controlled instead by the Active check box as described in Chapter 3).

To show/hide all layers:

◆ Click the Show/Hide Layers button.

Note that this button only works if you have audio in your project and it is visible in the Timeline.

To show/hide audio:

◆ Click the Show/Hide Audio button.

A new pane in the Timing pane appears with a drag bar, which allows you to adjust how many audio tracks versus layers are visible.

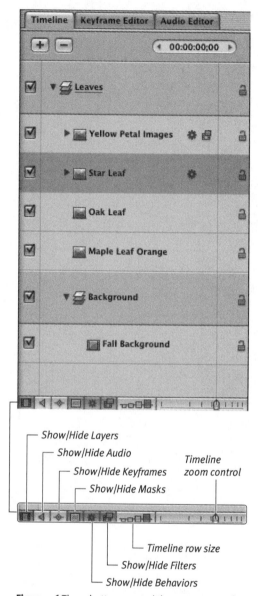

Show/Hide Layers
Show/Hide Audio
Show/Hide Keyframes
Show/Hide Masks
Timeline zoom control
Timeline row size
Show/Hide Filters
Show/Hide Behaviors

Figure 5.6 These buttons control the appearance of different items in the Timeline.

To show/hide keyframes:

◆ Click the Show/Hide Keyframes button.
   The keyframes appear as gray diamonds
   and turn white when selected.

To show/hide masks:

◆ Click the Show/Hide Masks button.

To show/hide behaviors:

◆ Click the Show/Hide Behaviors button.

To show/hide filters:

◆ Click the Show/Hide Filters button.

Zooming

When working in the Timeline, you'll find
it useful to be able to zoom in on an area,
perhaps just a few frames, to make fine
adjustments. Or you may want to zoom out
to get the big picture of how objects are
related to the full length of your composition.
Motion provides two tools for zooming: the
Zoom slider and the Zoom/Scroll control.
Both are available at the lower left of the
Timeline. There are also several shortcut
methods for quickly resizing the window to
the length of the play range or the full project.
See "Defining the Play Range" later in this
chapter for information on how to set a
play range.

To zoom in or out of the Timeline:

Do one of the following:

◆ Click and drag the Zoom slider; move
   left to zoom in and right to zoom out.
   While you are moving the slider, the
   playhead remains centered in the Timeline.

◆ Click and drag either end of the
   Zoom/Scroll control.
   Dragging toward the center zooms in;
   dragging toward the edges zooms out.

CHANGING THE TIMELINE'S APPEARANCE

To zoom the Timeline to fit the play range:

Do one of the following:

◆ Choose View > Zoom Time View > To Play Range.

◆ Control-click on the ruler and select Zoom to Play Range from the drop-down menu.

◆ Double-click on the Zoom to Fit button to the far right of the ruler.

To zoom the Timeline to fit the project:

Do one of the following:

◆ Choose View > Zoom Time View > To Project.

◆ Control-click on the ruler and select Zoom to Project from the drop-down menu.

◆ Click the Zoom to Fit button to the far right of the ruler.

✔ Tip

■ As you zoom in with the Zoom/Scroll control, it shrinks around its own center and not the playhead location. This means you may zoom in on a location that doesn't appear in the Canvas. Or, you can click the Zoom/Scroll bar and drag it to the playhead location to change the area that is displayed without changing the zoom amount (**Figure 5.7**).

Figure 5.7 Change the area that is displayed, but not the zoom amount, by dragging the Zoom/Scroll bar.

Track height

You can adjust tracks to four different heights. The taller tracks allow you to see icons for each object in the Track area, which makes the object easier to identify. If you use smaller tracks, on the other hand, you can fit more of them into the viewable area—this is quite handy when you are trying to adjust the timing of tracks in relationship to each other.

The track height of behaviors, filters, and keyframes is not adjustable.

To adjust the track height:

Do one of the following:

◆ Click the appropriate bar in the Resize Track Height button.

◆ Move the cursor into place between two tracks in the Layer list. When it changes into an adjustment pointer, drag up to make tracks smaller or down to make them larger.

✔ Tip

■ You can use this dragging method to adjust the height of audio tracks independently of layers.

Track display

You have several choices for how tracks appear in the Timeline: with just the name of the object, with the name and a thumbnail, or as a filmstrip. If the tracks appear as a filmstrip, a series of icons display. In the case of a video clip, you can use these icons to quickly identify specific frames of video.

To change the track display:

1. Choose Motion > Preferences (or press Command-, (comma).

2. Click the Appearance icon.

3. In the Timeline section, click the Timebar Display pop-up and choose from the list (**Figure 5.8**).

4. Click the Preferences window close box.

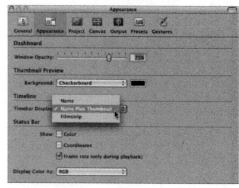

Figure 5.8 You can change how tracks appear in Motion's Preferences.

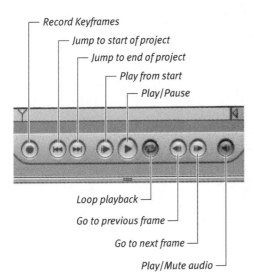

Record Keyframes
Jump to start of project
Jump to end of project
Play from start
Play/Pause

Loop playback
Go to previous frame
Go to next frame
Play/Mute audio

Figure 5.9 The Transport controls let you move around your project in different ways.

Navigating the Timeline

As you work on your composition, you need to be able to quickly move to different parts of the Timeline. Maybe you want to work on a specific frame, or a specific time location. Or maybe you want to get to the first frame of a certain object or effect. Wherever you want to go, Motion offers you several ways to get there: you can use the Transport controls, the Ruler area, and keyboard shortcuts. You can also set the specific area you are working on as a play range, add markers to identify key points in time or on objects, and set the overall project duration.

Transport controls

Just above the Timeline, at the bottom of the Canvas, you'll find the Transport controls (**Figure 5.9**). These allow you to play or pause your project, to move frame by frame, or to jump to the beginning or end of your project.

To play your project:

Do one of the following:

◆ Click the Play icon in the Transport controls.

◆ Press the space bar.

◆ Choose Mark > Play.

✔ Tip

■ If you want your project to play continuously, you can turn on Loop Playback by selecting Mark > Loop Playback or by pressing Shift-L.

To pause your project:

Do one of the following:

◆ Press the spacebar.

◆ Click the Pause icon in the Transport controls (the Play icon turns into a Pause icon while the project is playing).

To move one frame at a time:

Do one of the following:

◆ Click the Go To Previous Frame or Go To Next Frame icon in the Transport controls.

◆ Press the left or right arrow keys on the keyboard.

◆ Choose Mark > Go to > Previous Frame or Mark > Go to > Next Frame.

✔ Tip

■ To move forward or backward 10 frames, hold down the Shift key when pressing the left or right arrow keys.

To move to the beginning of the project:

Do one of the following:

◆ Click the Go to start of project icon in the Transport controls.

◆ Choose Mark > Go to > Project Start.

◆ Press Home on the keyboard.

To move to the end of the project:

Do one of the following:

◆ Click the Go to end of project icon in the Transport controls.

◆ Choose Mark > Go to > Project End.

◆ Press End on the keyboard.

NAVIGATING THE TIMELINE

Current Frame field *Ruler* *Zoom to Play Range button*

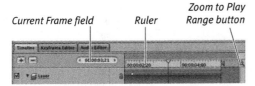

Figure 5.10 The Ruler area lets you set and adjust your play range and more.

Figure 5.11 You can toggle the Current Frame field so that it displays either timecode or frames by clicking the Current Time icon.

The Ruler area

At the top of the Timeline is the Ruler area (**Figure 5.10**). This area includes the ruler, the Current Frame field, and the Zoom to Play Range button. You can set and adjust your play range and scrub quickly through your Timeline in the ruler.

To move to a specific timecode or frame location:

1. Toggle the Current Frame field to display either timecode or frames by clicking the Current Time icon (**Figure 5.11**).

2. *Do one of the following:*

   ▲ Click in the Current Frame field, enter the frame or timecode location you want, and press Enter or Return.

   ▲ Click and drag in the Current Frame field to scrub to a new frame or timecode location.

   ▲ Click the top of the playhead in the ruler and drag it to the new location.

   ▲ Click in the ruler directly on the new location.

To scrub through the project:

◆ Click the playhead in the ruler and drag forward or backward.

NAVIGATING THE TIMELINE

Jumping to objects

Often you will want to navigate to the first or last frame of an object to view it in the Canvas and to make adjustments to its starting or ending location.

To move to the beginning of an object:

1. Select the object.

2. *Do one of the following:*

    ▲ Choose Mark > Go to > Selection In Point.

    ▲ Press Shift-I.

To move to the end of an object:

1. Select the object.

2. *Do one of the following:*

    ▲ Choose Mark > Go to > Selection Out Point.

    ▲ Press Shift-O.

Defining the play range

The *play range* identifies the portion of your composition that you see when you press the Play button. By default, the play range is set to the length of your project.

However, you can change the play range to start and end wherever you'd like to focus your attention. You change the play range by setting new in and out points in the Ruler area, which determine the beginning and end of the play range. You can also easily jump the playhead to these in and out points.

To set the play range:

1. Move the playhead to the beginning of the new play range.

2. *Do one of the following:*

   ▲ Select Mark > Mark Play Range In.

   ▲ Press Command-Option-I.

3. Move the playhead to the end of the new play range.

4. *Do one of the following:*

   ▲ Select Mark > Mark Play Range Out.

   ▲ Press Command-Option-O.

Now when you press the Play button in the Transport controls (or press the space bar), only the frames between the play range in and out points are played back.

✔ Tips

- In the ruler, you can click and drag the in point and out points to new locations.

- You can enter a duration value in the Duration window and the play range out point will move the new distance from the in point. The in point will not change.

- To reset the play range back to the project duration, choose Mark > Reset Play Range or press Option-X.

To jump to the play range in point:

Do one of the following:

◆ Choose Mark > Go to > Play Range Start.

◆ Press Shift-Home.

To jump to the play range out point:

Do one of the following:

◆ Choose Mark > Go to > Play Range End.

◆ Press Shift-End.

Setting project duration

When you launch Motion, the length of the project is 10 seconds by default. You can change the duration in the Project Properties window.

To change the project duration:

1. Choose Edit > Project Properties or press Command-J.

2. On the General tab, enter an amount in the Duration field.

   You can choose frames, timecode, or seconds from the drop-down menu.

✔ Tips

■ A much faster way to change the project duration is to enter the new value in the Duration field at the bottom right of the Canvas.

■ You may have noticed that you can set the project duration in the Project pane of Motion's preferences (Motion > Preferences or Command-,) (**Figure 5.12**). However this setting only affects *future* projects, not the current project.

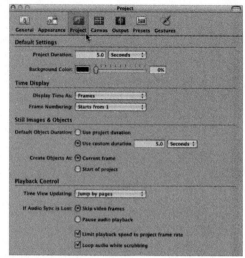

Figure 5.12 You can set your project's duration in Preferences, but the setting is only for new projects, not the current project. For the current project, use Project Properties (Command-J).

NAVIGATING THE TIMELINE

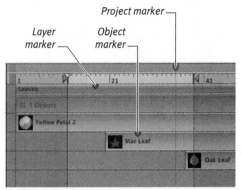

Project marker

Layer marker

Object marker

Figure 5.13 You can choose from three different types of markers for your projects and you can customize them.

Using Markers

If you use Final Cut Pro, you already know that markers are a powerful tool for adding notes, aligning tracks, or otherwise flagging specific points in the Timeline. Well, you can also use markers in Motion.

Markers are small icons that you add to the Timeline at specific frames. You can add as many markers as you need and quickly navigate to them. You can move them, give them names, and make comments about them. You can have them extend over a specified amount of time or a specified number of frames. You can even change their colors!

There are three types of markers you can add: object markers, layer markers, and project markers (**Figure 5.13**).

To add a marker:

1. Navigate to the frame where you want to place the marker.

2. For an object marker, select the object. For a layer marker, select the layer. For a project marker, make sure nothing is selected (Edit > Deselect All or Shift-Command-A).

3. *Do one of the following:*

   ▲ Choose Mark > Markers > Add Marker.

   ▲ Press M.

✔ Tips

- For a project marker, you can also Control-click in the gray area above the ruler and select Add Marker. Note that the marker is added where you click, not at the playhead location, so with this method, it's difficult to add a marker to a specific frame.

- Pressing Shift-M always adds a project marker, even if there are object(s) selected in the Timeline.

- Project markers are useful when you want to mark a specific time location that won't change as you move objects. Object markers, on the other hand, are useful for identifying a specific frame of content that you may want to sync up to another object or to a point in time.

- Clip markers from Final Cut Pro HD are retained and visible when you export from Final Cut into Motion. See Chapter 17 for more information.

Fly-By Markers

Markers are very handy for aligning a specific frame of one object to a specific frame of another. For example, you can use them to match the action in a video to the beat of a music track. And because you can add markers while your project is playing, or "on-the-fly," it's easy to lay down markers to the beat of the music! Just select the audio object in the Timeline, press play, and then tap the M key on each beat. Motion lays down markers as you go.

For more info on how to align markers to objects or to each other, see "Editing Objects in the Timeline" later in this chapter.

To move a marker:

◆ Click directly on the marker and drag it left or right.

To delete a marker:

Do one of the following:

◆ Drag the marker away from the object or ruler and release the mouse.

◆ Double-click the marker and click Delete Marker in the Edit Marker dialog.

◆ Control-click the marker and select Delete Marker.

◆ Park the playhead on the marker and select Mark > Markers > Delete Marker.

To delete all project markers:

1. Select Edit > Deselect All or press Shift-Command-A.

2. Select Mark > Markers > Delete All Markers.

To delete all object or layer markers:

1. Select the object(s) and/or layer(s) that have markers you want to remove.

2. Select Mark > Markers > Delete All Markers.

To edit a marker:

1. Open the Edit Marker dialog by *doing one of the following*:

   ▲ Double-click the marker.

   ▲ Choose Mark > Markers > Edit Marker.

   ▲ Press Command-Option-M.

2. In the Edit Marker dialog, enter a name for the marker (**Figure 5.14**).

You can also use the Edit Marker dialog to add comments to a marker, change it's location and duration, and assign a new color.

✔ Tips

- If you want to edit a layer or an object marker, you need to select the layer or object before you use the menu or keyboard shortcut to bring up the Edit Marker dialog.

- The name of each project markers appears in the Ruler area. The comments appear in the tooltip when you hover over a project marker. However, the only way to see the name and comment of a layer or object marker is to open the Edit Marker dialog.

- Project markers include a staff below the marker that makes it easier to align object markers to objects.

- Giving a marker a duration is a convenient way of marking a range of frames in a clip—to indicate, for example, the desired length of an effect or text (**Figure 5.15**).

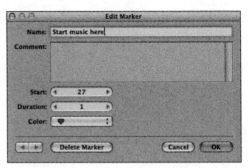

Figure 5.14 The Edit Marker dialog lets you name a marker, change its location and duration, and assign a color.

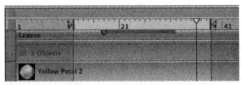

Figure 5.15 You can assign a marker a duration longer than the default of one frame.

USING MARKERS

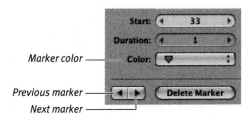

Marker color

Previous marker

Next marker

Figure 5.16 Jumping to markers is easy with the Edit Marker dialog.

To navigate to a marker:

1. Select the object or layer that contains the markers you want to jump to.

If you want to jump to project markers in the ruler, choose Edit > Deselect All or press Shift-Command-A.

2. *Do one of the following:*

▲ To navigate to the next marker forward in time, choose Mark > Go to > Next Marker or press Option-Command-Right Arrow.

▲ To navigate to the previous marker, choose Mark > Go to > Previous Marker, or press Option-Command-Left Arrow.

✔ Tips

■ To navigate to project markers, you can also Control-click in the gray area above the ruler and select Next Marker or Previous Marker .

■ You can jump to markers in the Edit Marker dialog (**Figure 5.16**). This can be useful if you dropped in several project markers while the project was playing, because you can name each marker and jump to the next one while remaining in the dialog window.

■ You can also assign markers specific colors in the Edit Marker dialog. For example, a set of markers that all indicate the placement of text could be purple.

Adding Objects to the Timeline

Becoming an expert at navigating in the Timeline isn't very useful if there isn't *anything* in the Timeline. So let's discuss the ways and means of getting objects into the Timeline and getting them organized.

Motion contains many editing functions that allow you to drag and drop objects directly into the Timeline at specific locations. In addition, you can specify exactly how the objects impact other objects already in the Timeline: Do you want to insert the object between others? Composite it on top? Exchange it with another object? With drag and drop editing, Motion lets you choose how the object is edited into the timeline.

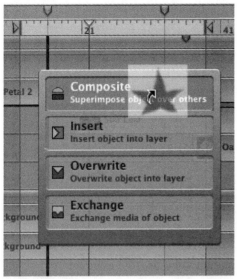

Figure 5.17 The drop menu appears when you drag an object to the Timeline.

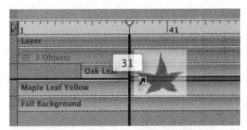

Figure 5.18 Compositing an object adds it to a new track above the object you target.

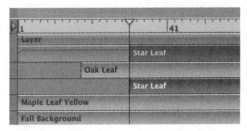

Figure 5.19 Notice how the name of the selected object, Star Leaf, appears in both the object row and in the Layer row.

Drag and Drop Editing

When you drag an object to the Timeline, a drop menu appears (**Figure 5.17**). If you drag to a layer, the available options are Composite, Insert, and Overwrite; if you drag to an object, you get an additional option called Exchange. Note that it's not only important where you drag *vertically*, meaning which track the mouse is over when you let go, but it's also important where you drag *horizontally*, meaning where the mouse is located in time, because that determines the in point, or the beginning of the object.

Compositing objects

Composite adds the object to a new track above the object you drop onto (**Figures 5.18 and 5.19**). This works the same as when you drag an object to the Layers tab or the Canvas, except that you can determine the in point of the object by where you drop it.

To composite an object:

1. Drag an object from the File Browser or Library in the Utility pane or from the Media tab in the Project pane to the Track area of the Timeline.

2. Drag to the right and stop at the frame where you want the object to start (the tooltip indicates the current frame location of the cursor).

3. Then drag up or down and stop on the layer or object that you want the new object to appear above.
   Continue to hold down the mouse button.

4. When the drop menu appears, choose Composite.

✔ Tips

- To composite over the top object in a layer, drag onto the layer track itself.

- You can also drag to the Layer list to perform a Composite action. Move the mouse above the layer you want to composite on top of and let go (**Figure 5.20**). Note that the object's in point will be located at the current playhead location or at the beginning of the project, depending on your setting in Motion's Preferences—see "Setting Drag and Drop Preferences" later in this chapter (**Figure 5.21**).

Inserting objects

Insert pushes the object(s) already in the Timeline to the right to make room for the new object. If you let go somewhere within an object, Insert cuts the existing object(s) at the drop point and inserts the new object in between (**Figure 5.22**).

To insert an object:

1. Drag an object from the File Browser or Library in the Utility pane or from the Media tab in the Project pane to the Track area of the Timeline.

2. Drag to the right and stop at the frame where you want the object to start (the tooltip indicates the current frame location of the cursor).

3. Then drag up or down and stop on the layer or object that you want the new object to be inserted over.

4. When the drop menu appears, choose Insert.

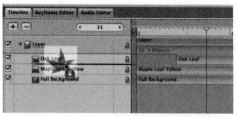

Figure 5.20 To perform a Composite action, move the mouse above the layer you want to composite on top of and let go.

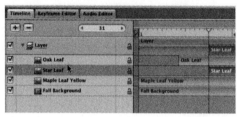

Figure 5.21 By dragging to the Layer list, you perform a Composite edit starting at the current playhead location (assuming you have set Motion's preferences to do so).

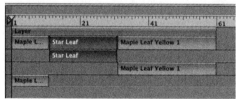

Figure 5.22 By letting go in the middle of an existing object, you split it to make room for the new object. The right side of the split object is moved to a new track on the same layer.

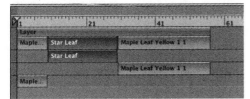

Figure 5.23 You can overwrite a portion of an object.

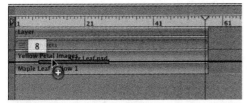

Figure 5.24 Make sure the thin bar is above the object to be overwritten.

✔ Tips

■ It can be difficult to see exactly where you are dropping an object before the drop menu appears. If you aren't sure, continue holding down the mouse and drag away from the drop menu until it disappears, then try again.

■ The top object does not move when you perform an insert edit.

Overwriting objects

Overwrite deletes the object or layer you drop onto and replaces it with the new object. If you drop into the middle of a layer, Overwrite deletes the part of the object(s) that the new object covers and places the existing object on a separate track (**Figure 5.23**).

To overwrite an object:

1. Drag an object from the File Browser or Library in the Utility pane or from the Media tab in the Project pane to the Track area of the Timeline.

2. Drag to the right and stop at the frame where you want the object to start (the tooltip indicates the current frame location of the cursor).

3. Then drag up or down and stop on the layer or object that you want to replace with the new object.

4. When the drop menu appears, choose Overwrite.

✔ Tip

■ When selecting the object to overwrite, make sure the thin bar that appears is above the selected object (**Figure 5.24**).

DRAG AND DROP EDITING

Exchanging objects

Exchange works like Overwrite except that the new object takes on the duration of the object it is replacing (**Figure 5.25**). If you drop the new object into the middle of an existing object, Exchange deletes the existing object from that point forward and places the new object on a new track, but only for the remaining duration of the deleted object.

To exchange an object:

1. Drag an object from the File Browser or Library in the Utility pane or from the Media tab in the Project pane to the Track area of the Timeline.

2. Drag to the right and stop on the object you want to exchange.

3. When the drop menu appears, choose Exchange.

✔ Tips

■ You can also perform the Exchange operation by dragging onto the object in the Layer list and letting go when you see the hooked arrow (**Figure 5.26**).

■ Exchange always start from the first frame of the new object and sets the duration based on the replaced object. If the replaced object's duration is longer than the new object, Exchange functions like an Overwrite, overwriting the old object with the full duration of the new object in a new layer and placing the rest of the old object on a new track.

■ You can only exchange objects, not layers themselves.

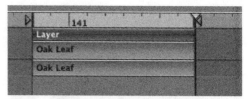

Figure 5.25 Exchange trims the new object to the duration of the object it is replacing.

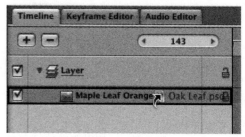

Figure 5.26 You can exchange an object in the Layer list. Release the mouse once you see the hooked arrow.

DRAG AND DROP EDITING

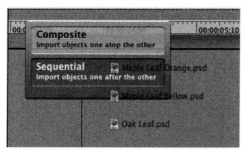

Figure 5.27 Select Composite or Sequential from the drop-down menu.

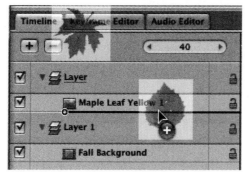

Figure 5.28 You can composite multiple objects by dragging to the Layer list.

Adding multiple clips

Just as you can add several clips at the same time to your project via the Canvas or the Layers tab, you can drag multiple clips to the Timeline. But by dragging to the Timeline, you have additional control over how the objects are added: you can now choose the in point where they start, and then choose whether you want to composite the objects on top of each other, or have them appear sequentially.

To add multiple clips to the Timeline:

1. Select the objects in the File Browser, Library, or Media tab.

   Hold the Command key down to select multiple objects.

2. Using the tooltip as a guide, drag the objects into the frame in the Timeline at which you want them to appear.

3. When the drop menu appears, select Composite to stack the clips on top of each other, or select Sequential to line them up one after the other (**Figure 5.27**).

✔ Tips

- To composite multiple objects, you can also drag to the Layer list in the Timeline (**Figure 5.28**). Letting go in between any object rows stacks the new objects between those two objects. Letting go on a layer places the objects at the top of the layer stack.

- The stacking order of the clips in a Composite edit or the sequence order in a Sequential edit is determined by the order in which you select the objects when you Command-click them. If you select a range of clips by Shift-clicking or drawing a marquee, they are stacked or sequenced in alphanumeric order (starting from the bottom of the stack or the beginning of the sequence).

Setting drag and drop preferences

You can modify the way drag and drop editing behaves in two ways through Motion's preferences: you can modify how long it takes for the drop menu to appear, and you can set where objects get dropped when you drag them onto the Layer list—either at the beginning of the project or at the current playhead location.

To change the delay for the drop menu:

1. Choose Motion > Preferences or Command-, (comma).

2. Click the General Icon.

3. In the Interface section, drag the slider to adjust the Drop Menu Delay.

To change where new objects appear in the Timeline:

1. Choose Motion > Preferences or Command-, (comma).

2. Click the Project Icon.

3. In the Still Images & Objects section, select Create Objects at Current Frame or Start of Project.

   This preference only affects objects dragged to the Layer list. Dragging to the Track area always results in the object starting at the frame on which you drop them.

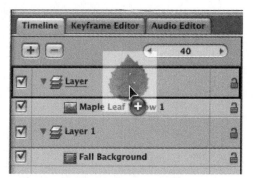

Figure 5.29 Place the mouse over the Layer row and release it to add an object to the top of a Layer stack.

Adding objects to layers

You can drag objects directly to the Layers list in the Timeline. The Layers list behaves just like Layers tab. Objects dragged to it appear at the beginning of the project or at the playhead location, depending on your choice in Motion's preferences.

To add an object to an existing layer:

1. Drag an object from the File Browser, Library, or Media tab to the Layers list.

2. *Do one of the following:*

   ▲ Place the mouse over the Layer row and release to add the object to the top of the layer stack (**Figure 5.29**).

   ▲ Place the mouse between any two object rows and release to place the object between those objects in the stacking order.

To add an object to a new layer:

1. Drag an object from the File Browser, Library, or Media tab to the Layers list.

2. Move the mouse to the top of an existing layer until the plus sign (+) position indicator appears and then release.

   A new layer is created above the existing layer and the object is placed in the new layer.

To replace an object in an existing layer:

1. Drag an object from the File Browser, Library, or Media tab to the Layers list.

2. Move the mouse over the object row you want to replace until a black box appears around the object row and a hooked arrow appears; then release the mouse button.

   This operation is the same as the Exchange edit in the drop menu: it replaces the current object but keeps its duration.

DRAG AND DROP EDITING

Managing Layers

As you add objects, create new layers, and begin applying masks, filters, and behaviors, your project increases in complexity. As a result, it can become difficult to stay organized and focused.

Here we explore ways you can organize your project and streamline the interface: by naming objects and layers, and by putting them in proper order; by enabling, locking, and collapsing tracks; by hiding effects; and by grouping tracks. You can perform all of these operations in either the Layers tab of the Project pane or the Layer list of the Timeline. For more information on working with the Layers tab, see "Working with Layers" in Chapter 3.

To rename an object or layer:

◆ Double-click the object name in the Layer list and type the new name.

✔ Tips

■ The object name is updated in both the Layer list and the Layers tab of the Project pane. Note that the name of the source file in the Media tab is unchanged. That's because this is the name of the underlying source file. Renaming the object only renames that specific instance of the object in the project.

■ Renaming objects in the Layers tab has the same result as renaming them in the Timeline.

MANAGING LAYERS

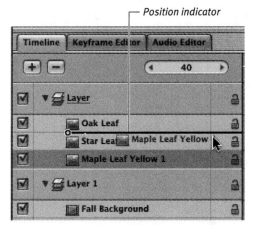

Position indicator

Figure 5.30 To change the stacking order of objects in a layer, simply click and drag.

To change the stacking order of objects in a layer:

1. Click the object row in the Layers list and drag the object up or down.

2. When the position indicator appears, release the mouse (**Figure 5.30**).

To move an object to another layer:

1. Click the object in the Layers list and drag it to another layer.

2. *Do one of the following:*

   ▲ Release the mouse on the layer itself to place the object at the top of the layer stack.

   ▲ Move the mouse so that the position indicator appears between two object rows and release.

To change the stacking order of layers:

◆ Select the layer to move and drag it above or below other layers.

✔ Tips

■ You can use the commands under the Object menu to move objects and layers one row up (forward), one row down (backward), all the way to the bottom (back), or all the way to the top (front). For details, see Chapter 3.

■ You can move multiple objects and/or layers at the same time. Just select them all first by Command-clicking (or Shift-click to select a range), then drag as usual.

MANAGING LAYERS

To disable a track:

◆ Click the check box on the left of the object row to toggle its visibility in the Canvas off and on.

To lock a track:

◆ Click the lock icon to toggle the lock status of a track on and off.

You can't modify locked tracks.

To collapse a layer:

◆ Click the disclosure triangle to the left of the layer name.

When you do so, all objects in the layer are hidden in the Layer list (but not in the Canvas).

Linking audio and video

If you import a QuickTime movie that contains both audio and video, the audio is *linked* to the video—when you move or trim one, the other is affected as well, and they stay in sync with each other. You can break the link if you want to change the relationship of the video and audio. For example, if you want to replace the audio that is linked to a video clip, you can unlink the current audio and then replace it with a new audio object.

To toggle linking:

◆ Click the link icon on the right side of the layer list for the object you want to link or unlink.

The link icon only appears if you have media linked to the object (typically audio linked to video).

MANAGING LAYERS

Hiding masks, filters, and behaviors

In both the Layers tab and the Timeline, masks, filters, and behaviors applied to clips appear as additional rows below the object to which they have been applied. You can hide all these effects to focus on the objects themselves, and then reveal them when you need to. Small icons for each effect remain in the object row of the Layer list to remind you of the effects that have been applied. Just as in collapsing layers, hiding effects in the Layer list does not impact their visibility in the Canvas—for that, use the visibility check box.

To hide and reveal effects:

◆ Click the disclosure triangle that appears next to the object icon in the Layers list.

✔ Tip

■ The same procedure works in both the Timeline tab and the Layers tab. But notice that collapsing the effects on one tab does not collapse them in the other. So you may find it useful to leave them open in the Layers tab so you can access them quickly, but keep them collapsed in the Timeline tab, or vice versa.

Grouping tracks with layer containers

When you add an object to the Canvas, it is always placed in a container called a *layer*. Layers are themselves objects, which means you can transform them (see Chapter 4), and apply effects to them (see Chapters 6, 8, and 9). Any transformations or effects you apply to a layer get applied to all the objects within the layer as if they were all one object—the objects act as if they are grouped together.

But the concept of grouping objects into a layer goes deeper. Because a layer is an object, you might ask the following question: Can I put layers inside of other layers? Yes, you can, with far-reaching implications. The process of placing layers within other layers is called *grouping* or *nesting*. If you are fluent in Final Cut Pro or other motion graphics applications, then this concept is quite familiar to you. You can build complex animations using grouping to collect objects that need to have all have the same effects or transformations applied. You can then group those layers into new layers—and there's really no limit to the number of layers you can create within other layers.

You can either create a new layer out of a subset of objects in a current layer, or you can group an existing layer into another layer. You can also ungroup layers that have been grouped together. And although we focus on performing these operations in the Timeline in this chapter, you can accomplish everything related to grouping in the Layers tab of the Project pane with the same procedures.

Figure 5.31 To group a layer into another layer, simply select the layer and drag it on top of another layer.

To group a layer inside another layer:

◆ Click the layer, drag it on top of another layer, and release the mouse (**Figure 5.31**).

The layer is placed into the first row of the containing layer. You can then move it up or down the stacking order of the containing layer like any other object.

✔ Tip

■ Collapsing layers by clicking the disclosure triangle can really come in handy when you are working with many objects in many layers.

To group a subset of objects in a layer:

1. Command-click to select all the objects to group.

2. *Do one of the following:*

   ▲ Select Object > Group.

   ▲ Press Shift-Command-G.

   ▲ Control-click the layer and select Group from the drop-down menu (**Figure 5.32**).

   Motion creates a new layer within the current layer and places all the selected objects into it. If the selection is not contiguous (for example, if there are unselected layers between the selected layers), then the new layer is created in the row above the highest unselected layer (**Figure 5.33**).

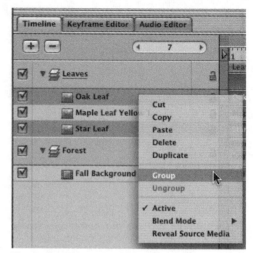

Figure 5.32 To group a subset of objects in a layer, Control-click the layer and select Group from the drop-down menu.

Figure 5.33 When grouping noncontiguous objects, Motion creates a new layer in the row above the highest unselected layer that is between the selected objects.

To ungroup a layer of grouped objects:

1. Select the layer that is grouped inside another layer.

2. *Do one of the following:*

   ▲ Select Object > Group.

   ▲ Press Option-Command-G.

   ▲ Control-click the layer and select Ungroup from the drop-down menu.

   Motion pulls the objects back out of the grouped layer and deletes the layer.

To remove a layer from another layer:

◆ Drag the contained layer to the top of the containing layer until the position indicator appears; then release the mouse.

To add a new layer in the Timeline:

◆ Click the Add new layer icon at the top of the Layer list.

To delete an object or layer in the Timeline:

1. Click the object or layer row to select it.

2. *Do one of the following:*

   ▲ Press the Delete key.

   ▲ Control-click the layer row in the Layer list and select Delete from the drop-down menu.

   ▲ Click the Delete icon at the top of the Layer list.

MANAGING LAYERS

Editing Objects in the Timeline

We've discussed how Motion allows you to perform basic editing operations when you are adding objects to the Timeline. We've also covered organizing the Timeline as it builds in complexity. Now it's time to really put the Timeline to work by examining how we can work with tracks: moving, trimming, and slipping media; copying, pasting, deleting, splitting, and soloing tracks; editing on layer tracks; editing regions; and inserting time. When combined with the ability to align objects to each other and specific points with snapping and markers, these operations form a powerful set of editing tools.

Moving objects in time

Moving an object in the Timeline changes its location without affecting its content or duration. For example, you could move a 5-second video clip from the beginning of the project to the middle so that it plays later in time. You can also quickly reposition objects by making them jump to the playhead location.

To move an object in the Timeline:

◆ Click the object in the Track area and drag it left or right.

A tooltip appears to indicate the new in and out points and the change from the starting location as you drag (**Figure 5.34**).

✔ Tip

■ If you hold down the Shift key as you drag, the object's in and out points snap to neighboring objects and markers—a dark vertical line appears to help identify the element with which you are aligning.

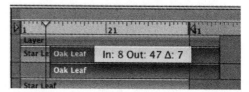

Figure 5.34 When you're moving an object, use the tooltip to help with exact placement.

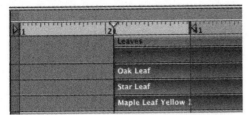

Figure 5.35 You can move multiple objects to the playhead at the same time using handy keyboard shortcuts.

To move an object to the playhead:

1. Place the playhead where you want the object's in or out point.

2. Select the object(s).

3. Select Mark > Move Selected In Point or Move Selected Out Point.

✔ Tips

■ The highly-recommended keyboard shortcut is Shift-[(Left Bracket) to move the object's in point to the playhead and Shift-] (right bracket) to move its out point to the playhead.

■ To move many objects at the same time to a specific location so they all line up, just select them all and use the keyboard shortcut (**Figure 5.35**).

Trimming objects in the Timeline

Trimming refers to changing the length, or *duration*, of an object by lengthening or shortening either its in point or out point. You can trim by dragging or by using a keyboard shortcut. The shortcut is useful when you want to trim to a specific location, or when you need to trim several objects by the same amount.

To trim by dragging:

1. Move the pointer to the end of the clip you want to trim.

   The pointer changes to a Trim pointer.

2. Click and drag in the direction you want to trim.

   A tooltip appears and displays the new in point location, the new duration of the clip, and the change from the current state.

✔ Tips

■ If you hold the Shift key down while dragging, the new in or out point snaps to neighboring objects and markers, and a black vertical line appears to indicate the alignment.

■ You can't extend the length of a clip beyond the available media. If there is any media beyond the in or out point, the unused frames appear semi-transparently when you click either point.

■ If you want to make a clip longer but there are no unused frames, you can make the clip repeat itself by altering its End condition in the Media tab of the Inspector.

■ If you want to change the tooltip display from timecode to frames or vice versa, click either the Current Time icon or the Project Duration icon located to the left and right of the transport controls.

To trim using the keyboard:

1. Move the playhead to where you want the new in or out point.

2. Select the object to be trimmed in the Track area of the Timeline.

3. *Do one of the following:*

   ▲ To trim the in point, choose Mark > Mark In, or press I.

   ▲ To trim the out point, choose Mark > Mark Out or press O.

✔ Tips

■ You can trim multiple objects at the same time with the keyboard method. To do so, just select all the objects, position the playhead, and press I or O.

■ If a particular clip doesn't have enough media to make it to the playhead, it is extended as far as possible.

■ Trimming works on other objects, like filter and behaviors, as well.

EDITING OBJECTS IN THE TIMELINE

Slipping media

Slipping is the process of changing which frames of a media clip are displayed without changing the clip's duration or location. As opposed to *moving* and *trimming*, which you can apply to any object, you can only apply slipping to a video or audio object. And even with audio or video, you first need to trim a clip before you can slip it.

To slip a clip:

◆ Hold down the Option key, then click anywhere on the clip and drag left or right.

The pointer changes to a Slip icon and the full length of the available media is temporarily visible as you drag (**Figure 5.36**).

You can only slip as far as you have extra media, or *handles*, beyond the in or out points.

✔ Tips

■ Slipping works on video and audio clips. Technically you *can* slip a graphic, but because a graphic's image doesn't change over time, there is no impact.

■ Slipping affects content only. Any masks, effects, or keyframes remain in their current timecode location.

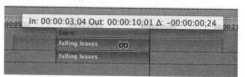

Figure 5.36 Slipping a clip. The underlying media moves left or right, but the location of the in and out points, and the duration of the visible section of the clip, stay the same.

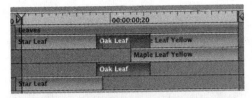

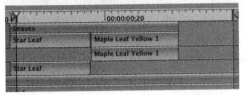

Figure 5.37 Ripple delete shifts objects over to fill the gap.

Deleting, cutting, copying, and Pasting

All the standard cut-copy-paste operations that you are probably familiar with are available to you when you are editing in the Timeline; in addition, some variations on these are also available. For instance, when you delete objects in the Timeline, you can choose whether to leave a hole or have the other objects slide over to close up the hole. This latter choice is known as a *ripple delete*.

To delete an object in the Timeline:

1. Select the object you want to delete.

2. *Do one of the following:*

   ▲ Choose Edit > Delete.

   ▲ Press the Delete key.

   ▲ Control-click the object and select Delete.

   The object and its track are deleted, but all other objects remain in their current locations.

To ripple delete an object in the Timeline:

1. Select the object you want to delete.

2. *Do one of the following:*

   ▲ Choose Edit > Ripple Delete.

   ▲ Press Shift-Delete.

   All other objects to the right of the deleted object that are in the same layer shift to the left to fill the gap (**Figure 5.37**).

To cut an object from the Timeline:

1. Select the object(s) you want to cut.

2. *Do one of the following:*

   ▲ Choose Edit > Cut.

   ▲ Press Command-X.

   ▲ Control-click the object and select Cut.

   All other objects remain in their current locations and the object(s) you cut are copied to the Clipboard for pasting.

To copy an object from the Timeline:

1. Select the object(s) you want to copy.

2. *Do one of the following:*

   ▲ Choose Edit > Copy.

   ▲ Press Command-C.

   ▲ Control-click the object and select Copy.

   Nothing changes in the Timeline, but the object(s) are copied into the clipboard for pasting.

To paste an object into the Timeline:

1. Copy or Cut the object(s) you want to paste.

2. Click the layer in the Layer list into which you want to paste the object(s).

3. Position the playhead where you want the object(s) to start.

4. Choose Edit > Paste or press Command-V.

✔ Tips

■ Objects are pasted into the top of the selected layer.

■ If any effects or keyframes are applied to the object(s), they carry over to the pasted object(s) (**Figure 5.38**).

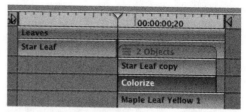

Figure 5.38 If effects are applied to an object, they are included in the Copy-Paste operation.

EDITING OBJECTS IN THE TIMELINE

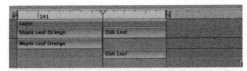

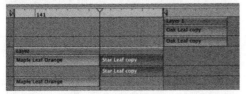

Figure 5.39 Paste Special with Insert performs an Insert edit.

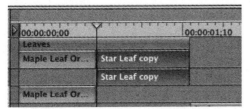

Figure 5.40 Paste Special with Overwrite deletes existing clips.

Working with Paste Special

Paste Special allows you to perform an insert, overwrite, or exchange edit when you're pasting the contents of the clipboard into the Timeline (see "Drag and Drop Editing" earlier in the chapter). An insert pushes all objects already in the Timeline over to the right to make room for the pasted clips (**Figure 5.39**). An overwrite deletes any objects that are in the way (**Figure 5.40**). An exchange replaces the selected object with the contents of the clipboard.

You can also use Paste Special in combination with Regions. See "Working with Regions" later in this chapter for more information.

To use Paste Special:

1. Load the desired object into the clipboard by copying or cutting.

2. Select the layer where you want the object pasted from the Layer list.

3. Choose Edit > Paste Special or press Option-Command-V.

4. Choose the paste method from the Paste Special dialog.

Splitting Object Tracks

When you split a track, you cut the object into two pieces that are then treated as separate objects and are placed in separate object rows (**Figure 5.41**).

To split an object track:

1. Select the object bar in the Track area.

2. Place the playhead on the frame where you want the split.

3. Choose Edit > Split.

✔ Tip

- Splitting a track is useful when you want an object that was behind another object to change stacking order and move to the front. For instance, you can make a moon object move behind an earth object, and then move in front of the earth object as if it were moving in 3D space, by splitting the moon track.

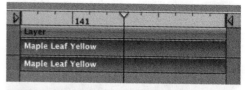

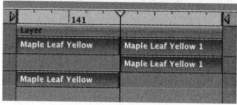

Figure 5.41 Splitting a track cuts the object into two pieces that are treated as separate objects and placed in separate object rows.

Soloing Object Tracks

When you want to focus all your attention on one object, you can turn off the visibility of all other tracks in one shot rather than clicking the visibility check box for all the other tracks. There's also a handy keyboard shortcut.

To solo an object track:

Do one of the following:

◆ Option-click the visibility checkbox in the Timeline list or the Layers tab.

◆ Select the object and choose Object > Solo.

◆ Select the object and press Control-S.

✔ Tips

■ Repeat the same procedure to unsolo an object.

■ If the object is a QuickTime movie with audio, you can choose to unsolo the audio, the video, or both by choosing Object > Unsolo > Video Only, Audio Only, or Video and Audio.

Editing with Layer tracks

Motion allows you to perform many of the editing operations, such as moving, trimming, and slipping, directly on the Layer track rather than by selecting the specific object or objects. Why would you want to do this? Well, it allows you to collapse your layers in the Timeline, which means you can view many layers simultaneously without needing to scroll up and down (**Figure 5.42**). It's a handy and powerful feature that can speed up your workflow.

In the illustrations for some of the examples that follow, the Layer track is expanded so that you can see how the operation affects the objects in the layer, but the idea is that you can move, trim, and slip individual and even multiple overlapping objects without even seeing them! Very slick. You can also move or trim the entire layer.

To move a single object on the Layer track:

1. Click the object in the Layer track to select it.

   If there several overlapping objects, Control-click and select the object you want to move from the shortcut menu.

2. Drag the highlighted section right or left to move the object forward or backward in time.

✔ Tips

■ When selecting one of several overlapping objects, the name of the object appears in the thicker, lower bar of the Layer track.

■ If you hold down the Shift key while dragging, the object snaps to neighboring in and out points and markers, indicated by a vertical black line (**Figure 5.43**).

Figure 5.42 Collapsing layers makes efficient use of screen real estate.

Figure 5.43 Holding down the Shift key while moving an object snaps the object to neighboring in and out points.

Figure 5.44 Select all overlapping objects by clicking the track where the overlap occurs.

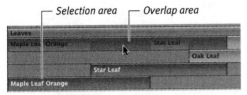

Figure 5.45 Objects that extend beyond the overlap area are fully selected.

Figure 5.46 Dragging the thin bar at the top of the Layer track moves the layer and all objects it contains.

Figure 5.47 To trim an object on the Layer track, click-drag the in or out point to extend it or shorten it.

To move all overlapping objects on the Layer track:

1. Click the area of the track where the overlap is indicated (**Figure 5.44**).

2. Drag the highlighted section right or left to move all the overlapping objects forward or backward at the same time.

✔ Tip

- The area that is selected (highlighted) may be wider than the overlap area if any of the overlapping objects extend beyond the overlap (**Figure 5.45**).

To move all objects and the layer:

- Click the thin blue bar at the top of the Layer track and drag it left or right.

  The layer with all of its contents moves (**Figure 5.46**).

To trim an object in the Layer track:

1. Click the object in the Layer track to select it.

   If there are numerous overlapping objects, Control-click and select the object you want to move from the shortcut menu.

2. Move the pointer to the edge of the selection until it changes to the Trim pointer.

3. Click and drag to extend or shorten the selected object (**Figure 5.47**).

✔ Tips

- If you select multiple overlapping objects, only the longest object is trimmed. If multiple objects have the same in point or out point, they are trimmed together.

- If masks, filters, or behaviors are applied to the object, they are trimmed as well. To trim the object and leave any applied masks or effects unchanged, hold down the Command key when trimming.

To trim the layer independently of layer objects:

◆ Hold down the Command key and click and drag the beginning or end of the thin blue layer bar.

The layer itself becomes longer or shorter without affecting the length of any of the objects it contains. Objects that exist outside the length of the thin blue layer bar are not visible in the Canvas on playback.

✔ Tip

■ Modifying the length of the layer without modifying it's contents is a convenient way to temporarily shorten a layer to test for timing purposes without affecting the objects in the layer.

■ Once you modify the layer length to be longer or shorter than the objects it contains, it no longer adjusts automatically as you add new objects to that layer. To restore this automatic updating, Command-click the layer bar and align it with the first and last clips in the layer. Holding down the Shift key while dragging snaps the layer bar into place (**Figure 5.48**).

Figure 5.48 Return the layer length to its original length to restore its ability to automatically update as objects are added.

Figure 5.49 Dragging a clip with the Option key slips the underlying media.

Figure 5.50 You can slip multiple objects at the same time. Note the playhead location—the second object isn't visible in the Canvas, so you can't see the effect of your slip operation on both objects.

To slip an object in the Layer track:

1. Click the object in the Layer track to select it.

   If there are several overlapping objects, Control-click and select the object you want to move from the shortcut menu.

2. Hold down the Option key, click, and drag left or right on the highlighted section of the Layer track to slip the object **(Figure 5.49)**.

✔ Tips

- Slipping affects content only. Any masks, effects, or keyframes remain in their current timecode location.

- Slipping only works if the object has been previously trimmed.

- You can slip overlapping objects simultaneously, but be careful, because they may not all be visible in the Canvas, depending on your playhead location **(Figure 5.50)**.

Working with Regions

In the Timeline, you can select a range of frames, called a *region*, to be affected by an editing operation. You can cut or copy all the content in a region in order to paste it into another section of the Timeline, or you can insert a blank section of a specific length into the Timeline. Regions are flexible in that they don't need to start or end at the in or out points of the objects they contain.

To create a region:

◆ Press Command-Option, and drag in the Ruler area of the Timeline to define the region.

A shaded blue area indicates the selected frames.

✔ Tips

■ Once you have defined a region, you can move it by placing the pointer over the region (below the Ruler area) until it turns into a hand icon; then click and drag left or right (**Figure 5.51**).

■ To resize the region, mover the pointer to the edge of the region (below the Ruler area) until it changes to the Trim pointer; then drag left or right.

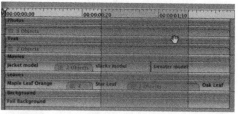

Figure 5.51 Move a region by dragging it with the hand icon.

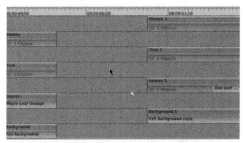

Figure 5.52 When you cut a region, the objects are split onto separate tracks before and after the cut, and the names of the objects and layers have a numeral 1 added to the track after the cut.

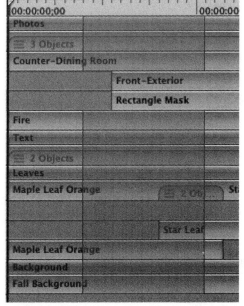

Figure 5.53 You can easily deselect masks and effects.

To cut or copy a region:

1. Create a region.

2. Choose Edit > Cut (Command-X) to cut or Edit > Copy (Command-C) to copy.

   If you cut a region, Motion deletes all the material in the region and leaves a gap in its place (**Figure 5.52**).

   Note that any objects that are split due to the cut operation are placed onto separate layers before and after the cut area. For more information on splitting clips, see "Splitting Tracks" earlier in this chapter.

✔ Tip

- If you want to perform a ripple delete of the region so that the gap is closed, choose Edit > Ripple delete or press Shift-Delete.

Deselecting parts of a region

Once you create a region, you can exclude specific objects from the selection before you delete, cut, or copy it.

To deselect objects from a region:

◆ Command-click the layer that contains the object(s), then Command-click each object.

   The shading disappears for the deselected object(s).

✔ Tip

- You can also deselect filters, behaviors, and masks (**Figure 5.53**).

WORKING WITH REGIONS

Pasting into regions

If you have content in the clipboard from a previous cut or copy operation, you can paste that content into a region in three different ways using the Paste Special command as an insert, an overwrite, or an exchange edit.

To paste into a region:

1. Select the object(s) to be pasted.

2. Copy (Command-C) or Cut (Command-X).

3. Press Command-Option and drag in the Ruler area of the Timeline to create a region.

4. Choose Edit > Paste Special or press Command-Option-V.

5. Select Insert, Overwrite, or Exchange from the Paste Special dialog.

Inserting time

A unique type of insert edit, Insert Time allows you to add blank frames anywhere in the Timeline based on the location and duration of the region. Inserting time splits all the tracks at the beginning of the region and pushes all the content to the right of the split by the width of the region.

To insert time:

1. Press Command-Option and drag in the Ruler area of the Timeline to create a region that is as wide as the amount of time you want to insert.

2. Choose Edit > Insert Time.

   Each layer is split, meaning Motion creates a copy of each layer after the split with the number 1 added to the layer name (**Figure 5.54**). For more on splitting objects and layers, see "Splitting Tracks" earlier in this chapter.

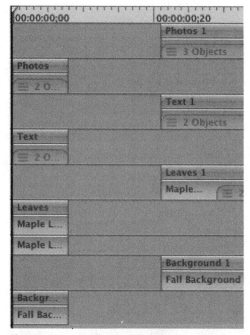

Figure 5.54 Inserting time splits layers and objects. Motion creates a copy of each layer after the split with the number 1 added to the layer name.

The Mini-Timeline

Creating a motion graphics project can get complicated very quickly. As you add objects, filters, masks, behaviors, particles, and keyframes, it can become difficult to locate specific items on which you want to focus your attention. Motion's mini-Timeline is one of the elegant solutions to this interface clutter (another is the Dashboard, introduced in Chapter 2).

The mini-Timeline, located at the bottom of the Canvas, only displays the currently selected object, mask, or effect (**Figure 5.55**). Many of the editing operations that you perform in the Timeline can also be performed in the mini-Timeline, so you don't even need to open up the Timeline as you work. In addition, the mini-Timeline contains a playhead area analogous to the Ruler area in the Timeline for scrubbing and navigation.

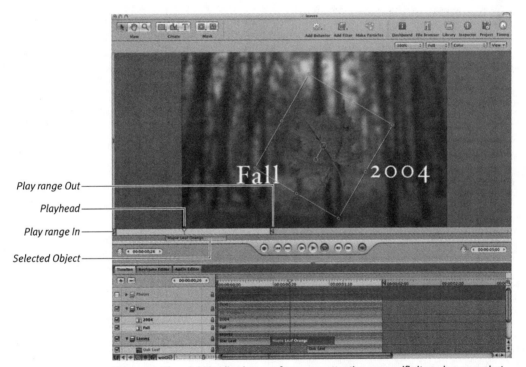

Play range Out

Playhead

Play range In

Selected Object

Figure 5.55 The mini-Timeline lets you focus your attention on specific items in your project.

As a general rule, when you need to place, move, trim, slip, copy, or paste a single object or effect, you can do it in the mini-Timeline. When you need to add objects to specific layers or you need to align one object or effect with another, then press F6 to open the full Timeline, perhaps resize the layers to fit more into the view, and work away.

To add an object to the mini-Timeline:

◆ Drag the object from the File Browser or Library to the mini-Timeline and release the mouse at the desired location.

A blue bar appears in the mini-Timeline along with a tooltip as you drag to identify the location of the object's in point.

✔ Tips

■ If the mini-Timeline is empty when you add an object, it means that no objects are currently selected, and Motion places the object into a new layer at the top of the layer stack.

■ If an object is selected before you drag, the object you add to the mini-Timeline is added below the selected object in the same layer.

■ If an effect is selected, however (a purple bar appears in the mini-Timeline for filters and behaviors; a gray bar for masks), then the new object is treated as if there were nothing selected; therefore, it is placed in a new layer at the top of the layer stack.

Figure 5.56 Use the tooltip to add multiple objects to the mini-Timeline.

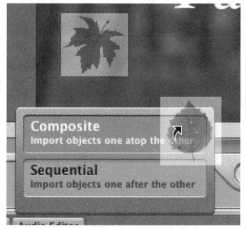

Figure 5.57 The drop-down menu appears.

To add multiple objects to the mini-Timeline:

1. Select the objects in the Utility pane (see Chapter 4 for how to select multiple objects).

2. Drag the objects to the mini-Timeline and stop at the desired frame, which is indicated by the tooltip until the drop-down menu appears (**Figures 5.56** and **5.57**).

3. Select either Composite or Sequential from the drop menu (see "Drag and Drop Editing" earlier in this chapter).

To move an object in the mini-Timeline:

◆ Click and drag the object, using the tooltip to determine the new in and out points, as well as the change from the current location.

To trim an object in the mini-Timeline:

◆ Click and drag either end of the object and use the tooltip to determine the amount of media being added or subtracted.

✔ Tips

■ As in the Timeline, when you move or trim an object in the mini-Timeline, the operation also affects any masks or effects that may be applied to the object.

■ Also just as in the Timeline, you can hold down the Command key when you trim an object to trim just the object and leave the duration of any masks or effects untouched.

■ You can also move and trim masks and effects in the mini-Timeline. The location or duration of the object to which they are applied isn't affected.

THE MINI-TIMELINE

To slip an object in the mini-Timeline:

1. Select the object to slip.

2. Hold down the Option key and click and drag the object bar.

✔ Tips

- The pointer changes to a slip icon and the total amount of media beyond the clip's in and out points becomes temporarily visible as you drag.

- Note that you can't slip unless you have previously trimmed a clip. In other words, you need media beyond the in and out points.

THE MINI-TIMELINE

WORKING
WITH BEHAVIORS

You accomplish animation in Motion with either of two very different methods: by using keyframing or behaviors. *Keyframing* is the process of setting specific values for the parameters of objects, masks, and effects at specific points in time. The software then calculates, or *interpolates* values between those keyframes to create animation as the value changes over time. The process of working with keyframes is discussed in Chapter 7. *Behaviors*, on the other hand, are procedural animations—each behavior has built-in instructions, or procedures, that tell the object to animate in a specific way, without using keyframes at all.

Motion's real-time playback makes the process of adding and adjusting behaviors downright addicting. Add an object, press play, drop on a behavior—instant animation! You can then adjust the behavior while the composition continues to play, and continue to add behaviors, filters, and other objects. The whole process of building an animated composition becomes fluid, interactive, and fast. And behaviors aren't just for objects—you can apply them to masks, filters, text, and even particles to create incredibly complex and interesting animations in very short order.

Behaviors are a type of *effect* in Motion. Other effects include filters (Chapter 9) and particles (Chapter 11). Effects are usually applied to objects, but you can also apply them to layers (which are also objects, remember?), masks, filters, and even other behaviors.

There are five categories of behaviors in Motion:

Basic Motion behaviors such as Fade In/Fade Out, Throw, and Spin, animate a single parameter.

Parameter behaviors such as Ramp, Oscillate, and Random, can animate just about any parameter of an object or effect.

Simulation behaviors such as Gravity, Attractor, and Spring, create natural forces.

Particle behaviors include just one behavior, called Scale Over Life, but it's a darn good one.

Text behaviors include a stunning array of behaviors and presets for animating text.

In this chapter, I focus on Basic Motion, Parameter, and Simulation behaviors; I save Particle and Text behaviors for Chapters 11 and 13, respectively).

WORKING WITH BEHAVIORS

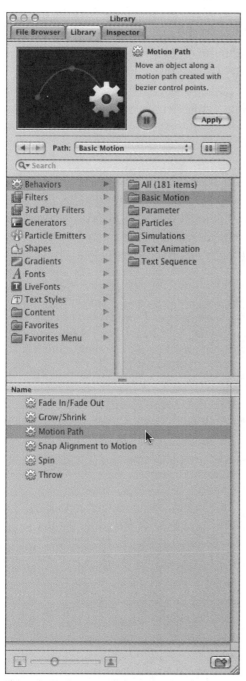

Figure 6.1 Motion stores behaviors in the Library. When you select a specific behavior, an animation appears in the Preview Area at the top of the Library to show how the behavior will work.

Choosing Behaviors

Motion stores behaviors in the Library, organized into six different category subfolders. When you select a specific behavior, an animation appears in the Preview Area at the top of the Library to illustrate how the behavior animates an object (**Figure 6.1**).

Behaviors vs. Keyframes

So if you can use either behaviors or keyframes to animate the parameters of an object, what's the difference? And when should you use one over the other?

Behaviors animate object parameters without any keyframes by creating a range of values over the life of the behavior (for example, a ball grows a little during the 5 seconds it is on the screen). Keyframes, on the other hand, establish a specific, precise value for a parameter at an exact point in time (the ball is 50 percent of it's full size at 0 seconds and 100 percent at 5 seconds).

Behaviors can be quite a bit faster to apply and adjust. In addition, you can create complex animations with behaviors that would be nearly impossible to create with keyframes.

On the other hand, keyframes give you very precise control, especially when you are starting or stopping animations, or coordinating multiple animated objects.

So which should you choose to use? There are no hard and fast rules, but here are some general guidelines:

◆ Use behaviors in animations for which you don't need precise values (I want this object to move to the right, grow in size, and spin and shake a little, and then I want it to move toward this other object.), for which you want a repeating animation (I want the pendulum to swing back and forth.), or for which you want a complex natural or random animation (I want the ball to fall and bounce.).

◆ Use keyframes when precise values are critical (These three objects need to be at these exact locations at 10 seconds.), or when you need precise motion control (I want the object to decelerate more slowly before coming to a stop.).

But you can have your cake and eat it too! You can combine behaviors and keyframes to get the best of both worlds—see "Behaviors and Keyframes" in Chapter 7 for details.

CHOOSING BEHAVIORS

Figure 6.2 Applied behaviors appear underneath the object to which they are applied in the Layers tab.

Behavior icon

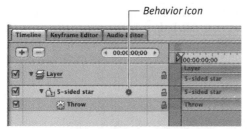

Figure 6.3 Applied behaviors also appear in the Timeline.

Applying Behaviors

Applying behaviors is quite straightforward: you just select the object and then select the behavior from either the Library or the Toolbar to apply it. An exception is parameter behaviors, which need to be applied to a specific parameter of an object rather than to the object itself (see "Applying Parameter Behaviors" later in this chapter).

To apply a behavior to an object:

1. Select the object in the Canvas, the Layers tab, or the Timeline.

2. *Do one of the following:*
   ▲ Drag the desired behavior from the Library to the object in the Canvas, Layers tab, or Timeline.
   ▲ Select the behavior in the Library and click the Apply button.
   ▲ Choose a behavior from the Behavior icon on the Toolbar.

3. Once you apply a behavior, it appears underneath the object in the Layers tab (**Figure 6.2**) and the Timeline (**Figure 6.3**). In addition, Motion adds a small gear-shaped icon to the object row, so even if you have collapsed all the effects, you can still tell that a behavior has been applied to the object.

✔ Tips

■ You can apply a behavior to multiple objects at the same time. Just select all the objects before applying the behavior.

■ You can apply multiple behaviors to an object at the same time by Command-clicking them in the Library and then clicking the Apply button or dragging them onto the object.

■ Remember, layers are objects too, so you can apply a behavior to a layer to affect all the objects contained in the layer.

APPLYING BEHAVIORS

Customizing Behaviors

Some behaviors, such as Fade In/Fade Out or Edge Collision, create an animation as soon as they are applied. Others, such as Throw or Spin, don't have any impact until you customize their settings. You can make these adjustments in either the Dashboard or the Inspector.

Customizing parameters in the Dashboard

The Dashboard provides quick access to the parameters you are most likely going to want to change, and it gives you an intuitive graphical interface to boot.

To customize a behavior with the Dashboard:

1. Select the object that has the behavior applied to it.

2. *Do one of the following:*

   ▲ Click the behavior in the Layers tab, the Timeline, or the Behaviors tab of the Inspector.

   ▲ Control-click the object in the Canvas and select the desired behavior from the drop-down menu.

3. If the Dashboard is not already visible, press the D key or F7 to reveal it.

4. Use the controls in the Dashboard to customize the behavior settings (**Figure 6.4**).

✔ Tips

■ If you have more than one behavior applied to an object, you can choose which behavior is displayed in the Dashboard by using the drop-down menu at the top of the Dashboard (**Figure 6.5**). Or, you can press D to cycle through each behavior.

■ To hide the Dashboard, click the X in the top left corner, or press F7.

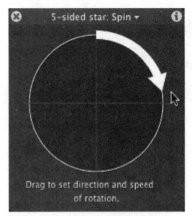

Figure 6.4 Various controls in the Dashboard let you customize behavior settings. With the Spin control, click the arrow and drag it around the circle to set the direction and speed of the spin.

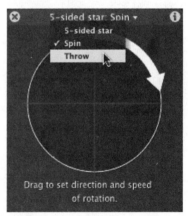

Figure 6.5 If an object has more than one behavior applied to it, you can choose which behavior is displayed in the Dashboard via the drop-down menu at the top of the Dashboard. Pressing D cycles through all effects applied to the object.

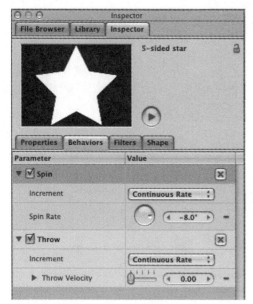

Figure 6.6 The Behaviors tab of the Inspector contains every behavior applied to the selected object.

Customizing parameters in the Inspector

The Behaviors tab of the Inspector (**Figure 6.6**) contains every behavior that has been applied to the selected object. As opposed to the Dashboard, it includes *all* of the adjustable parameters for each behavior.

To customize a behavior with the Inspector:

1. Select the object that has the behavior applied to it.

2. Open the Behaviors tab of the Inspector by clicking it or by pressing F2.

3. Adjust the parameters as desired.

Modifying Behaviors

You can modify behaviors just as you can objects and other effects in the Layers tab and the Timeline: you can rename them, turn them on and off, and lock them so that you don't change them accidentally once you have them working the way you want (**Figure 6.7**). You can also move, copy, paste, and duplicate them.

To rename a behavior:

◆ Double-click the name in the Layers tab or the Layer list in the Timeline and enter the new name.

The name of the original behavior in the Library is not affected.

To turn a behavior on or off:

◆ Click the visibility check box for the behavior in the Layers tab or the Timeline.

✔ Tips

■ To toggle the visibility of all the behaviors applied to an object, click the gear-shaped icon on the object row.

A red slash appears through the icon when the behaviors are disabled (**Figure 6.8**).

■ Control-clicking the gear icon reveals a drop-down list of all behaviors applied to the object (**Figure 6.9**). Choosing one opens the Behaviors tab of the Inspector.

■ To hide all behaviors in the Layers tab or the Timeline, click the Show/Hide Behaviors button at the bottom of the window. This button only hides the behaviors from view in the list; they are still enabled in the Canvas.

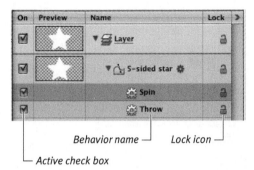

Behavior name — Lock icon —

— Active check box

Figure 6.7 You can rename behaviors, turn them on and off, and lock them in the Layers tab.

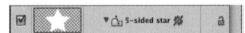

Figure 6.8 You can easily tell that a behavior has been disabled by the red slash through the icon.

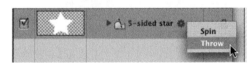

Figure 6.9 Simply Control-click the gear icon to reveal a drop-down list of all behaviors applied to an object.

To lock a behavior:

◆ Click the lock icon in either the Layers tab or the Timeline.

You can't change the parameters of a locked behavior.

To cut a behavior:

◆ Select the behavior and choose Edit > Cut or press Command-X.

To copy a behavior:

◆ Select the behavior and choose Edit > Copy or press Command-C.

Just as is the case when you cut or copy any other object, the behavior with all its current parameter values is loaded into the Clipboard so you can paste it if you want to.

To paste a behavior:

◆ Select the object to receive the behavior and choose Edit > Paste or press Command-V.

✔ Tips

■ The duration of the pasted behavior is the same as it is for the cut or copied behavior. If the object you are pasting onto is longer or shorter than the object the behavior came from, you may need to trim the behavior (see "Trimming Behaviors" later in this chapter) to get the expected result.

■ You can also Control-click a behavior and select cut, copy, or paste from the drop-down menu.

MODIFYING BEHAVIORS

To move a behavior to another object:

◆ Drag the behavior to the target object.

To delete a behavior:

1. Select the behavior.

2. *Do one of the following:*

   ▲ Choose Edit > Delete.

   ▲ Control-click the behavior (in the Layers tab or the Timeline) and select Delete from the drop-down menu.

   ▲ Press the Delete key.

To duplicate a behavior:

1. Select the behavior.

2. *Do one of the following:*

   ▲ Choose Edit > Duplicate.

   ▲ Press Command-D.

   ▲ Control-click the behavior and select Duplicate from the drop-down menu.

✔ Tips

■ You can duplicate a behavior and move the copy to another object all in one step by Option-clicking the behavior in the Layers tab and dragging it to the new object (**Figure 6.10**).

■ If you duplicate an *object* with behaviors applied, the behaviors get duplicated as well. If you need the same behavior applied to many different objects, you could apply the behavior once and adjust its parameters. Then, duplicate the object as many times as you need to, and exchange the content of each copied object with other objects (see "Drag and Drop Editing" in Chapter 5 to learn how to perform an exchange edit).

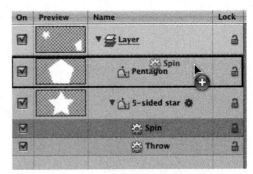

Figure 6.10 In just one step, you can duplicate a behavior and move the copy to another object. Simply Option-click the behavior in the Layers tab and drag it to the new object.

MODIFYING BEHAVIORS

Trimming Behaviors

When you apply a behavior to an object, by default, its duration matches the duration of the object (which means, by the way, that it doesn't matter where your playhead is located when you add the behavior). You can change a behavior's duration by *trimming* it in the Timeline so that it begins after the object starts or ends before the object ends. For example, if you apply a Spin behavior and then trim the behavior to half the length of the object, it stops spinning at the halfway point (**Figure 6.11**). There are some exceptions to this process—check out the sidebar "Hey, That's Not What I Wanted" on the next page.

To trim a behavior:

◆ Click and drag the in or out point of the behavior.

A tooltip indicates the new in or out point location, the new duration of the behavior, and the amount of change you are making in timecode or frames.

✔ Tip

■ You can trim multiple behaviors at the same time if they have the same in or out point. Just select them all and drag.

Figure 6.11 By trimming the out point of the Spin behavior in the Timeline, the star object stops spinning half-way through the play range.

Hey, That's Not What I Wanted!

If you try to trim the out point of a behavior to make it stop before the end of the object, you may get an unexpected result. This is because, although trimming the in point of a behavior can be a useful method for changing when a behavior starts, trimming its out point can have an unintended effect: with some behaviors, the object reverts to its original state after the end of the effect.

The solution? Rather than trimming, use the parameter behavior called Stop. The Stop behavior suspends the animation of a specific parameter (like Position, Rotation, and so on) at a specific point in time. To use it, first place the playhead at the location where you want to stop the animation. Then, in the Properties tab of the Inspector, Control-click the parameter you want to freeze and choose Stop from the drop-down menu. Stop is the one behavior that Motion adds to the object at the playhead location.

The Stop behavior freezes the parameter you choose for every behavior already applied to the object that uses that parameter. See "Applying Multiple Behaviors" on the next page for a tip on selecting which behavior is affected by the Stop behavior.

To change the parameter that the Stop behavior is freezing, switch to the Behavior tab in the Inspector, click the Go button under the Stop parameter, and choose the parameter from the Properties > Transform fly-out menu. To change the point in time when the Stop behavior kicks in, trim it in the Timeline.

For more information on working with parameter behaviors, see "Applying Parameter Behaviors" later in this chapter.

Finally, you can also change the start and end of behaviors with the Start Offset and End Offset parameters in the Inspector.

Applying Multiple Behaviors

Motion lets you add an unlimited number of behaviors to an object. Behaviors that affect the same parameter are usually added together for the combined effect (**Figure 6.12**).

The stacking order of behaviors doesn't usually have any impact on the animation, so changing the order is something you may want to do just to keep organized.

To change the order of behaviors:

◆ In the Layers tab or the Layer list in the Timeline, drag the behavior up or down. When the position indicator is in the desired location, release the mouse.

✔ Tip

■ The one behavior that does change depending on the stacking order is the Stop parameter behavior (see the "Hey, That's Not What I Wanted!" sidebar on the previous page). Any behaviors that are above it aren't impacted. Very handy!

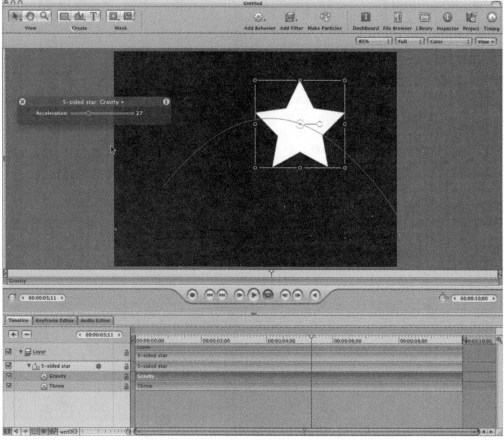

Figure 6.12 Behaviors work together for the final effect. Here, a Throw behavior from the Basic Motion category is combined with a Gravity behavior from the Simulation category. The result is that the object moves in a realistic arc similar to how a ball would travel if thrown.

Using Basic Motion Behaviors

The group of *Basic Motion* behaviors includes six behaviors: five of them animate a single parameter, and one modifies how an object travels along a motion path.

Fade In/Fade Out animates the opacity parameter of an object from 0 percent up to 100 percent at the beginning, and from 100 percent down to 0 percent at the end. You can modify the duration of the fade in and the fade out by dragging on the handles in the Dashboard, which are set to 20 frames by default (**Figure 6.13**).

Grow/Shrink animates the Size parameter. It is not animated by default. In the Dashboard, drag outward on the box to enlarge it or drag inward to shrink it (**Figure 6.14**).

Spin animates the rotation parameter. It is not animated by default. In the Dashboard, click and drag around the ring to determine the direction and rate of spin (**Figure 6.15**).

Throw animates the position parameter. It is not animated by default. In the Dashboard, click and drag in the circle to set the direction and rate of the movement. The further out you drag, the faster the object moves.

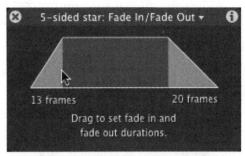

Figure 6.13 You can modify the duration of a fade in/fade out by dragging the handles in the Dashboard in or out.

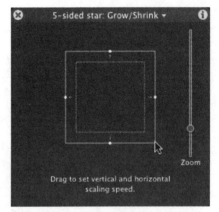

Figure 6.14 Grow/Shrink animates the size parameter. In the Dashboard, drag the box outward to expand the size and inward to shrink it.

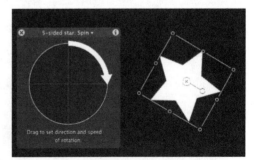

Figure 6.15 Spin animates the rotation parameter. In the Dashboard, click and drag the arrow around the ring to set the direction and rate of spin.

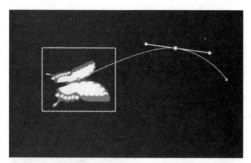

Figure 6.16 Bezier handles allow you to modify the shape of the path.

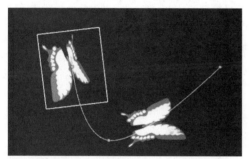

Figure 6.17 Snap Alignment to Motion animates the Rotation parameter as the object moves along the path so that it always points in the direction of the path.

Motion Path, like Throw, animates position, but it does so by creating a *path* along which the object travels. By default the path is a straight line with two *points*, one at the beginning and one at the end of the path. You can change the location of each point by clicking and dragging, and you can create additional points along the path by either double-clicking or Option-clicking the path (I find it's easier to Option-click). Each new point has *Bezier* handles, which allow you to modify the shape of the path (**Figure 6.16**). For more information on working with Bezier points, see Chapter 12.

Snap Alignment to Motion is used on an object whose position is already animated by a motion path or keyframes. It animates the rotation parameter as the object moves along the path so that the object always points in the direction of the path (**Figure 6.17**). The Dashboard provides control over which object axis follows the motion path and allows you to invert the axis.

✔ Tips

- You can eliminate one side of the Fade In/Fade Out behavior by dragging the number of frames in the Dashboard down to zero.

- If you have already changed an object's opacity, the Fade In/Fade Out behavior multiplies the effect setting by the current opacity. In other words, if you have opacity set at 60 percent, it fades in from 0 percent to 60 percent and out from 60 percent down to 0 percent.

- If you want the object to grow or shrink non-proportionally (for example, you want it to get taller or fatter), then click directly on the dots around the square in the Dashboard. There is no way to do this in the Behaviors tab of the Inspector!

continues on next page

USING BASIC MOTION BEHAVIORS

- An object grows or shrinks around its anchor point, so moving the anchor point allows you to pin the object down on one edge and animate it from that point (**Figure 6.18**). See Chapter 4 for information on working with the anchor point.

- To increase the rate of spin using the Spin behavior, drag around the circle multiple times.

- When you're using the Spin behavior, the object rotates around its anchor point, so moving the anchor point (see Chapter 4) causes the entire object to rotate around in a circle rather than just spinning.

- For the Throw behavior, use the Zoom control on the Dashboard to adjust the scale. When you zoom all the way in, dragging the arrow makes small moves; when you zoom out, you can make very large moves.

- If you hold down the Shift key while dragging, the direction of movement of the Throw behavior is constrained to 45 degree increments.

- With the Throw behavior, when you hold down the Command key, you can change the direction of the movement without changing the speed.

- You can change the speed at which the object moves along the motion path either by trimming the behavior in the Timeline or by adjusting its End Offset parameter in the Inspector.

- Control-clicking a motion path point reveals a drop-down menu in which you can toggle the point type between linear and smooth, delete the point, lock it, or disable it.

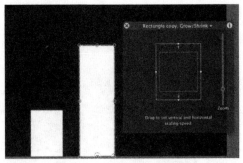

Figure 6.18 Animation is based on the anchor point location. With the anchor point repositioned to the bottom of the bar, the Grow/Shrink behavior, when stretched vertically, causes the bar to grow up from the base rather growing both upwards and downwards from the center.

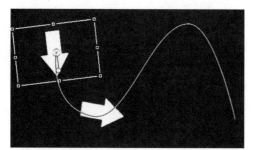

Figure 6.19 Align to Motion (Simulation) is not as precise as Snap Alignment to Motion—as the arrow moves along the path, it adjusts to point in the direction of travel, but it continuously overshoots as it does so.

Using Simulation Behaviors

Simulation behaviors are a group of behaviors that mimic the real-world movement and interaction of objects. You can apply some of these behaviors, like Gravity or Wind, to a single object. Others, like Attracted To or Orbit Around cause objects to interact with each other.

You can use combinations of these behaviors to create extraordinarily complex animations that are difficult, if not impossible, to create with keyframes (see Chapter 7 for information on working with keyframes).

You apply and modify simulation behaviors in the same manner as Basic Motion behaviors (see "Using Basic Motion Behaviors" earlier in the chapter). Below is brief description of each behavior and it's primary parameters.

Align to Motion (Simulation) is similar to the Snap Alignment to Motion behavior found in the Basic Motion group in that it causes an object that is already animated along a motion path to rotate so that it points along the path as it travels. The difference is that Align to Motion isn't as precise; as the object rotates, it moves past the path alignment, then it springs back, with the same amount of overshoot depending on how much Drag is applied (**Figure 6.19**).

Attracted To makes an object move toward a specified object. You control how strong the attraction is, where the attraction starts to affect the attracted object, and how much the object overshoots the object it is attracted to before it gets pulled back toward it again.

Attractor causes all objects in the Canvas to move toward the object that has the Attractor behavior applied. You can adjust the distance from the object where the attraction starts and the strength of the attraction.

Drag simulates the effect of friction on an object that is already animated with other behaviors or keyframes.

Drift Attracted To is like Attracted To except that the object doesn't bounce back and forth if it overshoots the object. How close it comes to the object or how far it overshoots is determined by the Drag control.

Drift Attractor works like the Attractor behavior except that objects moving toward the object with the behavior applied don't bounce around if they overshoot. How close they come to the object or how far they overshoot is determined by the Drag control.

Edge Collision causes already animated objects to stop or bounce when they come to the edge of the Canvas, depending on the setting of the Bounce Strength slider. You can determine which edges of the Canvas cause the collision to occur.

Gravity makes an object accelerate downward, simulating the effect of gravity. You can adjust the amount of acceleration.

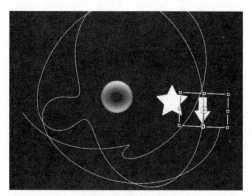

Figure 6.20 By orbiting objects around other orbiting objects, you can create complex animations.

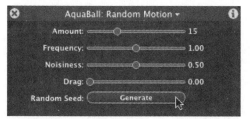

Figure 6.21 The path created from the Random Motion behavior is random, but it is also unchanging. Create a new random motion path by clicking the Generate button in the Dashboard.

Orbit Around does pretty much what you'd expect: it makes the object move in a circle around the object you choose. By default, the Strength is set to allow the object one full rotation for the duration of the effect. You can adjust the direction of the orbit, and you can make the orbit spiral into the object with the Drag control. By orbiting objects around other orbiting objects, you can create complex animations (**Figure 6.20**).

Random Motion applies a random motion path to an object. Although the motion is random, once applied, it is unchanging. You can create a new random motion by clicking the Generate button in the Dashboard (**Figure 6.21**).

Repel is the opposite of the Attractor behavior, and it pushes all objects away from the object to which it is applied. You can choose which objects are repelled by dragging them from the Layers tab or Layer list in the Timeline to the Behaviors tab of the Inspector.

Repel From causes an object to move away from a specified object.

Rotational Drag works just like Drag, but it slows down rotation instead of the position.

Spring makes one object behave as if it were attached to another object, set in the Attracted To control, by a spring. It moves toward that object, bouncing back and forth, in a spring-like fashion.

Vortex is the opposite of Orbit Around. It makes other objects rotate around the object to which it is applied. Vortex is a bit of a misnomer because by default, the objects just orbit. But by increasing the Drag control, you make the objects fall toward the center of the object to which the behavior is applied.

Wind makes an object move in a particular direction with a particular velocity. It differs from the Throw behavior in that it applies a constant force that you can vary over time with keyframes or parameter behaviors.

✔ Tips

- You can apply the Attracted To behavior to the same object multiple times, and you can define a different attracting object for each instance. This causes the object to get pulled in different directions at the same time.

- By default, Attractor affects all objects, but you can use the drop-down list in the Inspector to have it affect just the objects in the same layer (which Motion calls related objects) or you can choose specific objects by dragging them to the Affected Objects list.

- Other objects continue to be attracted to the object with the Attractor behavior even when it is moving, which creates a "follow the leader" effect.

- By default, objects attracted to the Attractor object never come to a rest, thus continuing to overshoot the target. To make them come to a stop, use the Attractor behavior's Drag control.

- If an object has multiple behaviors applied, the Drag behavior is an easy way to slow an object down because it acts universally on the combination of all behaviors animating the object, rather than on just one behavior.

- Edge Collision only works at the very edge of the Canvas.

- With the Edge Collision behavior, the bounding box of the object is usually what determines when an object hits the edge of the Canvas (the exceptions are text and particles, which use the object's center as the point that hits the edge of the Canvas). You can alter the bounding box with the Crop tool, which you may find useful for objects with an alpha channel—you can tighten up the bounding box so that the object appears to touch the edge of the Canvas before bouncing back.

- Normally with the Gravity behavior, objects continue to move off the edge of the Canvas. If you apply the Edge Collision behavior in combination with Gravity, the object bounces when it hits the bottom of the Canvas.

- If you combine Gravity with Throw set to an upward direction, you can create a realistic arcing motion path.

- With the Gravity behavior, you can apply a negative acceleration amount to make an object fly up and away. You can only do this in the Inspector, not the Dashboard, and only by scrubbing in the value field, not by dragging the slider. Sneaky!

- If there are other forces impacting the object, like Attractor or Repel, they affect the Orbit Around path.

- If the target object is moving, the object with the Orbit Around behavior attempts to follow it as it orbits.

- You can quickly animate multiple objects by applying Random Motion to the layer that contains the objects. Each object has a unique random path.

- Animating the object to which the Spring object is attracted can create interesting and complex motion.

- Throw applies a one-time force at the first frame of the animation, so it can't be changed later in time. Wind is useful when you want to change the velocity and/or direction of the object over time.

Those Tricky Wells

Many of the simulation behaviors such as Attracted To, Repel From, and Orbit Around include a well for identifying a target object (**Figure 6.22**). To use the well, you need to drag an object from either the Layers tab in the Project pane or the Layer list in the Timeline into it. But be careful! When you click the object to select it, make sure you keep holding the mouse down and don't let go until you are over the well. If you click and let go, the object becomes selected, and the well disappears from both the Dashboard and Inspector.

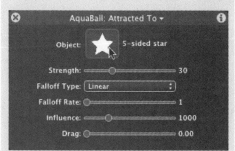

Figure 6.22 Many simulation behaviors include a well for identifying a target object. You must drag an object into the well for the animation to have any effect.

Using Common Simulation Controls

Many of the simulation behaviors have similar controls that adjust the physics of the movements and interactions of objects.

Working with the Object Well

The Object well appears for any simulation behavior that needs a target object, such as Attracted To or Orbit Around.

To use the Object well:

1. Select the behavior.

   The Object well appears in either the Dashboard or the Behaviors tab of the Inspector.

2. Drag the object from either the Layers tab or the Layer list in the Timeline to the well.

3. Release the mouse when you see the hooked arrow (**Figure 6.23**).

The Affect Objects check box

The Affect Objects check box only appears when you apply a behavior to a layer (**Figure 6.24**). When this box is checked, the behavior acts as if it were applied to each object individually. When it is unchecked, the objects behave as if they are all one object. Note that Affect Objects is available for all behaviors, not just simulation behaviors.

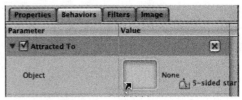

Figure 6.23 When dragging an object into the well, hold down the mouse until you see the hooked arrow.

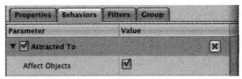

Figure 6.24 The Affect Objects check box only appears when a behavior is applied to a layer. When checked, objects in the layer are affected individually. Unchecked, the objects all act at one.

Figure 6.25 You can choose which objects are affected by a behavior by selecting Specific Objects from the Affect pop-up menu.

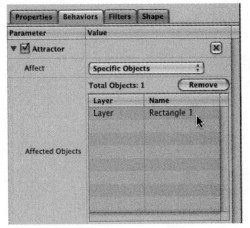

Figure 6.26 Next, drag the objects into the list box from the Layers tab.

The Affect parameter

The Affect parameter, which is contained in several simulation behaviors such as Attractor and Repel, determines which objects in the Canvas are affected by the behavior. By default, all objects are affected.

To affect specific objects:

1. Select the behavior.

2. *Do one of the following:*

   ▲ In the Affect drop-down list, choose Related Objects to affect all objects on the same layer as the object with the behavior applied. Objects on other layers will not be affected by the behavior.

   ▲ Choose Specific Objects from the Affect drop-down list, then drag objects from the Layers tab or the Timeline Layer list into the Affected Objects list that appears (**Figures 6.25** and **6.26**).

The Influence parameter

The Influence parameter determines the radius within which the behavior affects other objects. Objects outside the influence range are not affected by the behavior.

The Strength parameter

The Strength parameter adjusts the speed of objects as they influence or are influenced by other objects. For example, if you increase Strength for the Orbit Around behavior, an object will orbit around another object faster.

The Falloff Type parameter

If this parameter is set to Linear, then the attraction between objects falls off, or decreases, in proportion to the distance between the objects (within the area of influence). If it is set to Exponential, the strength of attraction decreases in proportion to the square of the distance, so it falls off much faster.

The Falloff Rate parameter

The Falloff Rate parameter determines how quickly the force of attraction between objects increases as objects move closer together. Higher values make objects accelerate more slowly.

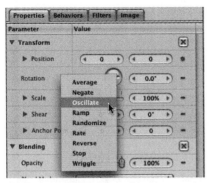

Figure 6.27 Control-click on the parameter you want to animate with a parameter behavior and choose from the drop-down list.

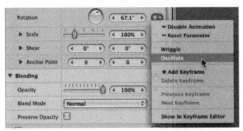

Figure 6.28 By clciking the gear-shaped icon that appears in the Animation menu in the Inspector next to the parameter that has been animated, you can see a list of all parameter behaviors that are applied to that parameter.

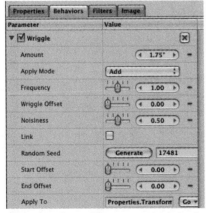

Figure 6.29 If you select a parameter behavior from the list associated with the gear-shaped icon, the Behaviors tab comes forward, so you can adjust the parameter behaviors.

Applying Parameter Behaviors

Parameter behaviors are aptly named: they are a group of behaviors that you apply to a specific parameter rather than to an object, and they only affect that parameter. They are incredibly powerful because you can apply them to just about any parameter of any object or of any effect, including filters, generators, particle systems, or other behaviors—even other parameter behaviors! Once you apply them, you can easily change which parameter a parameter behavior is animating.

To apply a parameter behavior:

1. Select the object that contains a parameter you want to animate.

2. In the Properties tab of the Inspector, Control-click the name of the parameter that you want to animate and select the parameter behavior from the drop-down list (**Figure 6.27**).

   A gear-shaped behavior icon now appears in the Animation menu in the Inspector, next to the parameter that has been animated.

3. Click the gear-shaped icon to reveal a list of all the parameter behaviors applied to that parameter (**Figure 6.28**); selecting from this list brings the Behaviors tab forward (**Figure 6.29**).

✔ Tips

■ The same gear-shaped behavior icon appears in the keyframe menu of the Keyframe Editor for each animated parameter. For more on using the Keyframe Editor, see Chapter 7.

■ Parameter behaviors also appear in the Layers tab and the Timeline, just like other behaviors.

■ You can animate the parameters of filters, masks, particles, and even certain behaviors with parameter behaviors. Select the appropriate object or effect, and Control-click the parameter in the Behaviors, Filters, or Object tab, depending on what you selected.

■ You can of course also add parameter behaviors to most of the parameters in the Properties tab for an object, such as position, scale, and rotation.

To change which parameter is affected by the parameter behavior:

1. Select the object.

2. In the Behavior tab of the Inspector, under Apply To for that behavior, choose a new parameter from the Go fly-out menu (**Figure 6.30**).

✔ Tip

■ All the parameters you can animate by parameter behaviors appear in the Apply To's Go menu. Some parameters can *only* be chosen here, so if you find that nothing happens when you Control-click a parameter name, apply the behavior to a different parameter and then see if you can change the parameter to the one you want in the Go menu.

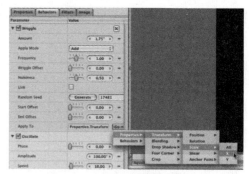

Figure 6.30 When changing which parameter is affected by the parameter behavior, choose the new parameter from the Go fly-out menu.

APPLYING PARAMETER BEHAVIORS

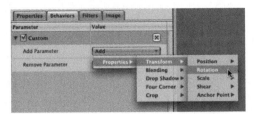

Figure 6.31 When creating a custom behavior, first apply it, then go to the Behaviors tab and choose the parameters you want to animate from the Add drop-down menu.

Using Parameter Behaviors

There are ten different parameter behaviors, including one that is designed just for building your own custom behavior that you can save in the Library for future use. Below is a short description of each parameter behavior and its controls.

Average smoothes the effect of other keyframes or behaviors applied to an object. For instance, it smoothes out a jagged motion path, or calms down a Random behavior. Adjust the Window Size to set the number of frames over which the value is averaged.

Custom lets you to create your own behavior by choosing and animating parameters.

To create a custom behavior:

1. Select the object to animate.

2. Apply the Custom parameter behavior by dragging it onto the object from the Library or choosing it from the Behavior icon in the Toolbar.

3. In the Behaviors tab, choose the parameters you want to animate from the Add drop-down menu (**Figure 6.31**).

4. Animate the selected parameters in the Keyframe Editor (see Chapter 7 for information on working with keyframes).

5. Save the completed behavior by dragging it to the appropriate folder in the Library (see "Saving Customized Behaviors" later in this chapter).

Negate multiplies the parameter to which it is applied by –1 with the result that the animation becomes reversed. For example, clockwise rotation becomes counterclockwise.

Oscillate moves back and forth between two parameter values, creating a repeated cycling effect. For example, imagine an object moving back and forth across the screen, expanding and contracting, or rotating back and forth. You choose an end-point value called the *amplitude* (the other end-point value is determined by multiplying the amplitude by –1), the speed of the change between those values (the *frequency*), and where in the cycle the animation begins (the *phase*).

Ramp changes the value of a parameter from a beginning value to an end value gradually over time based on the duration of the effect. Although it may seem just like Grow/Shrink if applied to the Scale parameter, or Throw if applied to the Position parameter, Ramp is more flexible in two key ways: first, you can adjust how the object animates between the two values with the *Curvature* slider (see "Using Common Behavior Controls" later in this chapter). Second, you can apply Ramp to just about any parameter or object.

Randomize creates random values of a parameter based on a range that you set. You can also set the number of times per second the values change (*frequency*) and the variance in the amount of randomness (*noisiness*).

Rate changes a parameter value continuously over time. Whereas Ramp starts at one value and ends at another, Rate continues for the duration of the effect with no ending value.

Reverse switches the starting and ending values of animated objects, as opposed to Negate, which inverts each value. For example, you can use Reverse to change the direction of a motion path.

Motion's Coordinate System

When Negate is applied to the Position parameter, is has the effect of moving the object to the opposite quadrant in the Canvas. This is because Motion's coordinate system places (0,0) at the center of the Canvas. Moving left from the vertical center creates negative x values, and moving down from horizontal center creates negative y values.

If you applied Negate to the position of an object that is animated along a motion path with the expectation that it will reverse the path, you'll find instead that Motion just moves the path to the opposite quadrant. To reverse the movement along the path, use the—you guessed it—Reverse parameter behavior.

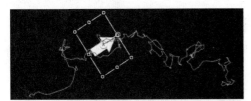

Figure 6.32 Applying the Wriggle parameter behavior to the position parameter of an object that has the Motion Path behavior applied causes the object to move erratically along the motion path. To see the path, select the object.

■ Applying Wriggle to the Position parameter of an object that is animated with the Motion Path behavior creates a more random motion that still starts and ends at the locations specified by the motion path.. When you select the object or the Wriggle behavior, the modified motion path is visible as a red line in the Canvas (**Figure 6.32**).

Stop freezes an animation at the point it's applied. Any behaviors that affect the same parameter and are stacked below it are suspended. Keyframes are also suspended. If you want the animation to start up again, trim the Stop behavior's out point.

Wriggle is similar to Randomize, but the effect is slower.

✔ Tips

■ When you apply Negate to the Scale parameter, the object gets flipped to a mirror image; the result is the same as if you dragged on the resize handles in the Canvas down past zero to a negative scale value.

■ When you apply Negate to a parameter that can't have a negative value, like Opacity, Blur, or Color, the parameter is forced to zero (which in the case of Color means black).

■ Like many other behaviors, the action created by Oscillate changes quite dramatically if you move the anchor point. For example, if you apply Oscillate to the Rotation parameter and move the anchor point outside, the behavior creates a pendulum-type swing.

■ Once you apply the Randomize parameter behavior, it does not change. In other words, every time you play your composition, the random movement is the same random movement. If you'd like to change it, you can generate a new random seed by clicking the Generate button in the Inspector.

■ To have Rate decrease rather than increase in value, enter a negative number.

Exploring Common Behavior Controls

Many behaviors contain similar controls for adjusting the way they impact the animation, whether in the Dashboard or the Inspector.

The Dashboard Zoom Level control

Several behaviors, such as Throw and Grow/Shrink, have a Zoom control in the Dashboard (**Figure 6.33**). By moving the slider, you adjust the field of view for the animated parameter, from making very small changes to very large ones.

✔ Tip

■ When using the Dashboard, you may find you can't make the value of a parameter go as high as you'd like. The fact is, the Dashboard limits not only the number of parameters that it displays but also the range of values that you can set for some of those parameters. If you can't go as high as you'd like, check out the same parameter in the Inspector and see if you can create a higher value there. Try Shift-dragging in the value field to change the value in larger increments.

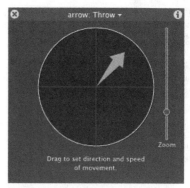

Figure 6.33 Some behaviors have a Zoom control in the Dashboard. This lets you adjust the field of view for the animated parameter.

The Curvature slider

Several parameter behaviors, like Rate and Ramp, have a *Curvature* slider, which affects how the animation starts and stops. As you increase the slider value, objects start and stop slower, but speed up in between. Curvature is essentially a combined ease in/ease out control.

The Apply Mode control

The Apply Mode control, used in Random and Wriggle, determines how the parameter values are combined with values from other parameters or keyframes that may be applied to an object. You can add to those values, subtract from them, multiply, or add *and* subtract.

The Offset controls

All parameter behaviors have Start Offset and End Offset controls, which adjust the point when a behavior starts and stops. Use the Start Offset to delay a behavior; use the End Offset to make it end sooner.

✔ Tip

- ■ End Offset can be a better tool than trimming the out point of a behavior because the object freezes at the last value rather than returning to its original state.

EXPLORING COMMON BEHAVIOR CONTROLS

Animating Behavior Parameters

Not only can you apply behaviors to animate the parameters of objects without using any keyframes, you can even animate the parameters of the behaviors themselves.

Earlier in this chapter, we looked at how you can animate an object's parameters, such as Position, Scale, Rotation, or Opacity, with parameter behaviors. But you can also apply parameter behaviors to the parameters of another behavior, or even of another parameter behavior! Confused yet? I'll now provide some examples to illustrate.

What About Basic Motion Behaviors?

You may have noticed that you can't apply parameter behaviors to the parameters of basic motion behaviors such as Throw, Spin, and Grow/Shrink. However, you can usually get the result you want with another method.

For example, say you want to have an object Spin, but then change the spin direction at a certain point. You might first try to apply the Reverse parameter to the Spin Rate parameter, but you'd find that it can't be done.

Instead, don't use Spin at all; just apply the Rate parameter behavior to the Rotation parameter to make it spin; then add the Reverse parameter behavior at the point where you want it to change direction. Better yet, apply Oscillate with a low frequency number and a high amplitude—this way you'll get a more natural slowing down and speeding up when the object changes spin direction.

In general, think about what parameter the Basic Motion behavior is affecting, and then animate it directly with a parameter behavior. At this point, you have full control to add other parameter behaviors to the same parameter, or even to the parameter behaviors themselves. You'll need to think about that one a bit!

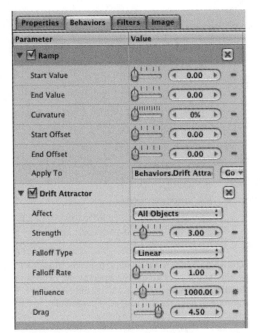

| Properties | Behaviors | Filters | Image |

Parameter	Value
▼ ☑ Ramp	☒
Start Value	0.00 —
End Value	0.00 —
Curvature	0% —
Start Offset	0.00 —
End Offset	0.00 —
Apply To	Behaviors.Drift Attra Go ▾
▼ ☑ Drift Attractor	☒
Affect	All Objects
Strength	3.00 —
Falloff Type	Linear
Falloff Rate	1.00 —
Influence	1000.0(✳
Drag	4.50 —

Figure 6.34 When you apply a parameter behavior, Motion automatically brings the Behavior tab forward so you can adjust the, um, parameters of the parameter behavior.

Applying parameter behaviors to a simulation behavior

You can animate pretty much any parameter of simulation behaviors that can take a range of values. You do this by applying parameter behaviors to the simulation behaviors in the same manner that you apply them to the parameters of objects. For example, if you apply a Ramp to the Drift Attractor's Influence parameter, you can cause objects that are more distant from the object with the behavior applied to remain stationary at first, but then move toward the object as the influence range grows.

To apply a parameter behavior to a simulation behavior:

1. Apply a simulation behavior to an object and select it.

2. In the Behaviors tab of the Inspector, Control-click the parameter you want to animate, and choose a parameter behavior from the drop-down list.

   The new behavior appears at the top of the Behaviors tab and is highlighted (**Figure 6.34**).

3. Adjust the parameter behavior controls as you desire (see "Using Parameter Behaviors" earlier in this chapter).

✔ Tip

■ If you want to change the behavior's parameter to which the parameter behavior is applied (read that three times!), click the Go button under the Apply To section of the parameter behavior and select a new parameter of that behavior from the fly-out menu.

ANIMATING BEHAVIOR PARAMETERS

Apply parameter behaviors to other parameter behaviors

Yes, that's what I said! You can create quite amazing animations by recursively applying parameter behaviors on top of each other.

For a simple example, let's say you have applied the Oscillate parameter behavior to the Rotation of an object. This creates a smooth rocking back and forth behavior. If you then apply a Ramp parameter behavior to the Amplitude of the Oscillate behavior, you can make the object's rocking increase or decrease over time.

To apply a parameter behavior to another parameter behavior:

1. In the Inspector, Control-click the parameter in the parameter behavior that you want to animate and select a parameter behavior from the drop-down menu (**Figure 6.35**).

   The new behavior appears at the top of the Behaviors tab and is highlighted.

2. Adjust the parameter behavior controls as you desire.

Of course, you can apply parameter behaviors to multiple behavior parameters. You can continue to apply parameter behaviors on top of each new parameter behavior as many times as you'd like. Just remember to stop to eat occasionally.

Keyframing behaviors

Sometimes you'll want to add keyframes to behaviors to get the results you want.

Converting behaviors to keyframes

You can take a behavior that you've applied and lock down the animation by converting the behavior into keyframes that you can then manipulate directly. See Chapter 7.

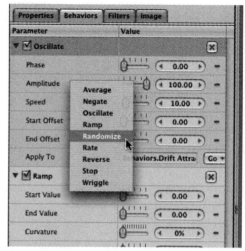

Figure 6.35 To apply a parameter behavior to another parameter behavior go to the Inspector and Control-click the parameter in the parameter behavior that you want to animate. Then select a parameter behavior from the drop-down menu.

Figure 6.36 To save a customized behavior, select the behavior and drag it to the File Stack in the Library.

Saving Customized Behaviors

Once you have adjusted a behavior to get it working just the way you like, wouldn't it be great if you could save all those setting so you could apply them to other objects without starting from scratch? No problem—Favorites to the rescue.

To save a customized behavior:

1. In the Library, select the Behaviors, Favorites, or Favorites Menu folder.

2. Select the behavior in the Layers tab, the Timeline, or the Inspector and drag it to the File Stack portion of the Library (**Figure 6.36**).

   In large icon view, the icon has a little person silhouette attached to indicate that it is a custom behavior.

✔ Tips

- You can create a new folder in any of the selected folders to better organize your custom behaviors.

- Before saving your custom behavior, give it a descriptive name that indicates what it does. Double-click the name in the Layers tab or the Timeline and type the new name. You can also name it after you save it by Control-clicking it in the File Stack and choosing Rename from the drop-down menu.

Custom or Customized?

Okay, it's time to clear up some confusing nomenclature. A *custom behavior* is a type of parameter behavior in which you choose which parameters to animate and then animate them with keyframes, as discussed in "Using Parameter Behaviors" earlier in this chapter.

A *customized behavior* is any behavior that you adjust by changing its default settings.

You can save both custom behaviors and customized behaviors in the Library.

ANIMATING WITH KEYFRAMES

7

In this chapter, I introduce the concept of keyframes, which are central to the animation process. Behaviors are amazingly fast and useful, but sometimes keyframes are the best way to go. And sometimes you'll want to use both.

After defining keyframes, I cover how to set them for parameters using different aspects of the Motion interface including the Canvas, the Dashboard, and the Inspector. Then I dive into how to modify keyframes, first exploring the Timeline, and then going deep into how to use the primary tool for working with keyframes, the Keyframe Editor.

I discuss how to interpolate the animation between keyframes, which Motion calls *curves*, and I explore how you can repeat keyframe data through extrapolation.

I explain how to use keyframe filters and then cover the different ways you can use behaviors and keyframes together. I finish up by describing how to create animation on the fly, leveraging the incredible real-time playback performance of Motion.

Understanding Keyframes

The concept of keyframes is quite straightforward. A *keyframe* is a fixed value of a parameter at a specific point in time (**Figures 7.1** and **Figure 7.2**). For example, you can set a keyframe so that an object's Scale parameter is set to 50 percent at 10 seconds. Or a Gaussian Blur filter's amount is set to 4 pixels of blur at 12 frames. Or an Oscillate parameter behavior's amplitude is set to 10 pixels at 1 minute.

Setting one keyframe, however, doesn't animate a darn thing; it just fixes the value of a parameter at a point in time. The magic happens when you have at least *two keyframes at different points in time with different values*. The parameter value then changes, or *animates*, between each keyframe.

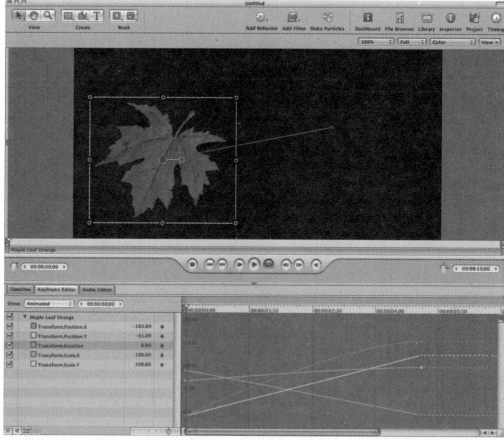

Figure 7.1 A keyframe represents a specific value for a parameter at a specific point in time. Here, values for the Position, Rotation and Scale of the leaf have been set at the first frame and at five seconds.

UNDERSTANDING KEYFRAMES

Once you have set keyframes, Motion provides some powerful tools for modifying them. You can make basic changes in the Timeline, or open the Keyframe Editor for full access to all the keyframe adjustment tools.

Because the value of the parameter is changing from one keyframe to the next, Motion needs to figure out how to change the value over time. The way in which Motion changes parameter values as it moves between keyframes is called *interpolation*. Normally Motion creates a steady transition between two keyframe values. So, for example, an object moves across the Canvas at a constant rate of speed, or scales up steadily over time, or gradually becomes blurrier. The process for changing keyframe interpolation is discussed in "Keyframe Interpolation" later in this chapter.

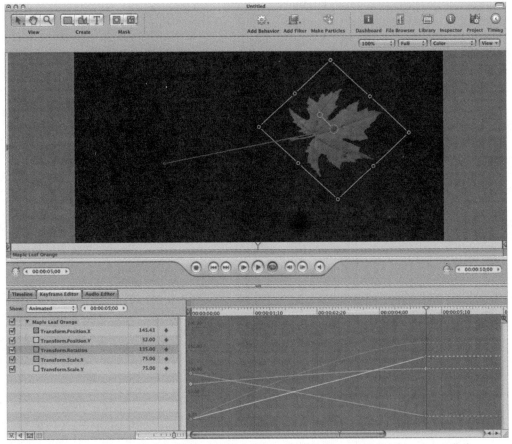

Figure 7.2 The leaf then animates between the keyframe values. The lines between the keyframes are called curves and represent how the animation changes over time.

Setting Keyframes

The simplest way to set keyframes with Motion is to use the Record Animation button, located with the transport controls at the bottom of the Canvas. With the Record Animation button, you can set keyframes in the Canvas, the Dashboard, or the Inspector. The Inspector also provides an alternate method for setting keyframes and provides some additional controls.

Setting keyframes in the Canvas

The quickest and easiest way to keyframe an object's Transform parameters (Position, Rotation, Scale, Shear, and Anchor Point) is to manipulate them directly in the Canvas while the Record button is activated. You can also keyframe the Drop Shadow, Four Corner, and Crop parameters in the Canvas. For information on making transformations in the Canvas, see Chapter 4.

To set keyframes on object properties in the Canvas:

1. Select the object and press Shift-I to move the playhead to the object's in point.

2. Enable keyframe recording by *doing one of the following:*

   ▲ Choose Mark > Record Animation.

   ▲ Press the Record button.

   ▲ Press the letter A on the keyboard.

3. Set your starting parameter values in the Canvas (Position, Rotation, Scale, and so on). If the values are already set, move to step 4.

4. Move the playhead to the time position for the second keyframe.

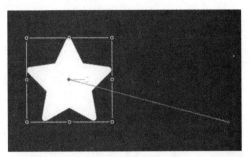

Figure 7.3 As the playhead moves between keyframes, the value of the parameter changes from the preceding keyframe to the next keyframe.

5. Adjust the appropriate parameters on the object in the Canvas.

For example, to change position, drag the object to the new position. To change Scale, drag one of the corner control handles. To change Rotation, drag the center control handle. To change Shear, Anchor point, Drop shadow, Four corner, or Crop, first select the appropriate tool from the Toolbar or Control-click the object and select the parameter you want from the drop-down list.

Now the parameter for which you have set keyframes changes as the playhead moves between them (**Figure 7.3**).

✔ Tips

■ You can keep adding as many keyframes as you like. Make sure Record Animation is turned on (the button glows with a pulsing red color), move to a new location in the Timeline, and adjust the desired parameter. Using this method you can, for example, very quickly create a motion path.

■ Record Animation always sets a keyframe at the beginning of the object. Therefore, it's not required to move the playhead to the object's in point before you record an animation; just place the playhead at the desired location for the second keyframe, turn on Record, and adjust the parameters.

■ If you don't want a keyframe at the beginning of the object, use the Inspector's Animation menu to set keyframes—see "Setting Keyframes in the Inspector" later in this chapter.

continues on next page

SETTING KEYFRAMES

- If you create keyframes for position, you'll see a red motion path. If you don't see the path, make sure that Animation Path has a check mark in the View menu on the Toolbar (**Figure 7.4**). You can create additional keyframes on the path either by the above method, or by Option-clicking any point of the path to add a keyframe (first click either end of the motion path to select it). Dragging immediately after Option-clicking while the mouse is still depressed creates a Bezier handle for smoothing and adjusting the motion path (**Figure 7.5**). To create Bezier handles for an existing point, Command-click on it and drag. For more information on working with Bezier handles, see Chapter 12.

- If you want an object to rotate more than once, continue to spin it around with the drag handle in the Canvas. To see how many times you have rotated it, open the Properties tab of the Inspector (press F1 to reveal it) and observe the Rotation parameter value as you rotate the object.

- If you change a parameter when Record Animation is turned off and the playhead is not parked on a keyframe, Motion adds the change every frame of the animation For example, for the Position parameter, this means that dragging the object moves the entire motion path (**Figure 7.6**). However, if the playhead is parked directly on a keyframe when you make the change, it only changes that particular keyframe value. For information on how to navigate to keyframes, see "The Inspector's Animation Menu" later in this chapter.

- You can also use Record Animation to, well, record an animation by making adjustments to an object on the fly while the Timeline is playing. See "On-the-Fly Keyframing" later in this chapter for details.

Figure 7.4 If you don't see a red motion path, check to see that Animation Path has a check mark in the View menu on the Toolbar.

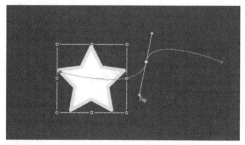

Figure 7.5 Option-click-drag to create a Bezier point on a motion path and set the length and angle of the handles, which determine the angle and amount of curvature.

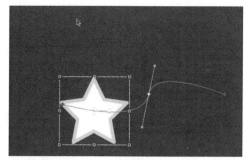

Figure 7.6 When Record Animation is turned on, dragging an object will create another point on a motion path. If Record Animation is turned off, as in this example, dragging the object simply moves the entire motion path along with the object—unless you happen to be parked directly on a keyframe, in which case you will only move that one keyframe.

SETTING KEYFRAMES

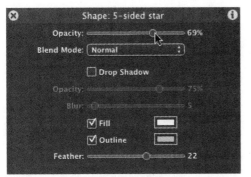

Figure 7.7 In the Dashboard, drag the slider for the parameter you want in order to set the initial value.

Setting keyframes in the Dashboard

Using the Dashboard rather than the Canvas to set keyframes provides more precise control over specific parameter values and allows you to keyframe parameters that aren't available in the Canvas, like Opacity, or parameters of effects such as filters and behaviors. You can even keyframe masks.

To set keyframes using the Dashboard:

1. Select the object, mask, or effect you want to keyframe.

2. Click the Record button or press A.

3. Position the playhead where you want the second keyframe (Motion automatically places a keyframe at the beginning of the object when using Record Animation).

4. If the Dashboard isn't visible, press D or F7. Drag the slider for the parameter you want to animate to set the initial value (**Figure 7.7**).

5. Move the playhead to the desired location of the next keyframe.

6. Change the parameter value using the slider in the Dashboard.

7. Repeat steps 4 and 5 as needed.

8. Click the Record button or press A to turn off Record Animation.

✔ Tip

■ You can only animate parameters that have slider controls in the Dashboard. This includes parameters for filters, behaviors, particles, and masks, so go crazy! Parameters with check boxes can be animated to turn on and off, but only by using the Keyframe Editor. You cannot animate parameters with drop-down lists.

Setting keyframes in the Inspector

To get the most control over setting keyframes, you'll want to use the Inspector, which contains the complete list of every parameter that can be keyframed and allows you to keyframe either with Record Animation or with the handy Animation menu, which contains a few extra controls. Every tab of the Inspector contains parameters that can be animated with keyframes—object properties, behaviors, filters, and the parameters on the Object tab.

To set keyframes using the Inspector with Record Animation:

1. Select the object or effect you want to keyframe.

2. Click the Record button or press A.

3. Position the playhead on the first frame of the object (press Shift-I).

4. Open the Inspector (press Command-3) and click the tab that contains the parameter you want to animate.

5. Set the parameter to the beginning value (**Figure 7.8**).

6. Move the playhead to the desired location of the next keyframe.

7. Change the parameter value in the Inspector.

✔ Tip

■ Just as when you're animating in the Canvas, Record Animation automatically sets a keyframe at the beginning of the object. If you want the first keyframe to occur later, you can set your second keyframe to have the same value as the beginning keyframe, or you can avoid this automatic behavior by using the Inspector's Animation menu that I cover next.

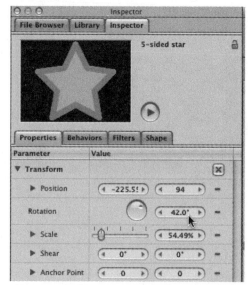

Figure 7.8 In the Inspector, set the parameter to the beginning value.

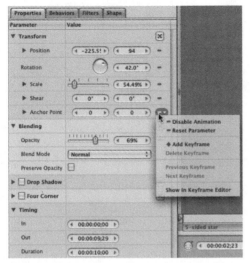

Figure 7.9 Every parameter that can be animated has an Animation menu in the Inspector.

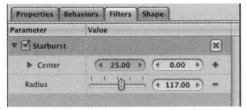

Figure 7.10 A solid gray diamond indicates that the playhead is parked on a keyframe.

The Inspector's Animation menu

Every parameter that can be animated has an Animation menu—represented by a tiny dash—in the Inspector (**Figure 7.9**). In addition to letting you set keyframes, the Animation menu allows you to delete keyframes, disable the animation, jump to keyframes, and view the keyframes in the Keyframe Editor.

However, you'll encounter one difference when setting keyframes with the Animation menu as opposed to using Record Animation: Motion doesn't automatically set a keyframe at the first frame of an object. So if you want an object to remain unanimated for some period before the first keyframe, the Animation menu is the way to go.

To set keyframes in the Animation menu of the Inspector:

1. Select the object or effect you want to keyframe.

2. Position the playhead where you want the first keyframe.

3. Open the Inspector (Command-3) and click the tab that contains the parameter you want to animate.

4. Set the parameter to the beginning value.

5. Click the Animation menu and select Add Keyframe.

   A solid gray diamond appears (**Figure 7.10**). It indicates that the playhead is parked on a keyframe. When the playhead is not on a keyframe, the diamond is hollow.

6. Move the playhead to the desired location of the next keyframe.

7. Click the Animation menu and select Add Keyframe.

8. Set a new value for the parameter.

To disable an animation:

◆ Choose Disable Animation from the Animation menu.

When you do, the values for the keyframes are ignored and the object reverts to its original parameter values. The keyframe information is hidden but not discarded, and you can turn the animation back on by selecting Enable Animation from the same menu.

To jump to a keyframe:

◆ Choose Next Keyframe or Previous Keyframe from the Animation menu.

If an option is grayed out, there are no more keyframes in that direction. Note that when the playhead is parked on a keyframe, the diamond in the Animation menu is solid; if the playhead is anywhere else on a keyframed parameter, the diamond is hollow.

To delete a keyframe:

◆ Choose Delete Keyframe from the Animation menu.

You must be parked on a keyframe to delete it from the Animation menu.

SETTING KEYFRAMES

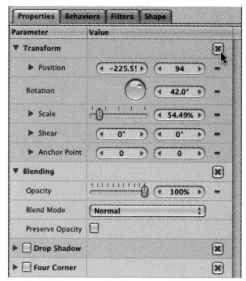

Figure 7.11 Clicking the Reset button resets all parameters in a parameter set.

To delete all keyframes for a parameter:

◆ Choose Reset Parameter from the Animation menu.

All keyframes are deleted and the parameter is reset to its default value.

To show a keyframe in the Keyframe Editor:

◆ Choose Show in Keyframe Editor from the Animation menu.

The Keyframe Editor opens and shows the keyframes for the chosen parameter. See "Using the Keyframe Editor" below for more information.

To reset all parameters in a parameter set:

◆ Click the Reset button to the right of the name of the parameter set (**Figure 7.11**).

✔ Tips

■ The Animation menu is also available in the Keyframe Editor, which is discussed below.

■ When setting keyframes with the Animation menu, it is critical to first add the keyframe, then set the value for the keyframe.

SETTING KEYFRAMES

Modifying Keyframes

Sometimes you can set a few keyframes and everything works just the way you want. But most of the time you will want to modify the keyframes to make them behave a little or a lot differently. Perhaps you need several keyframes on different objects to line up with each other. Or you want to change the value of a keyframe. Or you'd like to change the way the object animates as it moves between keyframes.

There are two tabs in the Timing pane that allow you to modify your object and effect keyframes: the Timeline and the Keyframe Editor (Audio keyframes are modified in the third tab, the Audio Editor, which is covered in Chapter 14). The Timeline allows you to view and change the timing of keyframes, whereas the Keyframe Editor provides tools to make more detailed, precise adjustments to keyframes and the paths between them, which are called *curves* in Motion.

Modifying Keyframes in the Canvas, Dashboard, or Inspector

If you just want to change the value of an existing keyframe, you can do so directly in the Canvas for an object property, or in the Dashboard or Inspector for other parameters. First you need to park the playhead on the keyframe in question. To do this, either drag the playhead in the Ruler area, or park it close to the keyframe; and choose Next Keyframe from the Animation menu in the Inspector. You'll know you are on the keyframe when the hollow diamond in the Inspector turns solid. When it does, adjust the value in the Canvas, Dashboard, or Inspector as appropriate.

For Position keyframes along a motion path, you don't even need to park the playhead on the keyframe—you can click directly on the keyframe in the Canvas and drag it to a new location.

Figure 7.12 To view keyframes in the Timeline, click the Show/Hide Keyframes button.

Modifying keyframes in the Timeline

The Timeline provides you with the ability to view how your keyframes are laid out over time, and it allows you to move them to new locations. It can be extremely useful for lining up keyframes with specific frames, objects, markers, or other keyframes. You can also delete keyframes directly in the Timeline.

When you trim effects that have keyframes applied, the keyframes get scaled by the trim amount by default, but you can override this behavior.

For an overview of the Timeline, see Chapter 5.

To view keyframes in the Timeline:

◆ Click the Show/Hide Keyframes button at the bottom of the Layer list in the Timeline (**Figure 7.12**).

If there are any keyframes applied to an object, they appear as hollow blue diamonds along a white line below the object bar. Keyframes applied to effects appear within the effect's bar itself.

✔ Tips

■ All keyframes applied to an object at a specific frame are represented by just one keyframe icon.

■ If two keyframes are located close together, it helps to zoom in close with the Zoom slider to see them. For more information on using the zoom controls in the Timeline, see "Changing Timeline Appearance" in Chapter 5.

MODIFYING KEYFRAMES

To view the keyframe value in the Timeline:

◆ Control-click the keyframe (**Figure 7.13**). The drop-down menu includes a list of all the keyframes applied at that frame along with their values at that frame.

To move a keyframe in the Timeline:

◆ Click the keyframe and drag it left or right to a new location.

✔ Tips

■ If more than one parameter has a keyframe at a specific frame, moving the keyframe icon moves all the keyframed parameters.

■ Holding down the Shift key while dragging causes the keyframe to snap to in and out points of objects and effects, the playhead, markers, and other keyframes.

■ You can move multiple keyframes from different locations and different objects at the same time by Shift-clicking them (to select contiguous keyframes) or Command-clicking them (to select non-contiguous keyframes) before dragging. Again, holding down the Shift key helps with alignment.

To delete a keyframe in the Timeline:

1. Select the keyframe.

2. *Do one of the following:*

   ▲ Control-click and choose Delete Keyframes from the drop-down menu (**Figure 7.14**).

   ▲ Press the Delete key.

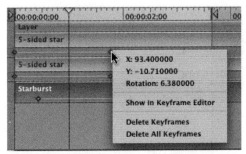

Figure 7.13 To view the keyframe value in the Timeline, simply Control-click the keyframe to reveal a drop-down menu.

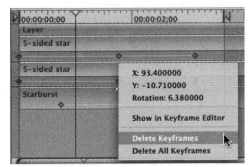

Figure 7.14 Control-click a keyframe and choose Delete Keyframes from the drop-down menu to delete a keyframe in the Timeline. Or, select the keyframe and press the Delete key.

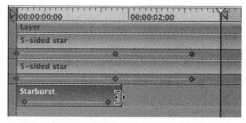

Figure 7.15 By default, when you trim an object or an effect, the keyframes scale to the new duration. To keep the keyframes in their original locations, hold down the Command key, then drag to trim the object or effect.

To delete all keyframes applied to an object or effect:

◆ Control-click one of the keyframes and select Delete All Keyframes from the drop-down menu.

The Show in Keyframe Editor option in the drop-down menu is covered in "Using the Keyframe Editor" later in this chapter.

To scale keyframes applied to an effect:

◆ Trim the effect in the Timeline.

When you do, the keyframes applied to the effect squeeze together or stretch out as you trim (**Figures 7.15**). Note that keyframes applied to objects do not change time location when the object is trimmed. If you want to trim an effect without scaling the keyframes, hold down the Command key as you trim.

✔ Tip

■ When you move a keyframe in the Timeline toward another keyframe, the animation on that parameter speeds up between the keyframes; moving away slows it down.

MODIFYING KEYFRAMES

Using the Keyframe Editor

Although the Timeline provides a condensed, simple view of your keyframes and allows for basic move and align operations, it has its limitations. For instance, when several keyframes occur at the same frame, you can't move just one, and you don't have any control over what is happening *between* the keyframes. Enter the Keyframe Editor—a powerful tool for manipulating keyframes and the curves that represent the animation between the keyframes.

The Keyframe Editor allows you to change the value of each keyframe (by dragging it up or down) as well as its location in time (by dragging it left or right). By viewing how the keyframes are laid out on curves and how curves of different keyframed parameters relate to one another, you can develop an understanding of how the animation unfolds without even seeing it play.

To reveal the Keyframe Editor:

Do one of the following:

◆ Open the Timing pane (press F6) and click the Keyframe Editor tab.

◆ Choose Window > Keyframe Editor.

◆ Press Command-8.

✔ Tips

■ If you have a keyframed parameter, from the Animation menu in the Inspector for that parameter, choose Show in Keyframe Editor. Or, Control-click the keyframe in the Timeline, and select Show in Keyframe Editor from the drop-down menu.

The Keyframe Editor contains a list of parameters on the left side; to the right is a graphical representation of keyframes and curves (**Figure 7.16**).

■ The Keyframe Editor displays a list of parameters for the currently selected object(s) or effect(s). To display the parameters for a different object or effect, select it in the Layers tab rather than the Timeline; this allows you to keep the Keyframe Editor visible.

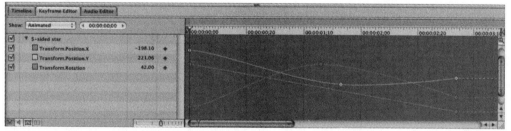

Figure 7.16 The Keyframe Editor contains a list of parameters on the left side and a graphical representation of keyframes and curves on the right.

Navigating in the Keyframe Editor

You move to specific frames or keyframes in the Keyframe Editor as you did in the Timeline.

To move to a frame:

Do one of the following:

- ◆ Click in the Ruler area or drag the playhead.

- ◆ Double-click in the value field of the Current Frame control and enter a value.

- ◆ Click and drag left or right in the Current Frame control.

To move to a keyframe:

1. Park the playhead near the keyframe.

2. In the Animation drop-down menu, choose Previous Keyframe or Next Keyframe (**Figure 7.17**).

✔ Tip

- ■ The Animation menu in the Keyframe Editor contains all the commands of the Animation menu in the Inspector, plus several more commands that are discussed throughout this chapter.

- ■ The Keyframe Editor has a ruler at the top and a Zoom slider and a Zoom/Scroll control at the bottom; these all work identically to the same controls in the Timeline (see "Changing Timeline Appearance" in Chapter 5). You can set the playback range (see "Defining the Play Range" in Chapter 5) and navigate to markers (see "Using Markers" in Chapter 5) as well.

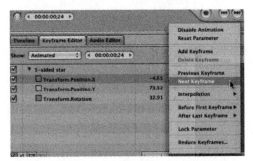

Figure 7.17 To move a keyframe, choose Previous Keyframe or Next Keyframe from the Animation drop-down menu.

Displaying keyframe parameters and graphs

When working in the Keyframe Editor, sometimes you want to focus on one parameter. Other times you want to look at keyframes on several different parameters to see how they relate to each other. When you have many different keyframed elements and parameters, the Keyframe Editor can become very difficult to decipher (**Figure 7.18**), so it's critical that you are able to choose which parameters and which graphs appear at any given time.

With the Curve Set List, Motion provides you with the ability to filter the list of all parameters to predefined subsets. You can also create your own custom sets and save them. And, when you view a list of parameters, you can turn individual graphs on and off.

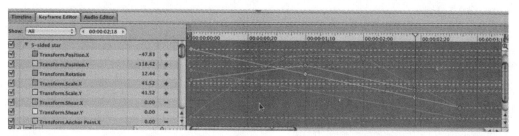

Figure 7.18 When you have many different keyframed elements and parameters, the Keyframe Editor can become quite a jumble.

To view all parameters for all selected items:

◆ Select All from the Curve Set List.

✔ Tip

■ Every parameter for every selected object is displayed in the parameter list, whether they have keyframes or not. Parameters without keyframes display straight dashed lines.

To display the keyframe graph for a parameter:

◆ Check the check box next to the desired parameter.

✔ Tip

■ Checking the check box next to the object name itself turns on the graphs for all the parameters for that object.

To view active parameters for selected items:

◆ Select Active from the Curve Set List.

✔ Tip

■ "Active" means any parameters that you are currently modifying—so if you aren't currently adjusting the value of any parameters, nothing appears. Each time you modify a parameter in the Canvas, Dashboard, or Inspector, that parameter will automatically appear in the Keyframe Editor.

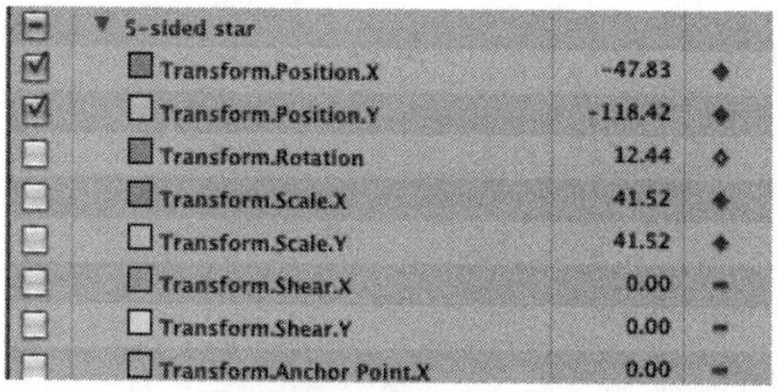

Figure 7.19 You can easily tell which parameters in the parameter list have keyframes applied because they have a diamond in the Animation menu.

To view all parameters with keyframes for all selected items:

◆ Select Animated from the Show drop-down list in the Curve Set list.

✔ Tips

■ You can tell which parameters in the parameter list have keyframes applied because they have a diamond in the Animation menu (**Figure 7.19**). Just as with the Inspector, the diamond is hollow unless the playhead is parked directly on a keyframe, at which time it becomes solid.

■ I find that Animated is the most useful choice from the Curve Set List—select Animated, then turn off the animated parameters you aren't working on by clicking the check box.

To create a new parameter set:

1. Choose New Curve Set from the Curve Set List.

2. In the resulting dialog, type a name for the parameter set and click OK.

   The custom set now appears in the Curve Set List.

✔ Tip

■ When you create a custom parameter set, it contains all the parameters that are in the parameter list when you create it. To start with an empty set, clear out the parameter list by deselecting all objects (Shift-Command-A).

MODIFYING KEYFRAMES

To add parameters to a custom parameter set:

◆ Drag the desired parameters from the Inspector to the parameter list of the Keyframe Editor (**Figure 7.20**).

✔ Tips

■ You can select parameters from any tab of the Inspector.

■ You can add only parameters that can be keyframed to the parameter list. For example, you cannot add the Blend Mode parameter.

To remove parameters from a custom parameter set:

◆ Drag the parameter off the list. It disappears in a puff of smoke.

✔ Tip

■ Be careful where you drag! If the Library is the active tab in the Utility pane and you drag to the File Stack, you will add the parameter to the Library.

To remove all parameters from a custom parameter set:

◆ Click the Clear curve list button at the bottom of the parameter list (**Figure 7.21**).

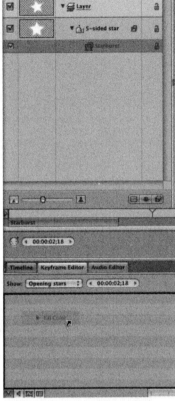

Figure 7.20 To add parameters to a custom parameter set, drag the desired parameters from the Inspector to the parameter list of the Keyframe Editor.

Figure 7.21 Click the Clear Curve List button at the bottom of the parameter list to remove all parameters from a custom parameter set.

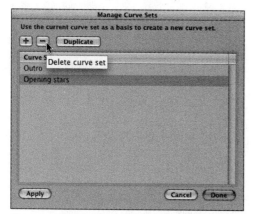

Figure 7.22 To delete a custom parameter set, select the curve set and click the Delete curve set button.

To delete a custom parameter set:

1. Select Manage Curve Sets from the Curve Set List.

2. In the dialog, select the curve set and click the Delete curve set button (**Figure 7.22**).

✔ Tip

■ You can create a new curve set while in the Manage Curve Sets dialog by clicking the Create new curve set button. Double-click the Untitled name to rename it.

To duplicate a custom parameter set:

1. Select Manage Curve Sets from the Curve Set List.

2. In the dialog, click the Duplicate button.

3. To change the name of the duplicate, double-click it.

✔ Tip

■ When you create custom parameter sets, they get saved with the project and are available at any time in the Curve Set List.

MODIFYING KEYFRAMES

Adjusting the graph view

As you manipulate keyframes on different graphs, you may want to zoom in tight to work on a particular section, or zoom out wide to see the overall picture. Motion includes several controls to manipulate your view of the parameter curves in the graph area.

To zoom in or out horizontally:

◆ Drag on either the Zoom slider or the ends of the Zoom/Scroll control at the bottom of the graph area (**Figure 7.23**). These tools work identically to the same tools in the Timeline, discussed in Chapter 5.

To zoom in or out vertically:

◆ Drag on the ends of the vertical Zoom/Scroll control at the right of the graph area.

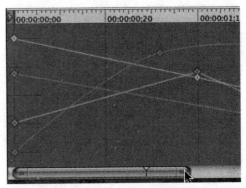

Figure 7.23 Drag the Zoom slider control to zoom in or out horizontally

To automatically fit all visible curves in the window:

◆ Click the Fit visible curves in window button at the bottom of the parameter list. The visible curves are resized both horizontally and vertically to fit (**Figure 7.24**). Very nice!

To dynamically scale vertically to fit curves in the window:

◆ Click the Auto-scale vertically to fit curves button at the top right of the graph area.

As you adjust the value of a keyframe, the window automatically resizes as you drag to fit the full curve into the window.

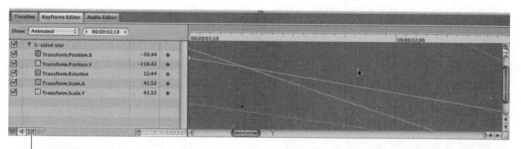

— *Fit visible curves in window button*

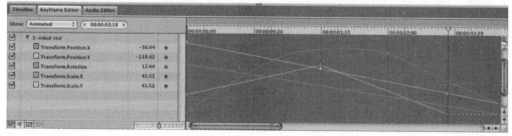

Figure 7.24 By clicking the Fit visible curves in window button, all curves that are currently at least partially visible (above) are automatically resized both horizontally and vertically to just fit in the viewable space (below).

Modifying keyframes in the Keyframe Editor

Once you know how to choose which parameters to include in the parameter list, how to select which graphs for those parameters you want to make active, and how to move around in the graph area, it's time to get to work making changes to your keyframes.

The Keyframe Editor gives you a great deal of control for setting the value and location of keyframes; for adding, deleting, copying, and pasting keyframes; and for adjusting the curves to change the way an animation unfolds in between keyframes.

To change the time location of the keyframe:

◆ Click the keyframe and drag it left or right. The keyframe turns white when selected and two numbers appear—the first indicates the new time location.

To change the value of a keyframe:

◆ Click the keyframe and drag it up or down. The second of the two numbers that appear indicates the new value.

✔ Tips

■ Holding down the Shift key while dragging constrains the motion either vertically or horizontally, so that you can change just the value or just the time location.

■ If you have a specific value in mind for the keyframe, it may be easier to type it in the value field in the Inspector. First make sure you are parked on the keyframe by choosing Next Keyframe or Previous Keyframe from the Animation menu drop-down list and verifying that the keyframe icon is solid.

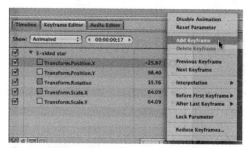

Figure 7.25 To place a keyframe at a precise frame, position the playhead on the frame and select Add Keyframe from the Animation menu.

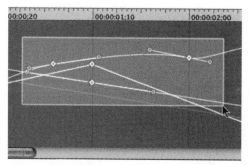

Figure 7.26 One way to select multiple keyframes is to drag a selection box around them.

To add a keyframe:

1. Hold down the Option key and move the pointer over the desired curve at the desired time location.

   The pointer turns into a crosshair.

2. Click the parameter curve.

3. If needed, drag the keyframe to change its value and/or time location.

✔ Tips

- To place a keyframe at a precise frame, position the playhead on the frame and select Add Keyframe from the Animation menu (**Figure 7.25**).

- You can add keyframes to parameters that don't already have any keyframes as well— just click on the "curve," which for a parameter without keyframes is a dashed line.

- New keyframes are added by default as linear keyframes. See "Modifying Curves" later in this chapter for more information on changing the keyframe interpolation method.

To delete a keyframe:

Do one of the following:

- Click the keyframe to select it, then Control-click and select Delete from the drop-down menu.

- Park the playhead on the keyframe and select Delete Keyframe from the Animation menu.

- Select the keyframe and press the Delete key.

✔ Tip

- You can move, adjust the value of, or delete multiple keyframes simultaneously by selecting them all first. To select multiple keyframes, Shift-click them or click and drag a selection box around them (**Figure 7.26**).

To lock a keyframe:

◆ Select the keyframe, then Control-click and select Lock from the drop-down menu.

  You can't change the value or time location of a locked keyframe. However, you can still change its interpolation method.

To disable a keyframe:

◆ Select the keyframe, then Control-click and select Disable from the drop-down menu.

  The keyframe icon in the graph dims and remains in the same location, but the graph no longer passes through it (**Figure 7.27**). To enable it again, first select it, then Control-click and select Enable from the drop-down menu.

To copy keyframes:

1. Select the keyframe(s). For multiple keyframes, either Shift-click or draw a selection box around them.

2. *Do one of the following:*

   ▲ Choose Edit > Copy.

   ▲ Control-click and select Copy from the drop-down menu.

   ▲ Press Command-C.

To cut keyframes:

1. Select the keyframe(s). For multiple keyframes, either Shift-click or draw a selection box around them.

2. *Do one of the following:*

   ▲ Choose Edit > Cut.

   ▲ Control-click and choose Cut from the drop-down menu.

   ▲ Press Command-X.

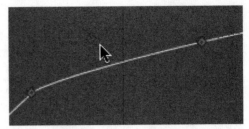

Figure 7.27 When you disable a keyframe, it's icon dims and remains in the same location, but the graph no longer passes through it.

MODIFYING KEYFRAMES

Aligning Keyframes

Because keyframes set precise values at exact points in time, it's very useful to be able to align them to other keyframes, project markers, or audio.

At the bottom left corner of the Keyframe Editor is a button that may look familiar to Final Cut Pro users: the Snapping button (**Figure 7.28**). Whereas Shift-dragging snaps objects in the Timeline, you enable Snapping in the Keyframe Editor to make keyframes snap to other keyframes and project markers.

Next to the Snapping button is the Show Audio button, which displays an audio waveform if the selected item contains audio. You can then align keyframes to the audio waveform.

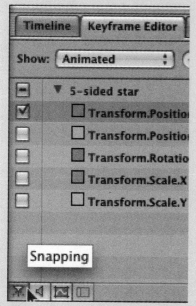

Figure 7.28 The Snapping button will look familiar to Final Cut Pro users.

To paste keyframes:

1. Click the parameter to which you want to apply the cut or copied keyframes in the parameter list.

2. Move the playhead to the time location where you want the first keyframe to be pasted.

3. Choose Edit > Paste or press Command-V.

✔ Tips

- Pasting keyframes can be handy when you want to apply the same animation to another object, to the same object at a different point in time, or even to another parameter.

- Different parameters use different value scales: some are measured as a percentage, like Scale; some as pixels, like Position; and some as degrees, like rotation. If you paste keyframes from one parameter to another with a different value scale, the results can be unpredictable.

MODIFYING KEYFRAMES

Modifying Curves

Motion lets you manipulate not just the keyframes themselves, but the curves *between* the keyframes. You can use preset interpolation methods that create more realistic animations by simulating momentum, inertia, or gravity, and you have full control to adjust the interpolation to fit your needs. You can also extrapolate a curve to create several types of continuing animation before the first keyframe or after the last one.

Changing keyframe interpolation

You can think of *interpolation* as the change in the velocity, or the *rate of change* of an animation between keyframes. By default, Motion animates values between keyframes in a linear fashion with no acceleration at all. This means, for example, if an object is animated to move 100 pixels across the Canvas over the course of 5 seconds, it moves at a steady, linear rate of 20 pixels per second— it never speeds up or slows down, it's either at rest or it's moving at a constant rate. By changing the interpolation method for a curve, you can cause the object to start out slowly, speed up, and then slow down again before coming to a rest, resulting in a much more natural, realistic animation.

✔ Tip

- The thing to remember about how Motion thinks about curves, especially if you have worked with keyframes in other applications, is that you select the keyframe to the left of the curve that you want to affect. So, for instance, if you want to ease into a keyframe, you actually select the *prior* keyframe and choose Ease In.

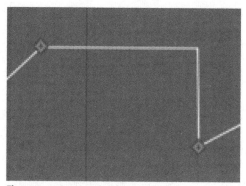

Figure 7.29 Constant holds the value fixed at the selected keyframe all the way through the curve.

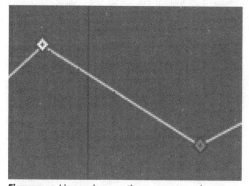

Figure 7.30 Linear changes the parameter value at a constant rate.

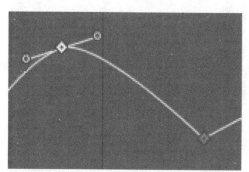

Figure 7.31 Bezier creates Bezier handles that allow you to manipulate the acceleration or deceleration into and out of the keyframe manually.

To change the interpolation method:

1. Select the keyframe to the left of the curve to be changed.

2. Control-click and select an interpolation method from the drop-down menu.

There are six different types of keyframe interpolation, and each one creates a different curve shape :

Constant holds the value fixed at the selected keyframe all the way through the curve. When the second keyframe is reached, the value changes instantaneously (**Figure 7.29**).

Linear is the default interpolation method and it changes the parameter value at a constant rate (**Figure 7.30**).

Bezier creates Bezier handles that allow you to manipulate the acceleration or deceleration into and out of the keyframe manually (**Figure 7.31**).

Continuous causes the parameter value to accelerate as it leaves the key frame up to the midpoint between the keyframes, then it cause the value to decelerate as it comes into the next keyframe (**Figure 7.32**).

continues on next page

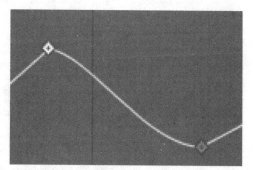

Figure 7.32 Continuous causes the parameter value to accelerate as it leaves the keyframe up to the midpoint between the keyframes, then it decelerates as it comes into the next keyframe.

Ease In slows down the rate of change of the parameter value as it approaches a keyframe. It works like the second half of the Continuous interpolation (**Figure 7.33**).

Ease Out speeds up the rate of change of the parameter value as it leaves a keyframe. It works like the first half of the Continuous interpolation (**Figure 7.34**).

✔ Tip

■ You can change the interpolation for all the keyframes applied to a parameter at once by choosing the interpolation method in the Animation menu rather than by selecting individual keyframes (**Figure 7.35**).

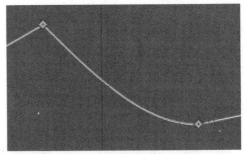

Figure 7.33 Ease In slows down the rate of change of the parameter value as it approaches a keyframe.

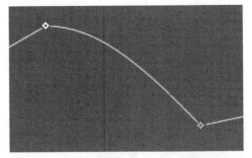

Figure 7.34 Ease Out speeds up the rate of change of the parameter value as it leaves a keyframe.

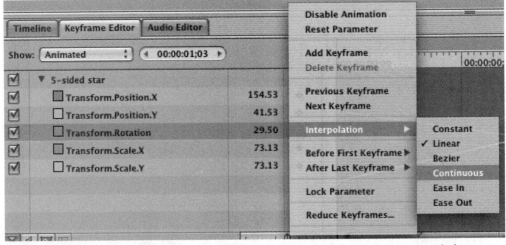

Figure 7.35 You can change the interpolation method for all the keyframes applied to a parameter at once in the Animation menu.

MODIFYING CURVES

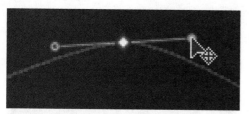

Figure 7.36 Convert linear position keyframes to Bezier directly in the Canvas by Command-clicking on them and dragging out Bezier handles.

Working with Bezier curves

Bezier is the most flexible of the interpolation methods because you can adjust the length and angle of the handles to change how the parameter value accelerates or decelerates.

To convert a keyframe to Bezier:

◆ Command-click and drag on the keyframe.

✔ Tips

■ You can convert Position keyframes to Bezier and adjust the handles directly in the Canvas by Command-clicking and dragging (**Figure 7.36**). Alternatively, you can Control-click and select Smooth from the drop-down menu.

■ Command-clicking a Bezier keyframe converts it back to a linear keyframe.

Working with Bezier handles

The Bezier handles are also called *tangents*. By default, the two handles are linked together—when you move one, the other moves. You can break this link so that you can change the animation on just one side of the keyframe.

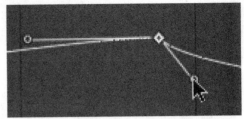

Figure 7.37 Command-click and drag a Bezier handle to adjust it independent of the handle on the other side of the keyframe.

To adjust one side of the Bezier handles:

Do one of the following:

◆ Command-click the handle you want to adjust and drag (**Figure 7.37**).

◆ Control-click the handle and select Break Tangent from the drop-down menu, then drag the handle (**Figure 7.38**).

Figure 7.38 You can also Control-click on a Bezier keyframe and select Break Tangent from the drop-down menu in order to manipulate each handle independently.

✔ Tips

■ The *angle* of the Bezier handle determines the amount of acceleration—the more vertical the handle, the greater the acceleration.

■ The *length* of the handle determines the influence of the acceleration—in other words, how much of the curve between the keyframes is affected by the acceleration.

■ To relink the handles, Command-click the keyframe and drag or Control-click and select Link Tangent from the drop-down menu.

MODIFYING CURVES

Extrapolating keyframes

Once you have set and adjusted several keyframes for a parameter, Motion can use those keyframes to create additional keyframes, either before the first one or after the last one, by extrapolating the keyframe data and repeating it over and over in several different ways to create an ongoing animation.

To extrapolate keyframes:

◆ Click the Animation menu, choose Before First Keyframe or After Last Keyframe, and then choose an extrapolation method from the fly-out menu.

The extrapolated curve appears as a dotted line in the graph area.

There are five different extrapolation choices:

Constant is the default behavior. The value of the parameter remains fixed at the first or last keyframe value.

Linear extends the curve along the last trajectory.

Ping Pong causes the same keyframe values to repeat over and over, but unlike Repeat, every other time, the animation is reversed (**Figure 7.39**).

continues on next page

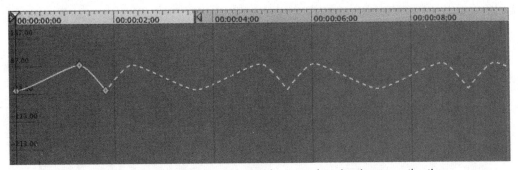

Figure 7.39 Ping Pong repeats the same keyframe values and reverses the animation every other time.

MODIFYING CURVES

227

Repeat causes the same keyframe values to repeat over and over (**Figure 7.40**).

Progressive repeats the same curve, but each time, it starts from the new ending value (**Figure 7.41**).

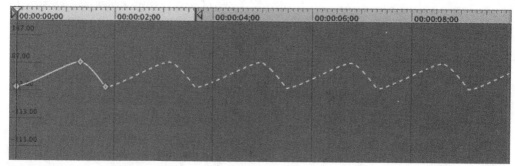

Figure 7.40 Repeat causes the same keyframe values to repeat over and over.

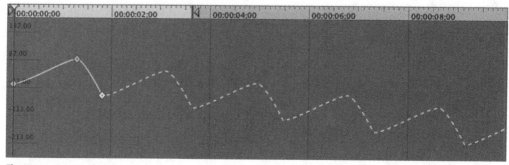

Figure 7.41 Progressive repeats the same curve, but each time it starts from the new ending value.

MODIFYING CURVES

Generating keyframes

By default, changing the extrapolation method creates a curve that contains hidden keyframes that you can't manipulate individually (you can, however, select and move the entire curve up or down). Ever flexible, Motion allows you to generate keyframes on the extrapolated curve so that you can make adjustments to individual keyframes. You can even select the range of the extrapolated curve for which you want to generate the keyframes.

To generate keyframes on an extrapolated curve:

1. For the extrapolated parameter, click the Animation menu and in the fly-out menu for either Before First Keyframe or After Last Keyframe, choose Generate Keyframes.

2. In the dialog that appears, use the slider to choose the number of cycles for which you want keyframes, and then click OK.

   Keyframes are now available along the extrapolated curve for the number of cycles you selected (**Figure 7.42**).

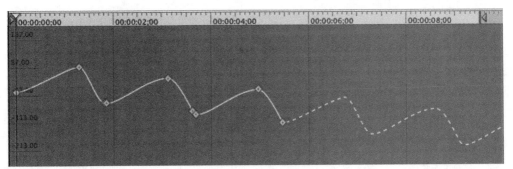

Figure 7.42 When you generate keyframes on an extrapolated curve, the new keyframes are fully adjustable just like keyframes you set yourself.

Saving Keyframed Parameters

Once you have carefully created the perfect animation by keyframing the parameters of an object and changing the keyframe inter-polation by modifying the curves, you may want to save all your work so that you can apply the same animated parameter to a dif-ferent object. You can accomplish this goal via two different methods.

First, you can either save the object itself into the Library, and all of the animated keyframes (as well as any other applied effects and masks) will be saved along with it. You can then add this object to a new project, and exchange the object itself with a new object, keeping the keyframes and other effects intact (the Exchange edit process is described in "Drag and Drop Editing" in Chapter 5).

An alternate method that we'll explore here is to save the animated parameters them-selves, separate from the object, to the Library. These animated parameters can then be applied to any object to recreate the animation quickly and easily.

To save a keyframed parameter:

1. Make the Library the active tab in the Utility pane by clicking it or pressing Command-2.

2. Choose the Favorites or Favorites Menu category.

3. In the Keyframe Editor, select the param-eter you want to save and drag it to the File Stack area of the Library.

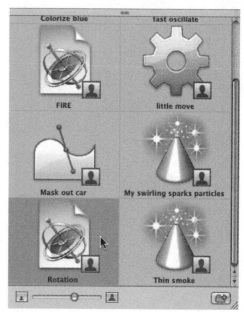

Figure 7.43 Custom parameters appear in the Library and include a user icon to indicate that it is a custom presets.

✔ Tips

■ The custom parameter appears in the Library as a Motion project icon with a user icon attached to indicate that it is a custom preset (**Figure 7.43**).

■ The custom parameter is named by default with the name of the parameter. To rename it, Control-click and choose Rename from the drop-down menu.

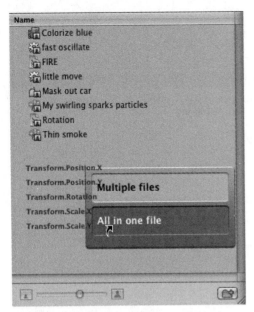

Figure 7.44 A drop-down menu lets you choose how to add multiple animated parameters to the Library at the same time.

To save multiple keyframed parameters:

1. Make the Library the active tab in the Utility pane by clicking it or pressing Command-2.

2. Choose the Favorites or Favorites Menu category.

3. In the Keyframe Editor, Shift-click to select a range of parameters or Command-click to select multiple non-contiguous parameters.

4. Drag the parameters to the File Stack area of the Library. Don't release the mouse yet.

   A drop-down menu appears (**Figure 7.44**).

5. *Do one of the following:*

   ▲ To save each of the parameters as its own file, drop the parameters into the Multiple files well.

   ▲ To save all of the parameters bundled into one file, drag the parameters into the All in one file well.

✔ Tip

■ When you save multiple files all as one file, the default name for the preset is "Untitled." To rename the file, Control-click it and choose Rename from the drop-down menu.

SAVING KEYFRAMED PARAMETERS

Keyframing Filters

Many filter parameters can be keyframed; the process is the same as keyframing object parameters.

To keyframe a filter:

1. Select the filter that has been applied to an object.

2. Click the Record button or press A to start recording keyframes.

   The button glows red to indicate that it is active.

3. Move the playhead to the frame where you want the animation to start.

4. In the Dashboard (press D or F6 to reveal), set the value (**Figure 7.45**). Motion automatically sets a keyframe at the beginning of the filter when using Record Animation.

5. Move the playhead to the location for the next keyframe.

6. Adjust the parameter value in the Dashboard.

7. Click the Record button or press A to stop recording.

✔ Tips

■ If the parameter you want to keyframe is not available in the Dashboard, change the value in the Inspector. If it's a check box parameter, add keyframes manually in the Keyframe Editor.

■ Filter parameter keyframes can be moved in the Timeline, and added, deleted, or modified in the Keyframe Editor, just like object parameter keyframes.

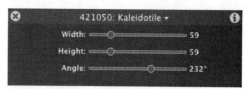

Figure 7.45 To animate a filter's parameters with Record Animation, set a value in the Dashboard.

KEYFRAMING FILTERS

Working with Behaviors and Keyframes

On the surface, it seems as if behaviors (discussed in Chapter 6) and keyframes represent entirely separate methods for creating animation, and never the twain shall meet. However, the reality is that they can coexist quite happily—in fact, you can create effects by leveraging the strengths of each, which isn't possible with just one or the other (**Figure 7.46**).

There are three ways to work with both behaviors and keyframes: first, you can keyframe a behavior parameter just as you would an object parameter or a filter parameter. Second, you can combine behaviors with keyframes. And third, you can convert a behavior into keyframes.

Keyframing behaviors

Many behavior parameters can be keyframed; the process is the same as keyframing object parameters.

To keyframe a behavior:

1. Select the behavior that has been applied to an object.

2. Click the Record button or press A to start recording keyframes.
   The button glows red to indicate that it is active.

3. Move the playhead to the frame where you want the second keyframe. (Motion sets a keyframe automatically at the beginning of the behavior when using Record Animation).

continues on next page

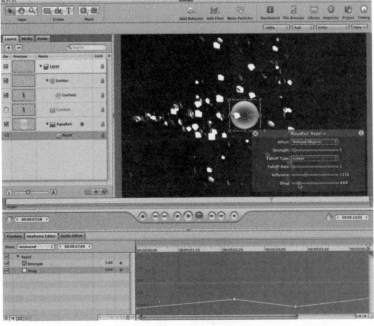

Figure 7.46 Keyframes and behaviors can work together as a team. In this example, the Drag parameter for the Repel behavior (applied to the ball) is keyframed to change over time so that the particles change how they react to the repelling force.

4. In the Dashboard (press D or F6 to reveal), set the keyframe value.

5. Move the playhead to the location for the next keyframe.

6. Adjust the parameter value in the Dashboard.

7. Click the Record button or press A to stop recording.

✔ Tips

- If the parameter you want to keyframe is not available in the Dashboard, change the value in the Inspector.

- You can move behavior parameter keyframes in the Timeline, and add, delete, or modify them in the Keyframe Editor, just like object parameter keyframes.

- Except for Motion Path, the parameters of Basic Motion behaviors are not keyframeable.

Combining behaviors with keyframes

If you add a behavior to an object and then keyframe the same parameter that the behavior is animating, you are telling Motion to do two different things with the same parameter. What happens? Your computer explodes!

Seriously, when Motion comes across this situation, it handles it by adding the two effects together to get a combined result.

For example, if you add a Spin behavior to an object that rotates it clockwise, and then set keyframes to the Rotation parameter to rotate it counterclockwise, Motion combines the two values. If the Spin behavior is set to a larger value than the keyframes, then the object still spins clockwise, but at a slower rate. If the keyframe values are larger, they overpower the Spin behavior and make the object spin counterclockwise.

You can combine keyframes with behaviors to modify behaviors in very specific ways. In the Spin example above, you can set keyframes that cause the rotation to slow and then reverse direction (**Figure 7.47**).

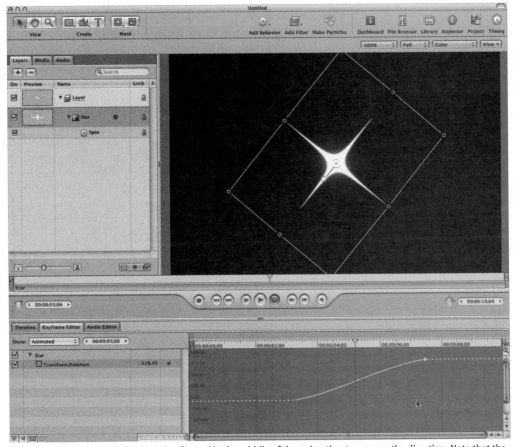

Figure 7.47 Here, a Spin behavior is keyframed in the middle of the animation to reverse the direction. Note that the curve has been set to Continuous to create a smooth transition when the rotation changes direction.

Converting behaviors to keyframes

If you find you need to combine a behavior and keyframes to get a specific result, it may be easier to just convert the behavior into keyframes and then adjust the keyframes or the curves (**Figures 7.48** and **7.49**).

To convert a behavior to keyframes:

1. Select the object with the behavior applied.

2. Choose Object > Convert to Keyframes or press Command-K.

3. Click the Convert button in the dialog that appears.

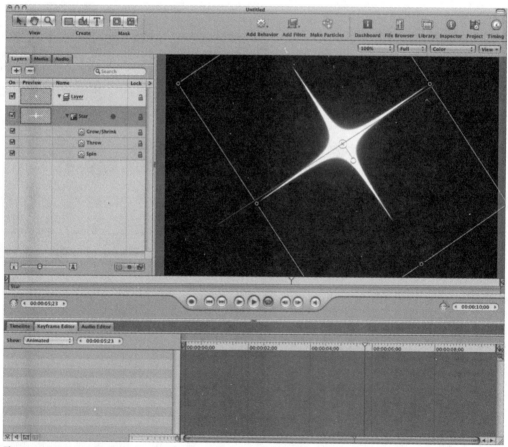

Figure 7.48 You can always convert behaviors to keyframes in order to tweak them.

✔ Tips

- If the selected object has multiple behaviors applied, they all get converted into keyframes—you can't select just one behavior to convert.

- If behaviors are applied to other objects that affect the selected object (like Attractor or Repel), then the effects of those behaviors are included in the keyframe conversion. The behaviors that are applied to other objects remain intact.

- Behaviors applied to the selected object that affect other objects aren't converted.

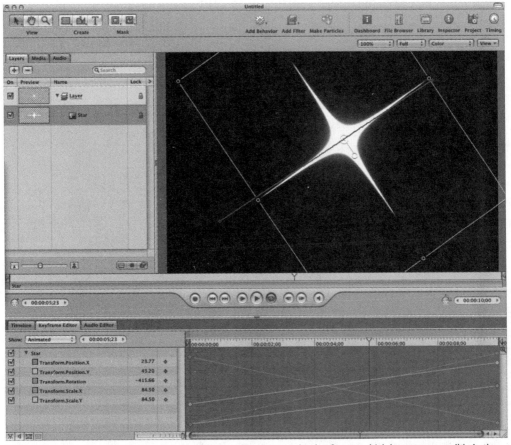

Figure 7.49 Here, three behaviors applied to an object are converted to keyframes which become accessible in the Keyframe Editor.

On-the-Fly Keyframing

Motion's capacity to playback your composition in real-time, even with multiple objects, filters, masks, behaviors, particles, and keyframes, creates a unique opportunity to set keyframes while your project is playing. Anyone who has used the keyframe automation feature of the Audio Mixer in Final Cut Pro knows right away the power of making changes to parameters on the fly. You can animate any keyframeable parameter in real-time as you watch, which allows you to make sure the animation is happening when you want. For example, you can create a shaky motion effect by dragging an object around the Canvas as your project plays, and Motion sets keyframes as you draw in real-time.

To keyframe a parameter on the fly:

1. Click the Record Animation button or press A to start recording.

2. Begin playback by pressing the Play button or hitting the spacebar.

3. Change the desired parameter value in the Canvas, the Dashboard, or the Inspector while the project plays,.

4. Click the Record Animation button or press A to stop recording.

   Keyframes are recorded in the Keyframe Editor based on the changes you made while recording (**Figure 7.50**).

✔ Tip

- If you find that you keep accidentally recording keyframes on the fly, you can turn this feature off in the Mark > Recording Options dialog.

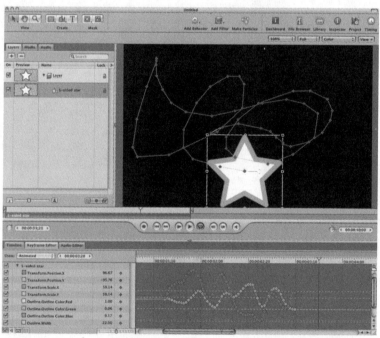

Figure 7.50 Keyframes can be recorded on the fly simply by dragging the object around the Canvas while the project plays with Record Animation turned on.

Thinning keyframes

When recording animation on the fly, it's possible to create keyframes at almost every single frame. That can be a lot of keyframes, especially if you want to modify them! You can reduce the number of keyframes that Motion creates during on-the-fly keyframing, which is called *thinning* keyframes, either before recording them, or after the fact.

To change how keyframes are recorded:

1. Select Mark > Recording Options or press Option-A.

2. In the dialog, select one of the thinning options:

   Reduced creates enough keyframes to keep the overall shape of the curve intact (**Figure 7.51**).

   Peaks Only just sets keyframes at the largest value changes (**Figure 7.52**).

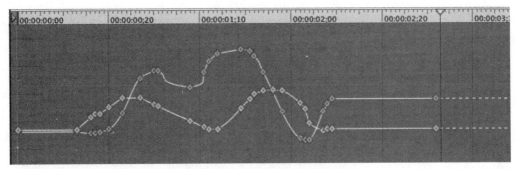

Figure 7.51 Reduced creates just enough keyframes to keep the overall curve intact.

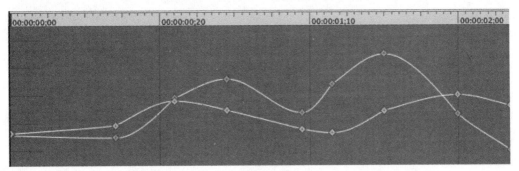

Figure 7.52 Peaks Only sets keyframes at the largest value changes.

To thin keyframes:

1. Click the Animation menu in the Keyframe Editor for the parameter whose keyframes you want to thin.

2. Choose Reduce Keyframes from the drop-down menu.

3. Adjust the Tolerance slider in the dialog that appears.

✔ Tip

■ Higher tolerance settings decrease the number of remaining keyframes.

USING THE LIBRARY

Motion's Library contains all the various effects, such as behaviors and filters, that you can apply to your objects to change their appearance or to animate them. You can also create a variety of objects directly in Motion, such as Shapes, Generators, and Particles. Just like any items you import, by adjusting their parameters and applying additional effects you can further customize and modify these Library elements in a virtually infinite number of ways. Many of these Library elements are preset effects, which takes the hard work out of setting up complex text styles or particle systems.

The Library is also the repository for your own collection of customized objects and effects that you can reuse at any time, in any project.

This chapter explores the functions of the Library: how to browse its contents and how to preview and apply Library elements. It also introduces the different types of elements that are available. Most Library categories have dedicated chapters covering how to use them in depth—for example, behaviors are covered in Chapter 6, filters in Chapter 9, and particles in Chapter 11.

Introducing the Library

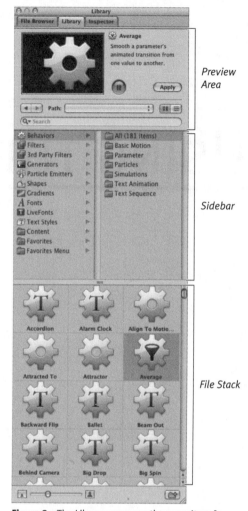

The Library is very similar in both form and function to the File Browser (see Chapter 3). You use both to browse, preview, and select items to add to your project. But whereas the File Browser is used to find media assets you have stored on local or networked hard drives, the Library serves as the repository for elements that are built into or supplied with Motion. These elements include Behaviors, Filters, Particles, Generators, Gradients, and Fonts, which are certain types of *effects* that are applied to objects; Shapes, Particle Emitters, and Text Styles, which are *objects* with predefined attributes; and Content, which includes various graphic and movie files. You can easily reorganize the Library to suit your needs, and you can add your own customized effects.

The Library is located on the second tab in the Utility Window, tucked between the File Browser and the Inspector.

The Library tab has three main areas, similar to the File Browser:

- **Preview Area.** The Preview Area at the top of the window allows you to preview a Library element before you add it to your project.

- **Sidebar.** The Sidebar in the middle section displays a folder hierarchy in which you can navigate to a specific Library element.

- **File Stack.** The File Stack at the bottom is where the specific Library elements in the currently selected folder display.

To reveal the Library:

Do one of the following:

- Click the Library tab in the Utility Window (**Figure 8.1**).

- Press Command-2.

Figure 8.1 The Library serves as the repository for elements that are built into or supplied with Motion.

INTRODUCING THE LIBRARY

Figure 8.2 Click and drag in the Preview window to see how Particle Emitters look when animated.

Using the Preview Area

Just as with the File Browser, once you select an element in the Library, you can preview how it will look in the Preview Area. If the object is animated, you can preview the animation. You can then apply the element to your project. Some elements that you preview are effects that you need to apply to an object already in the Canvas; others are objects that you can add by themselves.

To preview a Library element:

1. Select the element in the File Stack.

2. If applicable, click the Play button in the Preview Area.

✔ Tip

■ For Particle Emitters, click and drag directly in the window of the Preview Area to see how the emitter will behave if animated (**Figure 8.2**).

Effect or Object?

Every element in the Library can be categorized as either an *effect* or an *object*.

Objects are discrete, independent items that you can add to the Canvas by themselves. They have parameters that appear in the Properties tab of the Inspector (such as Position, Scale, and Rotation) that can be adjusted or animated. Objects in the Library include Shapes, Generators, and Particle Emitters. Each of these elements can be dragged directly to the Canvas, and effects can be applied to them.

Effects aren't independent—they need to be applied to an object. Effects in the Library include Behaviors, Filters (including 3rd Party Filters), Gradients, Fonts, LiveFonts, and Text Styles. Each of these elements can be applied to any object(s) already in the Canvas.

Using the Sidebar

The Sidebar contains a set of navigation controls and a collection of folders that group all of the Library elements available in Motion into the following 11 categories. There are also two additional folders for your own elements (**Figure 8.3**).

◆ **Behaviors.** This folder contains the following seven subfolders: All, Basic Motion, Parameter, Particles, Simulations, Text Animation, and Text Sequence. Each of these folders contains a specific type of behavior, except for All, which contains all of them. A *behavior* is an effect that must be applied to an object, and certain behaviors only work on certain objects. For example, the Text Animation behaviors only work when they are applied to text objects. For more on working with behaviors, see Chapter 7. For more on working with objects, see Chapter 3. For more on working with text behaviors, see Chapter 13.

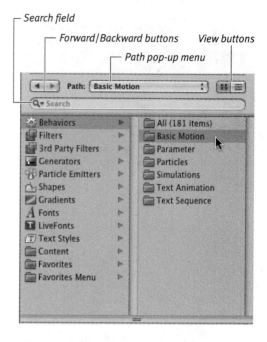

Search field

Forward/Backward buttons   *View buttons*

Path pop-up menu

Figure 8.3 The Sidebar contains the Library elements grouped into categories.

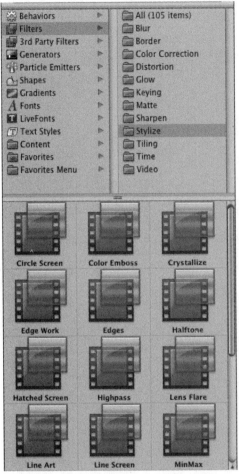

Figure 8.4 The Library contains all of Motion's filters divided into subcategories based on type.

◆ **Filters.** This folder contains all the filters available in Motion; they are divided into 12 subcategories based on filter type (**Figure 8.4**). A *filter* is an effect that must be applied to an object; in general, you can apply any filter to any type of object. For more information on working with filters, see Chapter 10.

◆ **3rd Party Filters.** Filters from third party vendors, usually called plug-ins, that work with Motion are available in this folder once Motion has been directed to "see" them. As with Motion's built-in filters, 3rd Party Filters are effects that are applied to objects. For more information on working with 3rd Party Filters, see Chapter 9.

◆ **Generators.** As opposed to behaviors and filters, generators are objects in and of themselves, similar to media objects you import into your project, except that they are computer-generated inside of Motion. They have unique parameters that you can change and animate. This folder contains the 13 types of generators. For more information on working with generators, see Chapter 10.

continues on next page

◆ **Particle Emitters.** This folder contains a set of particle presets organized into six subfolders based on emitter type (**Figure 8.5**). *Presets* are particle systems with specific emitter objects and parameters all saved together as a bundle. Particle Emitters technically consist of an effect applied to an object, but because the object is contained in the preset, they behave like objects. For more on working with particles, see Chapter 11.

◆ **Shapes.** A small collection of preset shape objects is contained in this folder. Shapes are objects that you can create and modify with the shape tools. For more on working with shapes and masks, see Chapter 12.

◆ **Gradients.** Gradients are specialized effects that you can apply only to objects that have a fill or an outline that can contain a gradient, such as shape or text objects. For more on working with gradients, see Chapter 10.

◆ **Fonts.** All fonts available in your system are found in this folder, organized according to your Font Book. You can only apply fonts to text objects. For more on fonts and working with text, see Chapter 13.

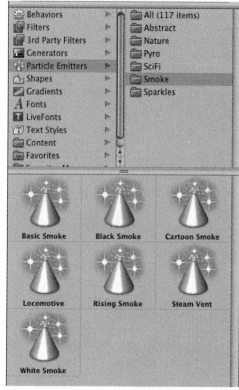

Figure 8.5 Particle presets such as those pictured here are contained in the Library.

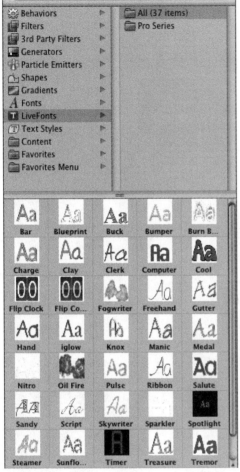

Figure 8.6 Fun and lively animated LiveFonts can be viewed within the Library's Preview Area.

◆ **LiveFonts.** This folder contains a list of all the animated LiveFonts that you have installed in your system (**Figure 8.6**). For more information on working with LiveFonts, see Chapter 13.

◆ **Text Styles.** This folder contains a collection of preset text parameters that you can apply to text objects. For more information on working with text styles, see Chapter 13.

◆ **Content.** This folder contains a large collection of graphics and movies for use in your projects, including every element used in the templates. For information on using templates, see Chapter 15.

◆ **Favorites.** Any time you create a custom version of an effect, you can store it in this folder so you can access it quickly. By default, the folder is empty.

◆ **Favorites Menu.** Custom effects that you create and place in this folder appear in the Favorites menu in the menu bar so you can access them easily.

Using the File Stack

The results of clicking folders, using the navigation tools, or entering a search term in the Sidebar are displayed in the File Stack. From here, you can change how you view the results, preview objects and effects, and apply selected elements to your project.

To change the view of icons in the File Stack:

◆ Click either the View as List button or the Icon View button in the navigation area of the Sidebar (**Figure 8.7**).

✔ Tip

■ When using Icon View, you can use the slider at the bottom of the Library pane to adjust the size of the icons.

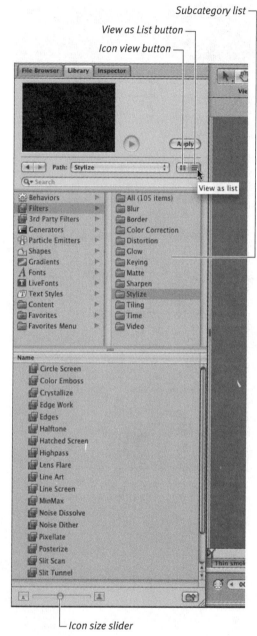

Subcategory list
View as List button
Icon view button

Icon size slider

Figure 8.7 You can view your Library items either as a list (shown here) or as icons by clicking either the Column or List view button.

Finding and Applying Library Elements

The method for finding a specific Library element to add to your project depends on what you are looking for. Are you simply browsing for ideas, searching for a specific category of element, or honing in on something for which you already know at least part of the name? In each case, you have a set of navigational tools such as a Search field, a Path drop-down list, and Forward/Backward buttons to assist you.

To browse for a Library element:

1. Click the folder for the category of elements you want.

2. If you chose a category that has subfolders, click the appropriate subfolder.

3. Click an item from the folder or subfolder that displays in the File Stack at the bottom of the Library pane. Then check the display in the Preview pane.

To navigate to a different location in the Library:

Do one of the following:

◆ Click the left and right navigation arrows.

    The left arrow takes you up through the current path; the right arrow takes you back down through the current path.

◆ Click the Path Shortcut menu, which displays the path to the currently selected folder.

FINDING AND APPLYING LIBRARY ELEMENTS

To search for a specific Library element:

◆ Type the name or several letters of the name of the element you are searching for into the Search field.

You do not need.to press Enter or Return.

✔ Tips

■ To start a new search, first click the "x" to the far right of the Search field to clear the current search; then type the new search term. This action ensures that you are searching the entire Library.

■ By using the Search field, you are filtering out all elements that do not meet the search criteria, but you still have access to all the folders because they remain visible and selectable in the Sidebar.

To apply a Library element:

1. Select the element in the File Stack.

2. If the element is an object, *do one of the following*:

   ▲ Drag the element from the File Stack into the Canvas.

   ▲ Click the Apply button in the Preview Area to add the element to the center of the Canvas.

3. If the element is an effect, select the object(s) in the Canvas to which the effect is to be applied (for more on selecting objects, see Chapter 3) and *do one of the following*:

   ▲ Drag the effect onto the selected object(s) in the Canvas (**Figure 8.8**).

   ▲ Click the Apply button in the Preview Area.

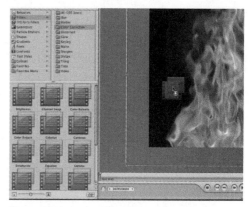

Figure 8.8 To apply a Library element to an object, simply drag it onto the object(s) in the Canvas.

Figure 8.9 To add your own customized element to the Library, simply drag it to the correct folder.

Adding Content to the Library

Just as new books are written and added to a real library, you can add your own new content to Motion's library. Any time you customize a filter, generator, particle emitter, gradient, shape, behavior, or text style, you can save your design as a new element to either that element's appropriate folder or to one of the two Favorites locations (or all of them!). In addition, you can even add your own imported media to the Library so it is always available for any future project.

To add a customized Library element to the Library:

1. Select the object or effect that you want to save in the Layers tab of the Project pane (press Command-4 to reveal this).

2. *Do one of the following:*

   ▲ Drag the object or effect to the appropriate subcategory list in the Sidebar (**Figure 8.9**).

   ▲ Drag the object to the Favorites folder in the Sidebar.

   ▲ Drag the object to the Favorites Menu in the Sidebar.

   The customized element is now available from the Favorites menu.

   ▲ Drag the object directly to the File Stack to place it in the currently selected folder.

✔ Tips

■ You can only place effects in the matching category. For example, you can place a customized filter in any of the Filter subcategories, but you can't placed it in a Behavior subcategory.

■ You can drag the same customized effect to more than one location. For example, you may want to create a new subcategory within Filters and place a customized filter in that folder as well as placing a copy in the Favorites Menu folder (see "Organizing Effects" below for information on creating and deleting folders).

■ If an object has more than one Library effect applied to it, you can save the combination of the object and all of its applied effects by dragging the object from the Layers tab to the Favorites or the Favorites Menu folder.

■ To rename a customized effect in the Library, Control-click it and select Rename.

Organizing Effects

Although you can't modify the existing folders and elements in the Library, you can create and delete new folders and move elements into different folders to reorganize them.

To create a new Library folder:

1. Click the Add Folder button at the bottom of the Library tab.

2. Double-click the name to change it.

To delete a Library file or folder:

1. Select the file(s) and/or folder(s).

2. *Do one of the following:*

   ▲ Choose Edit > Delete.

   ▲ Press Command-Delete.

Why Put Media in the Library?

When you import a media asset into your project (see Chapter 3), it is added to the Media tab in the Project pane, and remains there even if you delete the object from the Canvas. So why would you ever want to put a media asset into the Library?

The key difference between the Media tab and the Library is that the Media tab contents are specific to the current project only, whereas the Library content is available for *all* projects. So if you have some media assets that you expect to reuse over and over in different projects, add them to the Library. When you do so, they become part of your "permanent" collection and are easily accessible for your next project.

There's one caveat: even though an object is part of the Library, the underlying media file must be available to Motion in order for it to use that object. So if you move the object to another location, or open a project on another machine that does not have that object installed, it appears as offline when you launch the project.

USING FILTERS

The variety of effects you can achieve by applying, stacking, and animating filters is truly mind-boggling. Need to bring up the mid-tones in a video clip, create light rays on some text, key out the blue-screen background of a special effects shot, add a soft glow to a warm evening shot, or add a lens flare? You can correct, enhance, or radically change the look of video, graphics, and text by applying one or more of the over 100 filters included in the Motion Library. And if you have third-party filters that you use with other applications, you may be able to use those as well.

Filters alter the look of objects in your composition by blurring, shifting colors, distorting, tiling, making them glow, or by otherwise manipulating the visual information. You can enhance the look of an image or video or change it so dramatically that you'll be hard pressed to tell what the original object was.

Like behaviors, filters are *effects* in Motion, and you work with them in much the same way: you apply them to objects and make adjustments to their parameters.

Although filters don't animate objects like behaviors do, you can make a filter's parameters change over time with either keyframes or parameter behaviors to create animated effects.

Browsing and Previewing Filters

Filters are a category of elements in the Library, so browsing and previewing them works just like it does with behaviors, particles, and other Library elements.

A preview of how the filter affects a representative object and a short description of what the filter does appears in the Preview Area (**Figure 9.1**). Note that although some of the previews display an animation, the filter isn't animated until you apply keyframes or behaviors as described in "Animating Filters" later in this chapter.

To browse and preview filters:

1. Open the Library (Window > Library or Command-2).

2. In the Sidebar, select the Filters category.

3. On the right side of the Sidebar, select a subcategory.

4. In the File Stack, click a filter. A preview of how the filter affects an object appears in the Preview Area.

✔ Tip

■ You can toggle the view of filters between list and icons, you can change the icon size, and you can search on filters. For more information on how to use the Library, see Chapter 8.

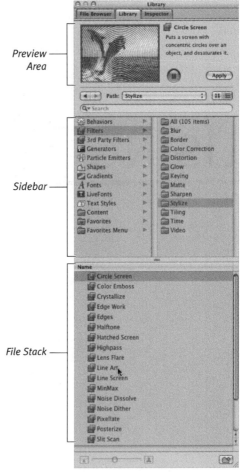

Figure 9.1 When viewing filters in the Library, you'll see a representation of how the filter affects an object as well as a short description of what the filter does.

Even More Filters!

As if Motion didn't have enough filters already, the ones described here include five additional filters that don't ship with Motion but are available for free from Apple's Web site (www.apple.com/motion/download). They are Channel Swap (in the Color Correction category), Noise Dither and Vectorize Color (in the Stylize category), and Scrub and Trails (in the Time category).

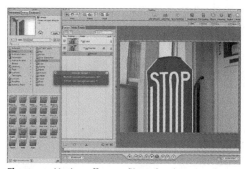

Figure 9.2 Motion offers 23 filters for changing the shape of an object.

Figure 9.3 Glow filters blur an object in addition to changing its brightness and color.

Figure 9.4 The Set Matte filter creates a matte on an object based on values from another object.

Filter Categories

Here are the 12 different categories of filters:

Blur contains 11 different filters that blur all, part, or channels of an object in different ways.

Border contains three filters that put different types of frames on an object.

Color Correction contains 17 different filters that give you an incredible amount of control over making an image appear more natural or creating dramatic color effects.

Distortion contains 23 filters for manipulating the shape of an object (**Figure 9.2**).

Glow contains eight filters that affect the image by blurring, changing brightness and color, and then combining the results back on the original object (**Figure 9.3**).

Keying contains five filters. You can use four of these five filters to remove the background around an object by isolating specific colors or luminance values. Usually, you do this to composite the object into another scene. You can use the fifth of these filters, Spill Suppressor, to help clean up a key. Keying is an art that takes practice and usually requires some additional filters and masks to completely isolate an object. See "Masks and Keys" in Chapter 12 for more information.

Matte contains two very useful filters: Matte Choker adjusts the edges of a matte, and Set Matte creates a matte on an object based on values from another object (**Figure 9.4**).

continues on next page

FILTER CATEGORIES

Sharpen contains two filters that create the illusion of sharpness by increasing the contrast along edges inside an image or video.

Stylize contains 21, count 'em, 21 different filters that manipulate objects to alter their appearance, sometimes radically (**Figure 9.5**).

Tiling contains six filters that create repetitions of an object and then combine those repetitions in various ways to create intricate patterns and mosaics (**Figure 9.6**).

Time contains five filters that, when applied to video, manipulate when and how frames of the video appear by moving, repeating, and combining them.

Video Filters contains Deinterlace, which removes interlace flicker from video, and Broadcast Safe, which ensures that video isn't too bright or too saturated to be broadcast.

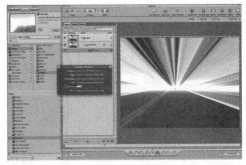

Figure 9.5 Motion provides a huge set of 21 filters for altering the appearance of an object, often quite radically.

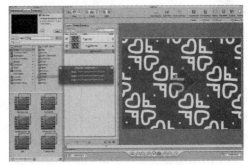

Figure 9.6 Tiling filters create repetitions of an object and then combine them in interesting patterns.

Figure 9.7 Filters show up in several places: below objects in the Layers tab and Timeline List area, as a purple bar in the Timeline, in the Filters tab of the Inspector, and in the Dashboard.

Figure 9.8 If you apply a filter to an object that is smaller than the Canvas size, the filter's effect is limited to the size of the object.

Figure 9.9 If you want a filter's effect to fill the Canvas, then you'll need to make sure the object is as large as the Canvas by changing its dimensions in a graphics application.

Applying and Removing Filters

You apply and remove filters the same as with behaviors (see Chapter 6).

Filters appear below objects in the Layers tab and Timeline list area, and appear as a purple bar in the Timeline. They also appear in the Filters tab of the Inspector, and in the Dashboard (**Figure 9.7**).

To apply a filter:

Do one of the following:

◆ Select the filter in the Library and drag it onto the target object in either the Canvas, the Layers tab, or the Timeline.

◆ Select the target object, then select the filter and click the Apply button in the Preview Area of the Library. Or, choose a filter by clicking on the Add filter icon in the Toolbar.

✔ Tips

■ Because Layers are also objects, you can apply filters to layers. Filters applied to layers affect all objects within these layers.

■ You can apply filters to a mask that is applied to an object.

■ You can, of course, apply multiple filters to an object. When you do so, Motion combines them for the final effect, with the topmost filter being applied last.

■ If an object to which you apply a filter has dimensions that are smaller than the Canvas size (set in Edit > Project Properties), then the filter's effect is limited to the size of the object (**Figure 9.8**). If you want the filter's effect to fill the Canvas, change the object's dimensions in a graphics application like Photoshop. You don't need to change the *scale* of the object, just the dimensions of the frame that contains it (**Figure 9.9**).

Adjusting Filters

Every filter has at least one *parameter* (such as its center, radius, angle, amount, or height) that has a default value you can change. Once you apply a filter, you'll likely want to change its default parameter values to dial-in a specific look. As with other elements, you can change some parameters in the Canvas, more parameters in the Dashboard, and all available parameters in the Inspector.

You can rename, move, copy, paste, enable, lock, and reorder filters like you do other Motion elements by using either the Layers tab or the Timeline.

Figure 9.10 If the filter has control points in the Canvas, you can simply drag on them to adjust the filter's parameters.

To change a filter's parameters:

1. Select the filter in the Layers tab or the Timeline.

2. *Do one of the following:*

   ▲ Some filters have control points. If there are one or more control points visible in the Canvas, drag the control point(s) (**Figure 9.10**).

   ▲ Reveal the Dashboard (press D or F7) and drag the parameter sliders.

   ▲ Reveal the Filters tab of the Inspector (press F3) and enter a new parameter value.

To rename a filter:

◆ Double-click the filter name in the Layers tab or the Timeline and type a new name.

Figure 9.11 Simply hold down the Option key while dragging a filter to create a duplicate.

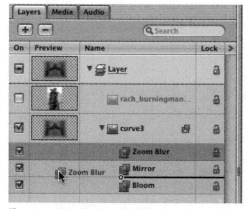

Figure 9.12 Here the Zoom Blur filter is being moved so that it sits between the Mirror and Bloom filters. Filters are applied to objects in the order they are listed.

To move a filter to another object:

◆ In the Layers tab or the Timeline Layer list, drag the filter onto the target object.

✔ Tips

■ Dragging a filter onto the object row places it at the top of the effects stack. If you want it below other effects, drag it there.

■ Holding down the Option key while dragging creates a duplicate of the filter, leaving the current one intact (**Figure 9.11**).

To copy a filter:

◆ Select the filter and choose Edit > Copy or press Command-C.

To cut a filter:

◆ Select the filter and choose Edit > Cut or press Command-X.

To paste a filter:

◆ Select the target object and choose Edit > Paste or press Command-V.

Any changes you have made to the parameter values carry over to the pasted clip.

To disable a filter:

◆ Click the Active (On) check box in the Layers tab or the Timeline.

You can't see disabled filters in the Canvas and they aren't rendered on output.

To lock a filter:

◆ Click the lock icon in the Layers tab or the Timeline.

You can't move, cut, trim, or change the parameters of locked filters. However, you can still copy them.

To change the stacking order of filters:

◆ In the Layers tab or Timeline, drag the filter up or down and release the mouse when the position indicator appears at the desired location (**Figure 9.12**).

ADJUSTING FILTERS

Adjusting Filter Timing

When you apply a filter to an object, by default, it lasts for the object's full duration. You can *trim* the filter so that it only affects the object for a specific amount of time, and you can *move* the filter so that it affects the object at a different point in time.

To trim a filter:

◆ In the Timeline, click and drag the in or out point of the filter to the desired location (**Figure 9.13**).

To move a trimmed filter:

◆ In the Timeline, click and drag the filter to the desired location.

Be careful not to click the ends of the filter or you'll trim it rather than move it.

Figure 9.13 You can change when a filter starts by dragging its in point in the Timeline.

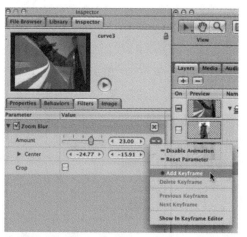

Figure 9.14 You can animate filter parameters by using the Animation menu.

Animating Filters

You can animate a filter by making just about any parameter change over time, using either keyframes or parameter behaviors. If you use keyframes, you can choose whether to record keyframes or set them with the Animation menu.

For a full discussion on using keyframes, see Chapter 7; for behaviors, see Chapter 6.

To animate filter parameters by recording:

1. Select the filter and set the parameter values you want for the first keyframe of the filter.

2. Move the playhead to the location for the second keyframe.

3. Click the Record button or press A.

4. Set the parameter value(s) for the new location.

5. Continue to move the playhead and set new parameter values until you are finished.

6. Click the Record button or press A to stop recording.

To animate filter parameters with the Animation menu:

1. Select the filter.

2. Move the playhead to the location for the first keyframe.

   Note: There won't be a keyframe at the beginning of the filter unless you add one.

3. In the Filter tab of the Inspector (press F3 to reveal it), click the Animation menu and select Add Keyframe from the drop-down menu (**Figure 9.14**).

continues on next page

ANIMATING FILTERS

4. Change the parameter to the desired value.

5. Move the playhead to the next desired keyframe location.

6. Repeat steps 3 through 5 until you are finished.

✔ Tips

■ Using Record always sets a keyframe at the first frame of the filter; if that's not what you want, set keyframes with the Animation menu.

■ When using the animation menu, it's critical that you *first* set the keyframe and *then* choose the parameter value for that keyframe. If you don't set the keyframe first, the new parameter value is added to the entire effect.

■ You can use the Animation menu in the Keyframe Editor to set keyframes as well.

■ You can move keyframes in the Timeline; you can move them, change their values, and change the curves between them in the Keyframe Editor. See Chapter 7 for more information on manipulating keyframes.

■ When you trim a filter with keyframes applied, the distance between the keyframes shrinks or expands proportionally. If you hold down the Command key while trimming, they remain stationary (**Figures 9.15a, b,** and **c**).

Figure 9.15a Here is the filter before trimming.

Figure 9.15b Trimming the filter shrinks the distance between the keyframes.

Figure 9.15c If you hold down the Command key while trimming, the filter's keyframes remain in their original locations. However, if the filter bar isn't visible over the keyframe, the filter won't be seen in the Canvas.

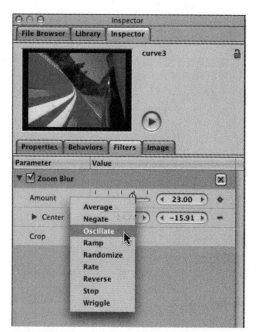

Figure 9.16 You can animate filter parameters with filter behaviors by going to the Inspector, Control-clicking the parameter you want to animate, and choosing a parameter behavior from the drop-down menu.

To animate filter parameters with parameter behaviors:

1. In the Filters tab of the Inspector (press F3 to reveal it), Control-click the name of the parameter you want to animate and choose a parameter behavior from the drop-down menu (**Figure 9.16**).

   As a result, the Behaviors tab of the Inspector comes to the front with the applied parameter behavior.

2. Adjust the parameters of the parameter behavior as desired.

   For more information on working with parameter behaviors, see Chapter 6.

Using Third-Party Filters

Many filters, called *plug-ins*, that are created by other vendors can be used in Motion if they are compatible with Adobe After Effects. To get these plug-ins to appear in the 3rd Party Filters folder in the Library, you just need to tell Motion where they are located.

To make third-party filters available in the Library:

1. Open Motion's Preferences by choosing Motion > Preferences or by pressing Command-, (comma).

2. If it's not already highlighted, click General at the top of the window (**Figure 9.17**).

3. Under the 3rd Party Plug-ins section at the bottom, click Choose.

4. Select the folder that contains your plug-ins and click Choose.

5. Quit and restart Motion. The plug-ins should now appear in the 3rd Party Plug-ins folder of the Library.

✔ Tips

- The specified folder can't be an alias.

- Third-party plug-ins are not accelerated, so you won't see the real-time performance that is available with Motion's filters.

- Not all After Effects–compatible plug-ins work with Motion. For current compatibility information, check Apple's Web site (www.apple.com/motion).

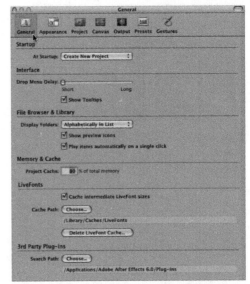

Figure 9.17 You can make third-party filters available in the Library from the General pane of Motion's Preferences.

10

USING GENERATORS

Need a stylish, animated background in a hurry? The Generators category in the Library contains a variety of useful patterns, gradients, and solids—some static and some already animated that can be used as background elements, masks, displacement maps, or other compositional elements. These generators all have parameters that you can adjust and animate, and you can save your modified generators into the Library for future use. By changing their default values, animating their parameters with behaviors (Chapter 6) or keyframes (Chapter 7), adding filters (Chapter 9), and changing blend modes (Chapter 4), you can dramatically alter how these generators look and behave.

Browsing and Previewing Generators

Generators are located in the fourth folder of the Library. Just like other Library elements such as behaviors and filters, you can preview generators to get a sense of what they look like before you add them to your project.

To browse and preview generators:

1. Open the Library (Window > Library or Command-2).

2. In the Sidebar, select the Generators category.

3. In the File Stack, click a generator.

A preview of how the generator appears with its default settings and a short description that explains which parameters you can change appears in the Preview Area. As opposed to filters, if the preview is animated, then the generator is already animated when you add it to the project, so you don't need to add keyframes or parameter behaviors (although you may want to animate it in other ways with these tools).

There are 13 different generators in the Library if you include the freebie mentioned in "The Freebie" sidebar:

Cellular creates soft moving blobs that resemble cells viewed under a microscope (**Figure 10.1**). You can change the size of the cells and the speed at which they move, and you can add a gradient to change the color.

Checkerboard creates a simple checkerboard pattern (**Figure 10.2**). You can change the size, color, and contrast of the pattern.

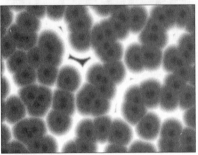

Figure 10.1 The Cellular generator creates soft, moving blobs that look like cells under a microscope.

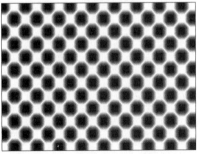

Figure 10.2 The Checkerboard generator can turn a straightforward checkerboard pattern into a work of art.

BROWSING AND PREVIEWING GENERATORS

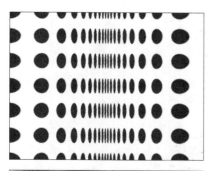

Figure 10.3 The Op Art 2 generator creates patterns of dots that can be squeezed and feathered.

Figure 10.4 The Op Art 3 generator is similar to Op Art 1, but it only uses one line and tosses in a skew parameter.

Clouds creates an animated cloud pattern that has four layers with independent strength controls. You can change the scale of the clouds, the speed at which they move, and apply a gradient.

Color Solid creates, well, a solid color of your choosing.

Gradient creates a static linear gradient between two colors by default. You can change it to a radial gradient, and you have a great deal of control over the number, type, and spread of color values and opacity with the Gradient Editor. This generator is discussed in more detail in "Using the Gradient Editor" later in this chapter.

Noise creates a static random pattern of tiny colored dots. You can change the random seed that generates the pattern.

Op Art 1 makes a pattern of wavy lines out of two different wavelengths that you can adjust independently. You can also change the amplitude, line thickness, roundness, and contrast of the wavelengths.

Op Art 2 makes a pattern of dots that are squeezed along a line. You can change the scale, angle, contrast, dot size, and compression (**Figure 10.3**).

Op Art 3 creates a pattern of wavy lines similar to Op Art 1, but with just one wavelength and an added skew parameter (**Figure 10.4**).

Soft Gradient makes radial gradient. You can adjust the color and radius.

BROWSING AND PREVIEWING GENERATORS

Star is a very spiky four-pointed white star that appears over a soft glow. You have several controls for the spikes and you can change the color of the glow (**Figure 10.5**).

Stripes makes stripes, no doubt about it. You can change the color, size, and contrast.

Swirly is an animated, multicolored spirography *thing* (thing is the technical term). You have many different controls over its shape and animation including three different styles, but you can't change its color (unless you add a filter) (**Figure 10.6**).

✔ Tip

■ You can modify generators to look quite different from their default state in the Preview Area, so don't pass one up just because it may not look like what you want at first glance.

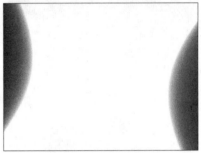

Figure 10.5 With the Star generator, you control the points as well as the color of the glow.

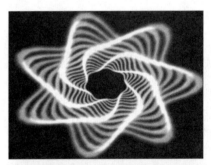

Figure 10.6 Use the Swirly generator to create animated spirals and swooshes.

The Freebie

The generators described here include the one called Clouds that doesn't ship with Motion, but is available for free (along with the four filters mentioned in Chapter 9) when you register Motion on Apple's Web site (www.apple.com/motion/download). It's a useful generator, so I recommend grabbing it!

BROWSING AND PREVIEWING GENERATORS

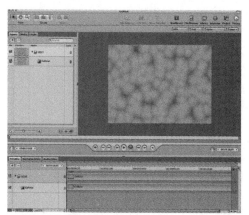

Figure 10.7 Generators appear in their own object row in the Layers tab and the Timeline.

Adding Generators

Because generators are objects, you import them into your project in the same manner as other objects. OK, technically you "apply" them rather than "import" them, but the steps are the same.

To add a generator:

1. Select the generator in the File Stack of the Library.

2. *Do one of the following:*

   ▲ Click the Apply button in the Preview Area of the Library.

   Clicking the Apply button automatically centers the generator on the Canvas.

   ▲ Drag the generator to the Canvas, Layers tab, or Timeline.

Generators appear in their own object row in the Layers tab and the Timeline (**Figure 10.7**). You can move, cut, copy, paste, lock, hide, solo, and reorder them just like you do with other objects. For more information on working with objects, see Chapter 3.

✔ Tips

■ Generators automatically adjust themselves to fit the Canvas size.

■ If you have Create Objects At set to Start of project in your preferences (select Motion > Preferences in the Project section under Still Images and Objects), the generator will have the same duration as the project. If you have Create Objects At set to Current frame, the generator starts at the playhead and continues to the end of the project.

■ You cannot add generators to the Media tab of the Project pane—because they are already part of Motion, they are considered already "imported."

Modifying Generators

Because generators are objects, they have transform properties that you can change directly in the Canvas, such as scale, position, and rotation. (For more on changing object properties, see Chapter 4.)

In addition, the generator-specific parameters are accessible in either the Dashboard or the Generator tab of the Inspector.

To modify generator parameters:

1. Select the generator.

2. *Do one of the following:*

   ▲ Adjust the parameters in the Dashboard (press D or F7 to reveal).

   ▲ Adjust the parameters in the Generator tab of the Inspector (press F4 to reveal)(**Figure 10.8**).

✔ Tips

■ The Dashboard usually contains a subset of all adjustable parameters, so check the Inspector for the full list.

■ If you want a colored solid that is smaller than the Canvas, create a Shape (see Chapter 12) rather than using the Color Solid generator because it takes less processing power to display (and it's much more flexible).

■ The Soft Gradient and Star generators both contain alpha channels (areas of transparency) so you can composite them easily.

■ Although adjusting the Scale parameter on the Properties tab of the Inspector has the same result as using the Width and Height controls in the Generator tab, it takes more system resources to calculate the change in the Scale parameter.

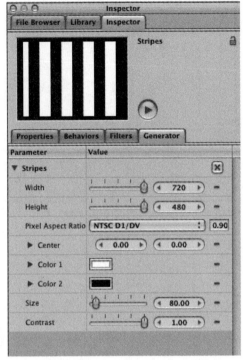

Figure 10.8 You can adjust the parameters for a generator via the Generator tab in the Inspector.

Hey, Where'd That Generator Tab Come From?

Surprised to see a Generator tab in the Inspector?

The fourth tab in the Inspector, called the Object tab, is *context-sensitive*. That means it changes its name and contents based on the object you have selected. If you have selected a text object, it becomes the Text tab; if a particle emitter is selected, it becomes the Emitter tab; and when a generator is selected, it becomes the Generator tab and contains all of the adjustable parameters for the selected generator.

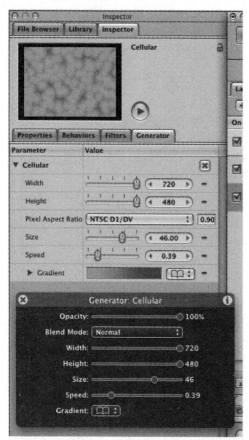

Figure 10.9 Cellular, Clouds, and Gradient generators each have a Gradient parameter.

Using Gradient Presets

The Cellular, Clouds, and Gradient generators each have a Gradient parameter (**Figure 10.9**). There are 14 preset gradient patterns that you can choose from in the Library.

To preview gradient presets:

◆ In the Library, click the Gradient category and select a gradient in the File Stack.

The gradient appears in the Preview Area.

To apply a gradient preset to a generator:

1. Select the generator that contains a Gradient parameter (Cellular, Clouds, or Gradient).

2. *Do one of the following:*
   - ▲ In the Dashboard, choose a gradient preset from the drop-down list.
   - ▲ In the Generator tab of the Inspector, choose a gradient preset from the drop-down list (**Figure 10.10**).
   - ▲ In the Library, select a gradient and drag it onto the generator in the Canvas, Layers tab, or Timeline.

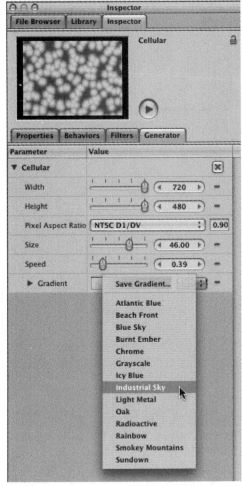

Figure 10.10 It's easy to apply a gradient preset to a generator. One way to do this is to choose a gradient preset from the drop-down list in the Generator tab of the Inspector.

Using the Gradient Editor

You can modify the default gradient or a gradient preset by changing the colors; the number, location, and spread of color *tags*; and the opacity at specific points and over specific ranges in the gradient. You can then save your settings as a new gradient preset in the Library.

To reveal the Gradient Editor:

◆ In the Generator tab of the Inspector, click the disclosure triangle for the Gradient parameter to reveal the Gradient Editor (**Figure 10.11**).

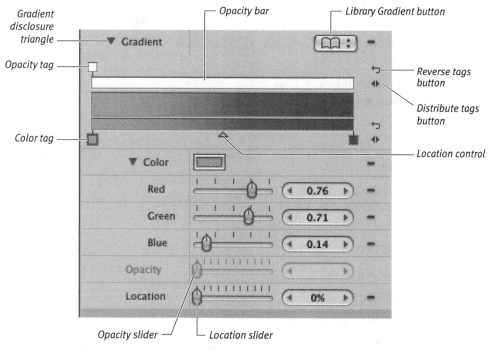

Figure 10.11 The Gradient Editor lets you modify the default gradient or a gradient preset and save your work as a custom gradient in the Library.

To change gradient colors:

Do one of the following:

◆ Double-click the color tag and select a new color from the color wheel (**Figure 10.12**).

◆ Click the color tag to select it, then Control-click the color swatch and sample a color.

◆ Click the color tag to select it, then use the Red, Green, and Blue sliders to enter values.

To change a color tag position:

1. Click the color tag to select it.

2. *Do one of the following:*

   ▲ Drag the color tag to the new location.

   ▲ Use the Location slider to specify the new location.

To change the spread of colors between two color tags:

◆ Drag the Location control between the color tags left or right.

To add a color tag:

◆ Click the lower color bar at the location where you want the new color tag placed (**Figure 10.13**).

To remove a color tag:

◆ Drag it away from the color bar.

To add an opacity tag:

◆ Click the opacity bar at the desired location for the new tag.

By default, the gradient is 100-percent opaque.

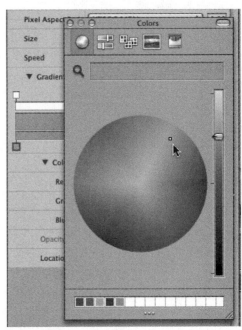

Figure 10.12 To change gradient colors, simply choose a new color from the color wheel.

Figure 10.13 To add a color tag, simply click the lower color bar at the location where you want the new tag to go.

Figure 10.14 To save a custom gradient, first click the Library Gradient button and then choose Save Gradient.

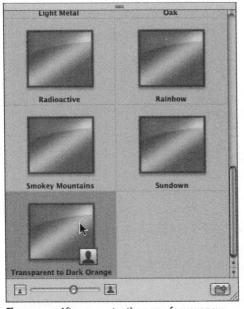

Figure 10.15 After you enter the name for your new gradient and click Save, the new gradient appears in the Gradient section of the Library.

To change the opacity of an opacity tag:

◆ Click the opacity tag to select it, then drag the Opacity slider.

White implies 100-percent opacity, black is 100-percent transparent, and shades of gray are varying levels of opacity. To change the range over which the opacity changes, drag on the Opacity location control.

To reverse the order of color tags or opacity tags:

◆ Click the appropriate Reverse Tags button.

To evenly distribute color tags or opacity tags:

◆ Click the appropriate Distribute Tags button.

To save a customized gradient:

1. Click the Library Gradient button and choose Save Gradient (**Figure 10.14**).

2. In the dialog that appears, enter the name for your custom gradient and click Save.

The gradient now appears in the Gradient section of the Library with a user icon attached (**Figure 10.15**), and it is available from the drop-down list in the Gradient Editor.

Other Objects That Use Gradients

The Gradient parameter is found in Text, Shapes, and Particle Cell objects as well as Generators, and it works almost identically for each type of object. You can choose the same preset gradients in the Library for any of these objects, and the same Gradient Editor is contained in the Inspector.

Animating Generator Parameters

You can bring a static generator to life by animating one or more of its parameters. Just as with other elements, you can either use keyframes or parameter behaviors to create animation. If you use keyframes, you can choose whether to record keyframes or set them with the Animation menu.

For a full discussion on using keyframes, see Chapter 7; for behaviors, see Chapter 6.

To animate generator parameters by recording:

1. Select the generator and set the parameter value(s) you want for the first frame of the generator.

2. Move the playhead to the location for the second keyframe.

3. Click the Record button or press A.

4. Set the parameter value(s) for the new location.

5. Continue to move the playhead and set new parameter values until you're finished.

6. Click Record or press A to stop recording.

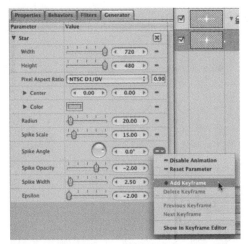

Figure 10.16 To animate generator parameters using the Animation menu, select Add Keyframe from the drop-down menu in the Generator tab of the Inspector.

To animate generator parameters using the Animation menu:

1. Select the generator.

2. Move the playhead to the location for the first keyframe.

    Note: There will not be a keyframe at the beginning of the generator unless you add one.

3. In the Generator tab of the Inspector (press F3 to reveal), click the Animation menu and select Add Keyframe from the drop-down menu (**Figure 10.16**).

4. Change the parameter to the desired value.

5. Move the playhead to the next desired keyframe location.

6. Repeat steps 3 through 5 until finished.

✔ Tips

- Using Record always sets a keyframe at the first frame of the generator; if that's not what you want, set keyframes with the Animation menu.

- When you're using the animation menu, it's critical to *first* set the keyframe, *then* choose the parameter value for that keyframe. If you don't set the keyframe first, the new parameter value is added to the current values at every frame.

- You can use the Animation menu in the Keyframe Editor to set keyframes as well.

- You can move keyframes in the Timeline; in the Keyframe Editor you can move them, change their values, and change the curves between them. See Chapter 7 for more information on manipulating keyframes.

ANIMATING GENERATOR PARAMETERS

To animate generator parameters with parameter behaviors:

1. In the Generator tab of the Inspector (press F3 to reveal), Control-click the name of the parameter you want to animate and choose a parameter behavior from the drop-down menu (**Figure 10.17**).

   The Behaviors tab of the Inspector comes to the front with the applied parameter behavior.

2. Adjust the parameters of the parameter behavior as desired.

✔ Tips

■ Remember, even animated generators like Swirly can have their parameters animated.

■ You can animate the colors and opacity of a gradient in the Gradient parameter with either keyframes or behavior parameters (or both!).

■ For more information on working with parameter behaviors, see Chapter 6.

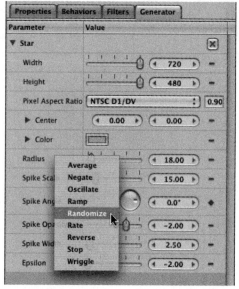

Figure 10.17 To animate generator parameters with parameter behaviors, Control-click the name of the parameter you want to animate and choose a parameter behavior from the drop-down menu in the Generator tab of the Inspector.

ANIMATING GENERATOR PARAMETERS

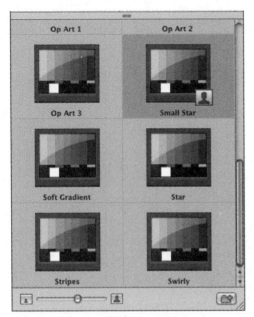

Figure 10.18 Custom generators appear in alphabetical order in the Library with a user icon attached to thems

Saving Customized Generators

Once you have spent time getting a generator looking just perfect, you can save your customized version back into the Library as a new generator. Then you'll always have access to it for any future project.

To save a customized generator:

1. Rename the generator by double-clicking the name in the Layers tab or Timeline, typing a new name, and pressing Return.

2. In the Library, select the Generator category in the Sidebar.

3. Drag the generator from the Layers tab to the File Stack of the Library.

    The custom generator appears in alphabetical order with a user icon attached to it (**Figure 10.18**).

✔ Tips

- Any keyframes or parameter behaviors that you add to a generator are saved along with it when you add it to the Library. Very cool!

- To rename a custom generator, Control-click it and select Rename.

- To delete a custom generator, Control-click it and select Move to Trash.

- You can also add custom generators to the Favorites and the Favorites Menu folders in the Library. You can even create your own folders. The only thing you can't do is save a generator into another Library category, like Filters or Behaviors.

WORKING WITH PARTICLES

With particle systems you can create an incredible variety of animated effects—you can make realistic natural phenomena like smoke, fire, explosions, clouds, and water; pattern-based animations like schools of fish or flocks of birds; or abstract animated backgrounds. The real-time viewing capability of Motion combined with the large number and variety of preset particles systems makes working with these complex effects easy and immediately rewarding.

In some ways, particles are the culmination of everything that is Motion because you can incorporate so many of Motion's features into a particle system. Behaviors, keyframes, blend modes, and filters can all be used to modify and enhance the animation and appearance of a particle system. You can even have particle systems interact with objects that are not part of the system by using simulation behaviors such as Attract, Repel, or Orbit Around.

In this chapter, I first break down a particle system into its components to understand how it works. Then, I take a look at how to use the preset systems in the Library. From there, I cover how to create a particle system from scratch, and how to customize it in detail. I look at applying filters, behaviors, and keyframes, and finally, I finish by covering how to save your customized particle systems for future use.

Understanding Particle Systems

Particle systems in Motion are made up of two primary components: an *emitter* and one or more *cells* (**Figure 11.1**). The emitter is the source from which all the cells emanate—like water from a fountain, arrows from a bow, or bullets from a gun. You adjust the parameters of the emitter to determine the number of cells and the direction they travel; you adjust the cell parameters to determine their characteristics, like their size, speed, and orientation.

The sheer number of parameters available for particle systems can be intimidating, but by examining them one by one, you'll find that they are all quite straightforward and easy to work with.

Once you grasp the basics of how to work with particles, the best way to learn what they can do is to play with them—take different presets from the Library, tweak their parameters, replace the particle cell source objects, and add some behaviors—Motion's real-time performance makes it down right addicting!

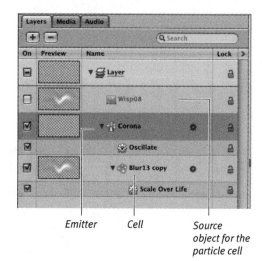

Emitter   Cell   Source object for the particle cell

Figure 11.1 A particle system contains an emitter and one or more cells. In this example, an Oscillate behavior has been applied to the emitter and the Scale Over Life particle behavior has been applied to the cell. Notice that the original source object for the cell is inactive—it's visibility check box is unchecked.

Figure 11.2 Abstract particle systems provide great otherworldly effects for animation.

Figure 11.3 Pyro particle systems include a set of 20 fire-based effects.

Figure 11.4 SciFi particle systems are often spacey looking.

Working with Preset Particle Systems

Particle systems can be very complex and sophisticated, but getting started with them is easy. Motion includes 117 preset particle systems in the Library, which are organized into the following six categories:

Abstract. These 24 systems are good for animated backgrounds and lower-thirds treatments (**Figure 11.2**).

Nature. This category contains 26 natural phenomena effects like rain, clouds, snow, dust, and bubbles.

Pyro. There are 20 different fire-based effects (**Figure 11.3**).

SciFi. This category is loaded with 27 effects, including some spacey-type effects like stars. Many effects in this category could belong in the Abstract category (**Figure 11.4**).

Smoke. There are seven different types of smoke effects.

Sparkles. These 13 effects use animated sparkling cells.

You can use these presets just as they come, or you can adjust a few parameters and replace or add objects to the sytstem. With these types of adjustments, you can very quickly create a sophisticated custom animation.

To browse and preview preset particle systems:

1. In the Sidebar of the Library (press Command-2 to reveal it), select the Particle Emitters category.

2. Select a subcategory.

3. Click a particle emitter in the File Stack.

   An animation of the particle systems plays in the Preview Area.

✔ Tip

- For some particle systems (for example, the Pyro and Sparkles categories), if you click and drag in the Preview window, you can see how the system behaves when the emitter is animated.

To apply a preset particle system:

1. Select a particle system preset in the Library.

2. *Do one of the following:*
   - ▲ Click the Apply button in the Preview Area.
   - ▲ Drag the particle emitter to the Canvas, Layers tab, or Timeline.

   The particle system plays in the Canvas in the same way it plays in the Preview Area (as opposed to some generators and behaviors, which are animated in the Preview Area, but aren't animated in the Canvas until you animate them with behaviors or keyframes).

Figure 11.5 When you create a custom particle system, Motion creates an emitter object and selects it.

Creating a Custom Particle System

Rather than starting with a preset particle system and modifying it, you can create your own system from scratch. In fact, you can do so with one click of the mouse!

To create a custom particle system:

1. Place the object that you want as the source for the cell of the system at the location in the Canvas from which you want the particles emitted.

2. Select the object.

3. Click the Make Particles icon in the Toolbar or press E.

When you click Make Particles, Motion creates an emitter object that appears in the Canvas with a bounding box because it is selected (**Figure 11.5**). Motion also creates a cell object that has the original object you selected as its source. The original object is inactive—that is, it is no longer visible—and the object that you see in the Canvas is now a cell from the emitter, not the original object.

If you play your project (click the Play button in the transport controls at the bottom of the Canvas or press the Spacebar), you'll see that the emitter spits out quite a few particles in all directions based on the default parameter settings.

Particles Everywhere!

What can you use as a cell source to create particles? Just about any object works—any type of graphic or even a QuickTime movie can be the source for the particle cells. Usually you want the object to have an alpha channel or areas of transparency so that it can be composited against a background.

Motion contains many elements that you can use as particles as well, such as Text (Chapter 13) and Generators (Chapter 10).

Also, an entire category of content in the Library, called Particle Images, contains over 100 images and QuickTime movies designed specifically to be used as particles.

For more information on creating your own particle cells, see the "Creating Objects for Cells" sidebar.

Creating Objects for Cells

By creating an object for use as a particle cell, you can build specific looks such as fog, smoke, sparks, fire, and so on. Here are a few helpful hints to keep in mind when you design your particle objects:

◆ Keep graphics small enough to improve particle system performance, but large enough so you won't need to scale them over 100 percent to avoid pixelization.

◆ Make sure you save the object with an alpha channel so that the background is transparent. If you create your object in Photoshop and you have removed the background, saving it as a .psd file automatically retains the alpha channel.

◆ Object edges with a gradual opacity falloff often look more organic than a hard edge.

◆ Remember that you have a variety of options to choose from to color your particle cells in the system, so for maximum flexibility, start with a white object.

◆ If you create a QuickTime movie to be used as a particle cell source, design it so that it loops seamlessly. You can create animations in Motion, export them as QuickTime movies, and then bring them back into Motion to use as particle cells.

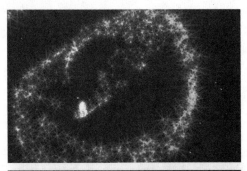
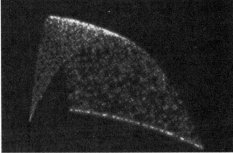

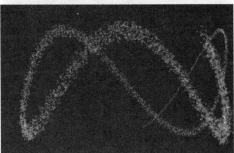

Figure 11.6 You can create many different types of particle systems from the same single particle cell by customizing the parameters of the system.

Customizing Particle Systems

Particles systems have a large number of parameters that you can adjust. The adjustments you make can result in drastically different animations, even with the same underlying object for the particle cell (**Figure 11.6**). Therefore, you'll want to build familiarity with all the controls. There are just a few parameters for the emitter, but their values have a very large impact on the look of the particle system. Parameters for particle cells, on the other hand, are much more numerous and nuanced.

As with other objects and effects, the Dashboard contains a subset of the most useful parameter controls, whereas the Inspector holds every adjustable parameter.

Customizing the Emitter with the Dashboard

When you create particles by clicking the Make Particles icon in the Toolbar, or by pressing E, the parameters of particle system that is created are populated with a set of default values. The first step in customizing the system is usually to adjust the parameters for the emitter to control the overall birth rate, life, scale, direction, spread, and speed of the particle cells—these parameters are all available in the Dashboard (**Figure 11.7**).

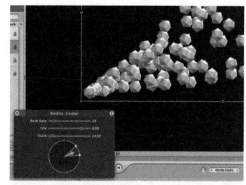

Figure 11.7 The Dashboard lets you adjust parameters for the emitter to control birth rate, life, scale, direction, spread, and speed of particle cells.

To modify emitter parameters with the Dashboard:

1. Select the emitter in the Layers tab, Canvas, or Timeline.

   Clicking any particle in the Canvas selects the emitter.

2. If the Dashboard isn't already visible, press D or F7 to reveal it.

3. Make adjustments to the controls as described below.

To change the Birth Rate, Life, and Scale parameters in the Dashboard

- Drag the appropriate slider control:

   Birth Rate controls how many particles appear each second, and it is set to 30 per second by default (which is a lot!).

   Life controls how many seconds each particle stays visible—if a particle hasn't moved off the Canvas by the end of its life, it disappears. The default is 5 seconds.

   Scale controls the overall size of the particles. It is set to 100 percent of the original object size by default.

Particle Feedback

It's helpful to set a play range (Command-Option-I sets an in point and Command-Option-O sets an out point) around the animation and loop playback (Shift-L) as you make changes to parameters to see how the changes impact the particle system. If you don't want to play the project, then place the playhead at a point far enough along in the animation so that you can see several emitted particles change in the Canvas as you make adjustments.

CUSTOMIZING THE EMITTER WITH THE DASHBOARD

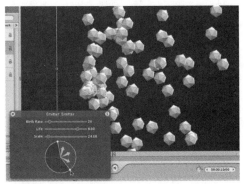

Figure 11.8 Drag along the outer edge of the Emission control (the circular item) to set the range over which particles are to be emitted.

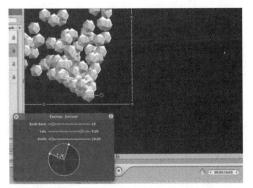

Figure 11.9 Drag anywhere inside the Emission control to change the direction of the Emission Range.

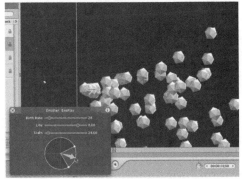

Figure 11.10 Drag the arrow inside the Emission control further outward or inward to increase or decrease the cells' speed, respectively.

To change the Emission Range parameter in the Dashboard:

◆ Click and drag anywhere along the outer edge of the Emission control to set the range over which particles are to be emitted (**Figure 11.8).**

To change the Emission Angle parameter in the Dashboard:

◆ Click and drag inside the Emission control to change the direction of the Emission Angle parameter(**Figure 11.9**).

To change the Speed parameter in the Dashboard:

◆ Click and drag one of the arrows in the Emission control (**Figure 11.10**). Dragging the arrow outward increases the speed.

✔ Tips

■ You can only increase the speed so far in the emitter's Dashboard. For more control, use the particle cell's Dashboard or the Inspector, both of which are discussed later in this chapter.

■ Technically, Birth Rate, Life, Scale, and Speed are actually not emitter parameters. Instead, they are cell parameters, as you'll see when we discuss the Emitter tab of the Inspector later on. They appear in the Dashboard when you select the emitter for convenience. Birth Rate, Life, and Speed also appear in the particle cell's Dashboard.

Customizing the Particle Cell with the Dashboard

There are six parameters available on the Dashboard when you select a particle cell; three of them, Birth Rate, Life, and Speed, are also available on the emitter Dashboard discussed previously. The other three provide some additional control, but you may find it's most useful to adjust these parameters in the Inspector.

To modify particle cell parameters with the Dashboard:

1. Select the particle cell in the Layers tab or the Timeline.

   Make sure to select the particle cell and not the original source object.

2. If the Dashboard isn't already visible, press D or F7 to reveal it.

3. Make adjustments to the controls as described below.

To adjust Birth Rate, Life, Speed, Spin, or Scale Range in the particle cell Dashboard:

◆ Drag one of the following sliders, whichever is appropriate:

   Birth Rate, **Life**, and **Speed** are discussed in "Customizing the Emitter with the Dashboard" earlier in this chapter.

   Spin controls how fast the particles spin, and it is set to zero by default.

   Scale Range defines an upper and lower limit to the size of the particle and is applied randomly so that each particle is created at a random size within the Scale Range. It is set to zero by default so that the particles are all the same size.

What About Emitter Properties?

Because an emitter is an object, it has properties that you can adjust just like those of any other object, such as Position, Scale, Rotation, Anchor Point, and Shear (Chapter 4 covers how to change these properties in the Canvas, the Dashboard, and the Properties tab of the Inspector). However, because a particle system involves a collection of independently generated objects, these properties for an emitter behave a little differently from ordinary objects.

If you change the Position parameter of the emitter, all the particles that it generates also change position as a group. But if you *animate* the Position parameter with either behaviors (Chapter 6) or keyframes (Chapter 7), then particles continue on the path based on the position of the emitter at the time they were emitted, creating a trail. You can force particles to follow the emitter by using the Attach to Emitter particle cell parameter, which is discussed later in this chapter.

If you change the other Transform properties (Rotation, Scale, Shear, and Anchor Point), the change affects the particle system as a whole, similar to making transforms on a layer (**Figure 11.11**).

Changing the blend mode for an emitter affects all particles in the system. Drop Shadow, Four Corner, and Crop work in the same manner.

The final parameter in the Properties tab, Timing, determines the duration of the entire particle system. It is usually more intuitive to adjust the duration by trimming the Emitter row in the Timeline (see Chapter 5 and the "The Show Must Go On" sidebar later in this chapter).

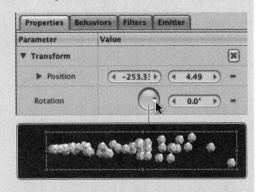

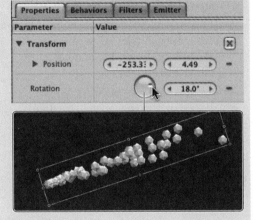

Figure 11.11 Changing a Transform parameter of the emitter, such as Rotation shown above, affects the particle system as a whole.

To change how the particles appear with the particle cell's Dashboard:

◆ Choose from the options in the Show Particles As drop-down list.

Each of these options can be useful if your composition is too complex for full real-time playback.

Points is the least processor intensive choice, and it replaces the object image with a white dot for each particle (**Figure 11.12**).

Lines replaces the object with a line that is oriented along the object's trajectory (**Figure 11.13**).

Wireframe draws an outline of the object's border with an "x" to give more visual clues about how the animation unfolds (**Figure 11.14**).

Image uses the object selected for the particle cell and is the default selection.

Figure 11.12 When you choose to show the particles as points, the source image is replace by a single white dot for each particle.

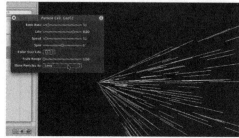

Figure 11.13 If you choose to show particles as lines, the source object is replaced by lines that indicate each particle's trajectory.

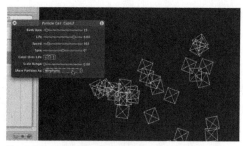

Figure 11.14 The wireframe choices lets you see how particles spin and change size in addition to their location and trajectory, yet without the full processor overhead required by using the source object.

CUSTOMIZING PARTICLE CELL WITH DASHBOARD

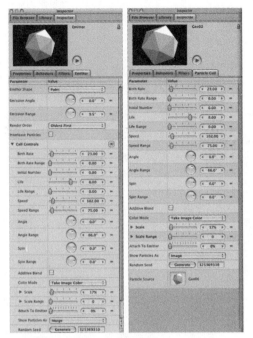

Figure 11.15 If you have just one particle cell source, then all the particle cell parameters are available in both the Emitter tab (left) and the Particle Cell tab (right).

Customizing Particle Systems in the Inspector

Although the Dashboard gives you quick and easy access to a few key particle system parameters, the Inspector is where you can really dig in and sculpt the animation in detail.

You need to consider two different sets of parameters when you're working with particle systems: those that modify the *emitter*, and those that modify the *particle cell*. These parameters are available on the Object tab of the Inspector—the tab furthest to the right that takes on the name of the element that is currently selected.

However, when you are working with a particle system that has just one object as its source for the particle cell, *all of the particle cell parameters are included on the Emitter tab*—notice how the same parameters are listed on each one (**Figure 11.15**). This consolidation makes it easier to adjust all of the parameters for the particle system in one location. Make sure you understand the difference between emitter parameters and particle cell parameters, because the contents of Emitter tab changes when there are multiple particle cells in a system (covered later in this chapter).

Customizing Emitter Parameters in the Inspector

There are only five parameters for the emitter, two of which are available in the Dashboard (Emission Angle and Emission Range, discussed earlier). The other three parameters determine how the particles appear as they are created.

To customize emitter parameters in the Inspector:

1. Select the emitter object.

2. Reveal the Emitter tab by opening the Inspector and clicking it, choosing Window > Show Inspector > Object, or by pressing F4.

3. Adjust the controls as desired.

✔ Tip

■ You may want to hide the Cell Controls in order to focus on the emitter parameters by clicking the disclosure triangle.

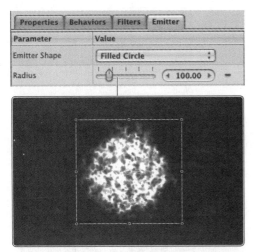

Figure 11.16 With a Filled Circle, particles emanate from anywhere inside the circle.

Customizing emission shape

The Emission Shape parameter determines the initial location of particles as they are created. By default, particles emanate from a point, but you have choices of five additional types of emitter shapes. Depending on your selection in the drop-down menu, different additional parameters appear.

To customize the emission shape:

1. Click the drop-down menu and choose one of the options.

   New parameters associated with your choice appear below the parameter.

2. Adjust the following new parameters as needed:

   Point defines a single point from which all particles emanate. It is the default choice and has no other parameters associated with it.

   Line makes particles emanate from a straight line. You can set the location of its end points and you can choose to have the particles emanate from a set number of points along the line.

   Circle causes particles to emanate from the edges of a circle whose radius you determine. You can also choose to have the particles come out of a fixed set of points.

   Filled Circle is the same as Circle but particles emanate from anywhere inside the circle, not just the edge (**Figure 11.16**).

   Geometry makes particles emanate from the edges of a shape that you determine by placing an object in the image well.

continues on next page

Image is similar to Geometry but particles emanate from the entire image, not just the edges. If the image has an alpha channel, you can have particles emanate from the edges of the alpha channel or between the alpha channel and the border of the image (**Figure 11.17**).

Several of the Emission Shape parameters have still more parameters associated with them:

Start Point and **End Point** are available only for the Line emission shape, and they determine the (x,y) coordinates for the line's end points.

Radius determines the size of the circle for the Circle and Filled Circle emmission shapes.

Shape Source determines the shape of the edges of the Geometry emission shape based on the Shape that you drag to the well.

Image Source determines the shape within which all particles emerge for the Image emission shape. Like Shape Source, you drag the object from the Layers list to the well. Unlike Shape Source, you can use any object, including movies.

Emit at Alpha is a parameter that appears with the Image emission shape. When you check the check box, particles emerge from the edges of the alpha channel.

Emission Alpha Cutoff is also available for the Image emission shape, and the slider determines how much of the transparency range is used to define the boundary for emerging particles.

Emit at Points is a parameter available for Line, Circle, and Geometry—all choices where particles emanate from an edge. When you select this check box, particles only come out of fixed points along the edge, the number of which is determined by the slider (**Figure 11.18**).

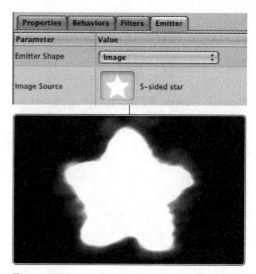

Figure 11.17 Image allows particles to emanate from an entire image based on whatever object you place in the image well.

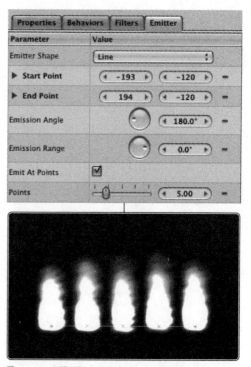

Figure 11.18 The Emit at Points parameter makes particles only come out of fixed number of points along the edge. You set the number of points with the slider.

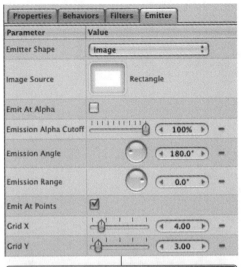

Figure 11.19 With the Grid X and Grid Y parameters, you choose the number of vertical and horizontal points at which particles will emerge.

Grid X and **Grid Y** are parameters for the Filled Circle and Image emission shapes, but *only if the Emit at Points parameter check box is checked*. They determine the number of horizontal and vertical points, respectively, from which particles emerge on a grid within the boundaries of the image (**Figure 11.19**).

✔ Tip

- You can use the shapes from the Shape category in the Library, or you can use the Shape tools to create a custom shape for the emitter. See Chapter 12 for more information on working with shapes.

Customizing Emission Angle and Emission Range in the Inspector

Although the interface isn't as intuitive as the Dashboard, when you want to enter specific values for these two parameters, the Inspector is the place to go.

To adjust the Emission Angle and Emission Range parameters in the Inspector:

1. Select the emitter and go to the Emitter tab in the Inspector.

2. *Do one of the following:*

   ▲ Click and drag on the dials.

   ▲ Click and drag in the Value fields.

   ▲ Click and enter a value in the Value fields.

✔ Tips

■ Hold down Shift as you drag in the Value field to scrub 10 times faster; hold down Option to scrub 100 times slower.

■ If the emission shape is a circle or a shape, a setting of 0 degrees for the Emission Angle parameter makes particles emerge only outside the shape. A setting of 180 degrees makes particles emerge only inside the shape.

■ If the emission shape is a line or a circle, setting the Emission Range parameter to 0 keeps particles perpendicular to the emitter when they emerge.

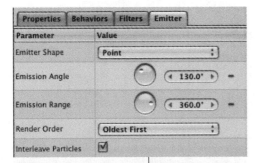

Figure 11.20 When you turn on Interleave Particles, the particles created from the different source objects are randomly stacked on top of each other, like shuffling a deck of cards.

Choosing the Render Order

The Render Order parameter determines whether particles are born in front of or behind previous particles.

To set the Render Order:

◆ Click the Render Order drop-down list and choose the desired order.

Oldest First makes new particles appear on top of older particles.

Oldest Last makes new particles appear underneath older particles.

✔ Tip

■ Use the Render Order parameter in combination with the Scale Over Life particle behavior (discussed later in this chapter) to make particles appear to be streaming toward or away from the viewer.

Interleaving particles

If you have multiple cells in a particle system, you can choose to have the particles that are generated from each cell mixed together so that some are below and some are above in the Canvas.

To interleave particles:

◆ Click the Interleave Particles check box (**Figure 11.20**).

If the check box is unchecked, which it is by default, particles generated from multiple cells stay in the same stacking order as the cells in the Layers tab. Using multiple cells is discussed later in this chapter.

Customizing Particle Cell Parameters in the Inspector

Particle cells have 21 different parameters that you can adjust to create diverse and unique particle systems (**Figure 11.21**).

If there is only one cell in the particle system, then all of these parameters are available in *both* the Emitter tab *and* the Particle Cell tab as discussed earlier.

To customize particle cell parameters in the Inspector:

Do one of the following:

◆ Select the emitter in the Layers tab or the Timeline and open the Emitter tab in the Inspector (press F4 to reveal it). Adjust each parameter as desired.

◆ Select the particle cell in the Layers tab or the Timeline and open the Particle Cell tab (press F4 to reveal it). Adjust each parameter as desired.

If the particle system has more than one cell, then the Emitter tab contains a set of *master controls* for all particles. If this is the case, you need to select the particle cell and go to the Particle Cell tab to adjust its individual parameters, as discussed in more detail on the next page.

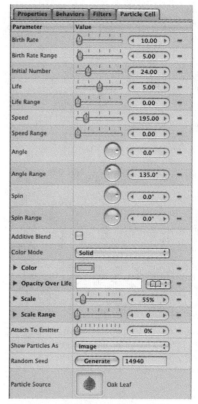

Figure 11.21 Particle cells have 21 different parameters which allow you to create incredibly diverse systems.

What About the Source Object?

When you create a particle system, the source object for the particle cells is made invisible in the Canvas. Any changes you make to its Position, Rotation, Scale, or Shear properties have no impact on the particle system.

However, other Properties tab parameters for the source object *do* change the look of the particles: changes to Anchor Point, Opacity, Four Corner, and Crop are passed through to the particles in the system. And of course you can animate these parameters with parameter behaviors or keyframes.

The particle cell parameters give you a great deal of control over how particles are born and how long they live; how fast they move; their angle and spin; their size, color, and more. And most parameters have a Range component that lets you apply a range of random values across particles, which can make the particles system appear much more variable, random, and organic. Here are the parameters and what they do:

Birth Rate determines how many particles are created every second.

Birth Rate Range allows you to create variability in the Birth Rate over time. The default value of zero results in a fixed birth rate.

Initial Number sets the starting number of particles before the Birth Rate starts. If the Birth Rate is set to zero, only the number of particles set in the Initial Number parameter emanates from the emitter.

Life sets for how long particles appear, in seconds. When a particle reaches the end of its life, it disappears.

Life Range creates variability so that different particles live for different lengths of time.

Speed sets how fast particles move away from the emitter. It is the same parameter that is controlled in the emitter's Dashboard by changing the size of the arrow.

Speed Range introduces variability so that different particles travel at different rates.

continues on next page

Isn't "Random Pattern" an Oxymoron?

Although particles are generated from an emitter in a random fashion to create an organic pattern, the randomness is actually fixed for a given set of parameter values. This means that, once you set all your values, any given frame of the animation has the same particles in the same location. This fact can be very useful for locking in an animation that you like, or for setting up other objects relative to particles in both space and time.

If you want to create a new random pattern, click the Generate button for the particle cell's Random Seed parameter.

Angle defines the fixed angle at which all particles are shown, as if you had transformed them with the Rotation parameter (note that rotating the source object for the particle cells has no impact on the particle cell angle).

Angle Range starts with the Angle value and then sets individual particle angles randomly by the value you set here (**Figure 11.22**).

Spin animates each particle by rotating it around its anchor point at a rate that you determine (in degrees per second) (**Figure 11.23**).

Spin Range causes each particle to spin at a different rate over the range you set with the slider.

Additive Blend, when checked, causes the particles' color values to add together when they overlap so that they get brighter.

Color Mode sets how particles are colored; this parameter is discussed in more detail in the "Working with Color Modes" later in this chapter.

Scale sets the size of the particles. You can set the x and y values independently (click the disclosure triangle to reveal the controls) to stretch or squeeze the particle shape.

Scale Range makes each particle randomly larger or smaller than the Scale setting based on the range set in this slider.

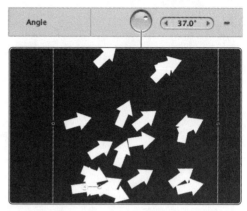

Figure 11.22 Angle Range changes individual particle angles randomly based on the value you choose.

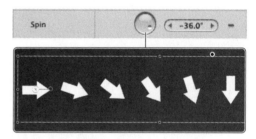

Figure 11.23 Spin animates each particle by rotating it around its anchor point at a rate you choose.

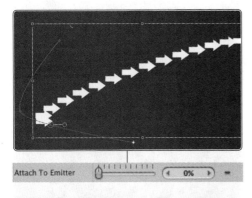

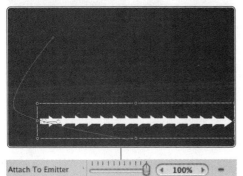

Figure 11.24 By changing the value in the Attach to Emitter parameter, you can force particles to follow the emitter after birth. Here, the emitter is animated along a motion path. In the first figure, particles ignore the emitter and travel their own path. In the second figure, the particles move as the emitter moves.

Attach to Emitter sets how closely particles follow a moving emitter. By default, this is set to zero and particles ignore the emitter after birth, following their own path. When this parameter is set to higher values, particles divert from their paths to follow the emitter (**Figure 11.24**).

Show Particles As provides several draft previews of the particles system to improve playback performance. These options are discussed in detail in "Customizing the Particle Cell with the Dashboard" earlier in this chapter.

Random Seed generates a new random value that determines how the particle cells are randomly generated in space and time.

Particle Source sets the object upon which all the particles for this cell are based. You can change the source by dragging a new object from the Layers tab to the well.

✔ Tips

- Changing the anchor point of the underlying source object (see Chapter 4) can have a dramatic impact on how the Spin parameter affects the particle system.

- If you are using a very small scale value for an image, set the anti-aliasing method in the Output preferences to Best. See Appendix B for more information.

Working with Color Modes

The color mode determines how particles are colored. There are five different options, several of which involve using a Gradient Editor, which is discussed in detail in Chapter 10.

To set the color mode:

◆ Click and choose a mode from the Color Mode pop-up menu in the Particle Cell tab in the Inspector.

Original retains the colors from the source object. When you select Original, you have the option of controlling how the opacity of the object changes with the Opacity Over Life parameter (**Figure 11.25**). You can add opacity tags along the bar and change their values with the Opacity slider. These controls are discussed in detail in Chapter 10.

Solid tints the particles based on a color you select either by clicking the color swatch or by using the RGB color sliders. You can set the overall transparency with the Alpha slider and make the transparency change over time with the Opacity Over Life control.

Over Life makes the particles change colors as they age. You can choose from any of the preset gradients in the Library using the Color Over Life drop-down list. The Gradient Editor works just as described in Chapter 10, except that the leftmost color value sets the color for the particle when it is created, and the rightmost value is the particle's color at the end of its lifespan. The color of the particle changes along the range of the gradient as it ages. As with the other color options, you have an Opacity Over Life parameter as well.

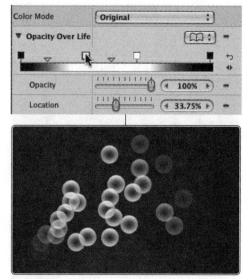

Figure 11.25 You can make particles fade in and fade out over time by editing the Opacity Over Life parameter.

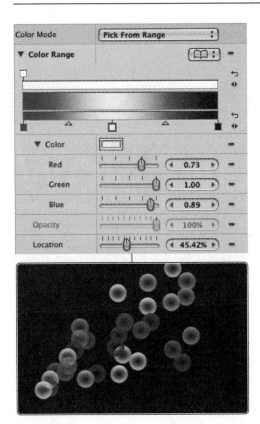

Figure 11.26 You can make each particle take on a random color from a fixed range of colors by choosing Pick From Range as the color mode.

Pick From Range assigns colors to particles randomly from the range you set in the Gradient Editor (**Figure 11.26**).

Take Image Color causes new particles to take on the color of the image at the point in time when the particle is generated.

✔ Tips

■ Clicking the color swatch brings up the Mac OS X Color Picker, which gives you many options, including sampling another color with the magnifying glass. However, to grab a color quickly, Control-click the swatch instead and, while continuing to hold the mouse button down, select a color from the pop-up Color Picker.

■ If you want a certain color to appear more frequently, create a large band of that color in the Gradient Editor.

Setting cell parameters for QuickTime movies

If you use a QuickTime movie as the source for your particle cell, several additional parameters appear in the Particle Cell tab (and in the Emitter tab if you only have one particle cell). These controls let you choose if and how the movie plays for each particle (**Figure 11.27**).

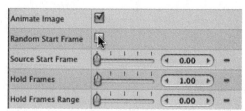

Figure 11.27 If you use a QuickTime movie as the source for your particle cell, then you'll have access to several additional parameters that let you choose if and how the movie plays for each particle.

◆ **Animate Image** determines whether the movie plays or not. It is checked by default, and the movie plays in a loop for every particle. When this box is unchecked, the particles take on the frame of the movie as determined by either the Random Start Frame parameter or the Source Start Frame parameter.

◆ **Random Start Frame**, also checked by default, chooses a random frame to start the animation for each particle. If Animate Image is turned off, then random still images from the movie are selected.

◆ The **Source Start Frame** slider appears if you uncheck the Random Start Frame check box. The Source Start Frame slider allows you to choose which frame of the animation each particle will start with. If the Hold Frames parameter is set to zero, the frame selected here will be a still image for the particles.

◆ **Hold Frames** slows down the animation by repeating each frame a number of times that you set with the slider. When set to 1, the animation plays at normal speed.

◆ **Hold Frames Range** plays each particle movie at a different speed based on the slider.

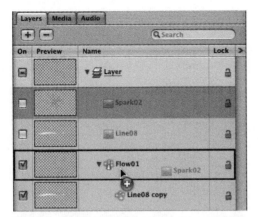

Figure 11.28 To add another particle cell to an emitter, simply drag the object on top of or just below the emitter.

The Show Must Go On

A particle system's duration is set by the duration of the emitter object, not the object that is the source of the particle cell. Trimming the emitter in the Timeline changes the duration of the overall system.

By default, particle cells match the duration of the emitter. However, if you have multiple cells in a system, you can change the timing for when the emitter begins and ends emitting particles for that cell by trimming the particle cell object in the Timeline (**Figure 11.29**).

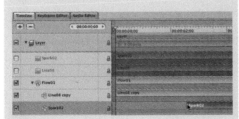

Figure 11.29 By trimming the in point of a particle cell in the Timeline, you can choose when the particles start to appear.

Using Multiple Cells

A particle system in Motion can contain more than one particle cell—this means that you can have several different objects set as the source for the particle cells that all emanate from one emitter. Motion provides a set of master controls over how these particles behave, and of course you can adjust the parameters of each particle cell individually.

To add another particle cell to an emitter:

1. Add the source object to your project by dragging it to the Layers tab, the Canvas, or the Timeline.

2. Turn off the object's visibility by unchecking the On check box.

3. Drag the object either on top of or just below the emitter (**Figure 11.28**). A new particle cell is created below the original particle cell.

Changing parameters for multiple particle cells

When a particle system has more than one particle cell, the Emitter tab contents changes to reflect a set of Master Controls for all the particles in the system.

To change parameters for multiple cells in a particle system:

1. Select the emitter for the system and open the Emitter tab in the Inspector (press F4 to reveal it).

2. Adjust the parameters as desired.

These controls affect all the particles cells in the system on a relative basis: for example, if you have set different birth rates for each particle cell in its own Particle Cell tab, then changing the birth rate in the Master Control applies the change proportionally, as a percentage of the rate for each individual cell.

Using Filters with Particle Systems

You can use filters with particle systems, but you can only apply them to the emitter, not individual particle cells. Therefore, the filter affects every particle in the system in the same manner. You can animate the parameters of filters applied to particle systems just as you would when filters are applied to other objects.

To apply a filter to a particle system:

1. Select the Emitter tab in the Layers tab.

2. *Do one of the following:*

   ▲ Select a filter from the Add Filter icon on the Toolbar (**Figure 11.30**).

   ▲ Select a filter in the Library and drag it onto the Emitter tab in the Layers tab.

For more information on applying, adjusting, and animating filters, see Chapter 9.

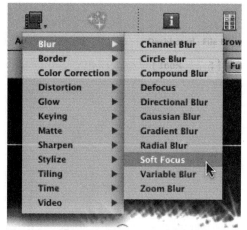

Figure 11.30 To apply a filter to a particle system simply select a filter from the Add Filter icon on the Toolbar.

Using Behaviors with Particle Systems

Particle systems, as complex and customizable as they are, can be made even more complex, customized, dynamic, organic, or just plain unique by throwing behaviors into the mix.

You can apply basic motion and simulation behaviors to emitters, and you can apply parameter behaviors to animate just about any parameter of emitters or cells.

Finally, one behavior is especially for particles—Scale Over Life—which allows you to change particles' size as they age.

To apply basic motion and simulation behaviors to emitters:

1. Select the emitter in the Layers tab.

2. *Do one of the following:*

   ▲ Select a basic motion or simulation behavior from the Add Behavior icon in the Toolbar.

   ▲ Drag the basic motion or simulation behavior from the Library onto the emitter in the Layers tab or Timeline.

✔ Tips

■ Although a subset of these behaviors can be applied to the particle cell rather than the emitter, the resulting animation is the same either way. Because not all behaviors work on cells, it can be easier to just apply them to the emitter.

■ Behaviors (and keyframes for that matter) only affect the position of particles at the point in time when they are created and do not affect the position and trajectory of existing particles. Therefore, if you animate the position of the emitter with a Throw behavior for example, the emitter leaves a trail of particles.

continues on next page

- Behaviors that affect parameters other than Position, such as Spin and Grow/Shrink, *do* continue to affect particles after they are created.

- You can force particles to follow the emitter with the Attach to Emitter parameter in the Particle Cell tab of the Inspector.

- If the source object for the particle cell has a directional shape, apply the Snap Alignment to Motion behavior to make the particles point in their direction of travel.

- For a less precise following of the path of travel, apply the Align to Motion (Simulation) behavior. Combine this behavior with other simulation behaviors for organic, complex systems (**Figure 11.31**).

- You can more easily create many Basic Motion behaviors by using the emitter and particle cell parameters, such as Emission Angle and Speed instead of Throw, or Spin (particle parameter) instead of, well, Spin (basic motion behavior).

- You can use simulation behaviors to cause multiple particles systems to interact with each other or with other objects.

Figure 11.31 By combining the Align to Motion (Simulation) behavior (above) with other simulation behaviors, such as Vortex, you can create complex, flowing particle movements (below).

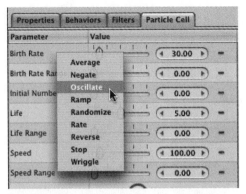

Figure 11.32 To apply a parameter behavior, simply Control-click the parameter you want to animate and select a parameter behavior from the drop-down menu. The parameter behavior gets applied with its default values, which may or may not have any impact. Tweak the parameter behavior parameters in the Behaviors tab.

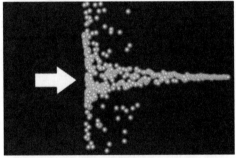

Figure 11.33 Here the Repel behavior has been applied to the arrow so that the particles, which have been aimed at the arrow, get pushed away.

To apply parameter behaviors to emitter and particle cell parameters:

1. Select the emitter or particle cell whose properties you want to animate.

2. In either the Properties tab, the Emitter tab, or the Particle Cell tab of the Inspector, Control-click the parameter you want to animate and select a parameter behavior from the drop-down menu (**Figure 11.32**).

3. In the Behavior tab that automatically comes to the front, adjust the parameters to taste.

For full coverage of working with parameter behaviors, return to Chapter 6.

✔ Tips

- By applying a parameter behavior to the Position parameter of the emitter (in the Properties tab), you can create a trail of particles.

- Apply parameter behaviors to the emitter parameters in the Emitter tab, such as Emission Angle and Emission Range, to affect the overall look of the system over time.

- By applying simulation behaviors to other objects or other particle systems in the project, you can create complex interactions between particles and objects (**Figure 11.33**).

- If you combine a parameter behavior that affects position with the Snap Alignment to Motion behavior (in the Basic Motion category), particles align themselves to the motion path.

Using the Scale Over Life behavior

The Particles behavior category contains one behavior that is designed just for particles—Scale Over Life. It's aptly named; it allows you to make particles change size over their lifespan.

To apply the Scale Over Life particles behavior:

1. Select the particle cell in the Layers tab or the Timeline.

2. *Do one of the following:*

   ▲ Select the Scale Over Life parameter from the Particles category in the Add Behavior icon in the Toolbar.

   ▲ Select the Scale Over Life behavior from the Particles category in the Library and drag it onto the particle cell in the Layers tab or in the Timeline (**Figure 11.34**).

3. Choose an Increment Type from the drop-down list.

4. Adjust the sliders as needed (**Figure 11.35**).

Figure 11.34 To apply the Scale Over Life particle behavior to a particle cell, drag it from the Library onto the cell.

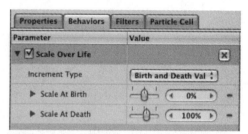

Figure 11.35 The Scale Over Life behavior has three parameters for adjusting how the particles change in size over time.

USING BEHAVIORS WITH PARTICLE SYSTEMS

You can employ three different ways of making the scale of particles change over time in the Increment Type pop-up:

Rate sets a constant rate for the particles to grow; use the slider to set the rate. To make particles shrink, use a negative Scale Rate.

Birth and Death Values allows you to set values for the size of the particles at their creation and their demise with the sliders as a percentage of the source object's size. Motion animates the scale in between these values.

Custom turns on the Custom slider, which you can then animate with either parameter behaviors, or with keyframes in order to animate the Scale Over Life parameter. For example, apply the Rate parameter behavior to make particles start out growing quickly over their lifespan, then start growing more slowly until they stop growing all together.

Keyframing Particle Systems

You can keyframe almost any parameter of an emitter or a cell, including the emitter's Properties parameters such as Position, Rotation, and Scale. You can also keyframe several of the source object's Property parameters such as Anchor Point, and Four Corner (see the sidebar "What About the Source Object?" earlier in this chapter).

You can choose whether to record keyframes or set them with the Animation menu.

For a full discussion on using keyframes see Chapter 7.

To animate particle system parameters by recording:

1. Select the emitter or particle cell and set the parameter values you want for the first frame of the animation.

2. Move the playhead to the location for the second keyframe.

3. Click the Record button or press A.

4. Set the parameter value(s) for the new location.

5. Continue to move the playhead and set new parameter values until you're finished.

6. Click Record or press A to stop recording.

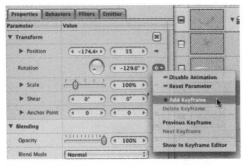

Figure 11.36 To animate emitter or particle cell parameters by setting Keyframes, simply click the Animation menu and select Add Keyframe from the drop-down menu.

To animate emitter or particle cell parameters with the Animation menu:

1. Select the emitter or particle cell you want to animate.

2. Move the playhead to the location for the first keyframe.

   Note: there will not be a keyframe at the beginning of the emitter or cell unless you add one.

3. In either the Properties tab (press F1 to reveal it), the Emitter tab, or the Particle Cell tab of the Inspector (press F4 to reveal either one depending on which object you selected), click the Animation menu and select Add Keyframe from the drop-down menu (**Figure 11.36**).

4. Change the parameter to the desired value.

5. Move the playhead to the next desired keyframe location.

6. Repeat steps 3 through 5 until you're finished.

✔ Tips

- Using Record always sets a keyframe at the first frame of the emitter or cell; if that's not what you want, set keyframes with the Animation menu.

- When you're using the animation menu, its critical that you *first* set the keyframe, and *then* choose the parameter value for that keyframe. If you don't set the keyframe first, the new parameter value is added to the entire effect.

- You can use the Animation menu in the Keyframe Editor to set keyframes as well.

- You can move keyframes in the Timeline; you can move them, change their values, and change the curves between them in the Keyframe Editor. See Chapter 7 for more information on manipulating keyframes.

Saving Custom Particle Systems

As you have seen, you can create highly customized particle systems by using multiple particle cell objects, adjusting parameters, and applying behaviors and/or keyframes. Once you have a system designed the way you like, you can save it in the Library for quick and easy access at any time. Your custom particle preset works just like any of the supplied presets.

To save a custom particle system:

1. In the Library (press Command-2 to reveal it), select the Favorites or the Favorites Menu category in the Sidebar.

2. Drag the emitter from the Layers tab to the File Stack area of the Library.

Items saved in the Favorites Menu folder become immediately available in the Favorites Menu (**Figure 11.37**).

✔ Tip

■ Particle presets are saved in the following folder on your hard drive:

/Home/Library/Application Support/ Motion/Library/Particle Emitters

If you used your own object source(s) for the particle cell(s), a copy is stored there as well. You can share these presets with other Motion users—they just need to copy the preset and any objects into the same folder on their system.

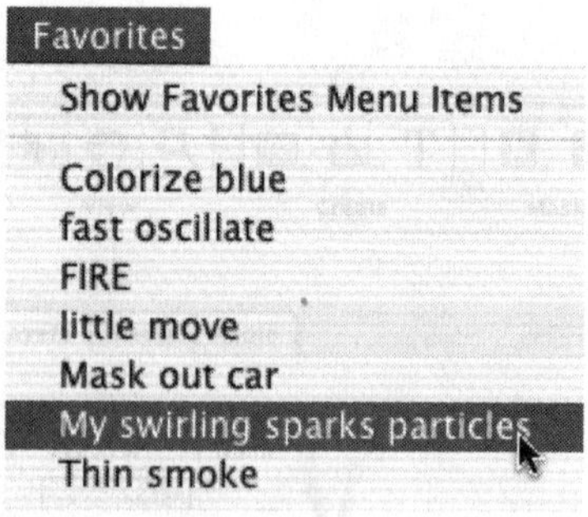

Figure 11.37 If you create a custom particle system and save it in the Favorites Menu folder, it will be immediately available in the Favorites Menu.

WORKING WITH SHAPES AND MASKS

Motion includes tools for creating simple and freeform *shapes*. Because shapes are another type of object, they can accept effects such as filters and behaviors. The same type of tools that create shapes can also be used to create *masks*. As opposed to a shape, which is a standalone entity, a mask is applied to an object to create transparency.

When drawing shapes or masks, you use pen tools to create *Bezier splines* or *BSplines,* which are lines connected by vertices called *control points*. These splines control the way the shape is created. You can animate the control points of shapes or masks to make them change form over time. And, because shapes and masks are vector objects, you can scale them to any size and still retain sharp edges.

In addition to drawing masks in Motion, you can create masks with image masks, blend modes, and certain types of filters. Masks are very flexible and are frequently used to remove an object from its original background by either *rotoscoping*—animating a mask— or *keying* out a solid background color.

In this chapter, I focus first on using the drawing tools. Although I discuss the tools in the context of shapes, masks are drawn in the same way. I then introduce the variations involved with drawing masks. From there, I look at other ways to create transparency with masks.

Drawing Shapes

Freeform shapes and masks are both drawn by creating control points connected by splines. As mentioned earlier, Motion includes two different methods for drawing splines: Bezier splines and BSplines.

Although you use separate tools for drawing shapes and masks, the process of working with control points and splines is almost identical for both.

In addition to allowing you to draw freeform shapes, Motion has tools for drawing rectangular and circular shapes. And, you can choose from a set of preset shapes in the Library.

To draw a Bezier shape:

1. Click the Bezier shape tool in the Toolbar or press B.

2. Click in the Canvas to establish the first control point.

3. Continue to click in the Canvas to create additional control points.

   By default, each point is connected by a straight line.

4. To finish the shape, *do one of the following:*

   ▲ To create a closed shape, click the first control point, or press C (**Figure 12.1**).

   ▲ To create an open shape, press Return to finish the shape or double-click to add a final control point (**Figure 12.2**).

Figure 12.1 Bezier shapes can either be closed...

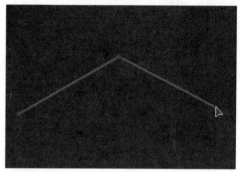

Figure 12.2 ...or they can be open.

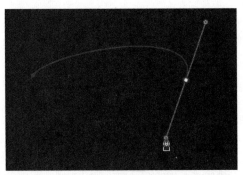

Figure 12.3 Click and drag to add a control point with Bezier handles, which control the curve through the control point.

✔ Tips

- If the shape is a closed shape, it is automatically filled with white. Open shapes have a white outline, with a default outline width of two pixels. Modifying the Fill and Outline parameters is covered in "Modifying Shapes" later in this chapter.

- If you click and drag when you are adding a control point, you create a curved Bezier point with handles (**Figure 12.3**).

- If you hold down Shift as you drag, a Bezier handle constrains the angle to 45-degree increments.

- To draw a straight line, create two control points—double-click to create the second point, or single-click and press Return.

- If you press Esc at any time while drawing a shape, the entire shape is deleted.

Bezier versus BSpline

A Bezier path can have hard corners or curves—and the curves are adjusted by using handles at the control point. BSplines, on the other hand, create a curve by moving tangential lines, and can be a little less intuitive until you've spent some time working with them.

No hard and fast rules exist for when you should use each type of spline, but in general, you'll find that Bezier splines are more suitable for creating shapes for illustration purposes, and that BSplines are easier to use for masking objects that have a lot of curves because they are inherently so smooth.

To draw a BSpline shape:

1. Click the BSpline shape tool in the Toolbar or press B twice.

   Pressing B toggles between the Bezier and BSpline tools.

2. Click in the Canvas to set the first control point.

3. Continue to click in the Canvas to create additional control points.

   Each point influences the shape of the curve (**Figure 12.4**).

4. To finish the shape, *do one of the following:*

   ▲ To create a closed shape, click the first control point, or press C.

   ▲ To create an open shape, press Return to finish the shape, or double-click to add a final control point.

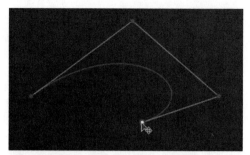

Figure 12.4 When you are drawing a BSpline shape, each point influences the shape of the curve.

✔ Tips

■ Try to keep the number of control points as low as possible—this makes the shape easier to edit and animate. You can always add more control points if you need them.

■ If you are used to creating Bezier splines in applications like Adobe Illustrator or Photoshop, BSplines can take some getting used to. When working with Bezier paths, the lines between the control points define the path itself, but with BSplines, the lines between the control points act as *tangents* to create the curve. When working with BSplines, it may be easier to first create several points and then move them to get the shape you want.

■ Just as with Bezier shapes, when drawing a BSpline shape you can press Esc while drawing to delete the shape entirely.

■ Once you create a shape, you can switch between Bezier and BSpline in the Shape tab of the Inspector (see "Modifying Shapes" later in the chapter for more information).

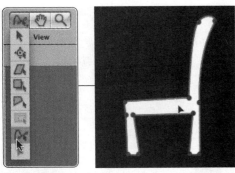

Figure 12.5 To reveal a shape's control points, choose the Adjust Control Points tool and click the shape.

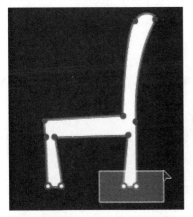

Figure 12.6 One way to select more than one control point is to simply Shift-click and drag a bounding box around the additional control points.

What Do Keyframes Have to Do with Shapes?

When you manipulate keyframe curves in the Keyframe Editor, you are actually working with Bezier control points—handles and all. The methods described in "Working with Control Points" and "Editing Bezier Control Points" apply to adjusting keyframe curves as well. These curves are discussed in Chapter 7.

Working with Control Points

You change the form of a shape by adjusting its control points with the Adjust Control Points tool. You can further manipulate the shape by moving, adding, deleting, locking, and disabling control points.

To reveal the shape control points:

◆ Select the Adjust Control Points tool from the Toolbar and click the shape (**Figure 12.5**).

✔ Tip

■ The Tab key cycles through the different transform tools.

To select a control point:

◆ With the Adjust Control Points tool and the shape selected, click the control point. The center of the point turns white.

To select more than one control point:

Do one of the following:

◆ Click the first control point, then Shift-click additional points.

◆ Drag a bounding box around the points to be selected.

◆ Shift-click and drag a bounding box to add to points to those already selected (**Figure 12.6**).

◆ To select all control points, choose Edit > Select All or press Command-A (with the Adjust Control Points tool active).

✔ Tip

■ To deselect points, Shift-click them or drag a bounding box around them.

To move control points:

◆ Select the points as described on the previous page, and drag them to a new location.

✔ Tips

■ Pressing Shift while dragging constrains the movement of the selected control points either horizontally or vertically.

■ Motion's dynamic guides can help you snap control points to each other, but if they get in the way of making small adjustments, press N to toggle them off.

To add control points to a shape:

1. Select the Adjust Control Points tool.

2. *Do one of the following:*

   ▲ Double-click the line between two control points where you want the new point.

   ▲ Option-click the line between two control points where you want the new point.

✔ Tips

■ When you hold down the Option key, the pointer icon changes to represent the current operation (**Figure 12.7**).

■ For a Bezier shape, if you Option-click and drag, you can immediately adjust the shape of the curve through the control point with the Bezier handles.

■ For a BSpline shape, make sure to double-click or Option-click the line that connects the control points, not the curve itself.

■ Adding a control point to a Bezier shape doesn't change the shape until you move the handles or the point itself; however, with BSpline shapes, just adding the control point changes the shape (**Figures 12.8** and **12.9**).

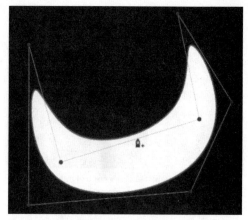

Figure 12.7 By holding down the Option key, the icon changes to a pen with a plus symbol, indicating that you are about to add a control point.

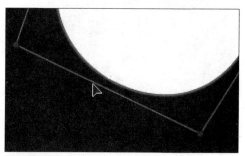

Figure 12.8 Adding a control point to a Bezier shape does not change the shape until you move the handles or the point.

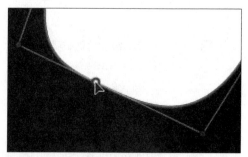

Figure 12.9 With BSpline shapes, simply adding a control point changes the shape of the object.

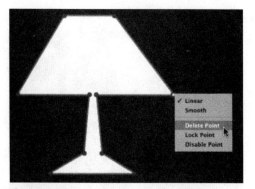

Figure 12.10 To remove a control point, simply Control-click it and choose Delete Point from the drop-down menu.

To add control points after the end of an open shape:

◆ Select the shape with the Adjust Control Points tool, then Option-click outside the shape to add a control point.

To close an open shape:

◆ Select the shape with the Adjust Control Points tool, then Option-click the first point.

✔ Tips

■ Don't remember which end point is the first point? The pointer tells you by adding a little circle icon when you hover over the first point.

■ When you close an open shape, it is not automatically filled with white as shapes that are created closed to begin with are.

To delete control points from a shape:

1. Select one or more control points with the Adjust Control Points tool.

2. *Do one of the following:*
   ▲ Choose Edit > Delete.
   ▲ Control-click one of the selected points and choose Delete Point from the drop-down menu (**Figure 12.10**).
   ▲ Press Delete.

To lock a shape's control points:

1. Select the point(s) with the Adjust Control Points tool.

2. Control-click a selected point and choose Lock Point from the drop-down menu. Locked control points turn from red to gray.

✔ Tips

■ To unlock a locked point, Control-click and select Unlock Point from the drop-down menu.

■ You can still move a shape with locked points, but you can't adjust the locked points themselves.

To disable a shape's control points:

1. Select the point(s) with the Adjust Control Points tool.

2. Control-click a selected point and choose Disable Point from the drop-down menu.

   The point remains on the Canvas and you can move it independently, but the shape no longer uses it to define the curve (**Figure 12.11**).

✔ Tips

■ To enable a disabled point, Control-click and select Enable Point from the drop-down menu.

■ If you move a shape with disabled points, the disabled points move with it, maintaining their relative position.

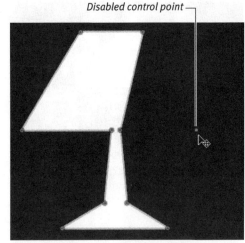
Disabled control point

Figure 12.11 When a control point is disabled, you can still see it in the Canvas, but the shape doesn't pass through it.

Figure 12.12 To change a curve with the Bezier handles, simply drag a handle to change the curve's length or angle. The opposing handle moves in tandem.

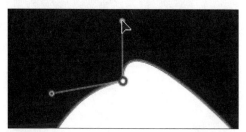

Figure 12.13 You can also change a curve with the Bezier handles by Command-clicking and dragging a handle to change its angle independently of the other handle.

✔ Tips

- If you can't see handles when you click a Bezier control point, make sure Handles is checked in the View pop-up menu in the Canvas.

- Press Shift while Command-clicking and dragging to constrain the movement to 45-degree increments.

Editing Bezier Control Points

If you have used Bezier tools to create shapes in other applications such as Photoshop or Illustrator, you will feel right at home editing shapes in Motion. You can easily create just about any shape you want by using either corner or curved control points and by manipulating the Bezier handles.

To change a corner control point to a curve and vice versa:

1. Select the Adjust Control Points tool.

2. *Do one of the following:*

   ▲ To change a curved point to a corner point, Command-click it.

   ▲ To change a corner point to a curved point, Command-click and drag it.

   Dragging creates the Bezier handles.

   ▲ Select one or more points, Control-click a selected point, and choose Linear or Smooth from the drop-down menu.

   Linear creates a corner point and Smooth creates a curve.

To change a curve with the Bezier handles:

Do one of the following:

- Drag a handle by the ball at the end to change its length and/or angle.

  The handle on the opposite side of the control point keeps its original length, but it moves in tandem with the handle you are adjusting to maintain a smooth curve (**Figure 12.12**).

- Command-click and drag a handle to change its angle independently of the other handle (**Figure 12.13**).

Editing BSpline Control Points

BSpline control points don't have handles—instead, you adjust the curve by moving control points closer to or farther away from each other. You can also adjust the amount of curvature at each control point either continuously or to three specific levels. At the extreme amount of curvature, the control point becomes similar to a corner point.

To change the amount of curvature through a BSpline control point:

1. Select the Adjust Control Points tool.

2. *Do one of the following:*

   ▲ Command-click the control point to toggle through three different levels of curvature (**Figures 12.14, 12.15, and 12.16**).

   ▲ Command-click and drag on a control point.

   Dragging to the right increases the level of curvature; dragging to the left decreases the level of curvature.

✔ Tip

■ If you select multiple points, the curvature is adjusted on all the selected points with either method.

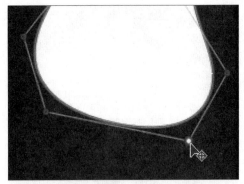

Figure 12.14 This is the default level of curvature.

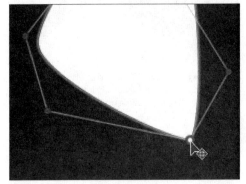

Figure 12.15 Command-clicking once on a control point increases the curvature angle.

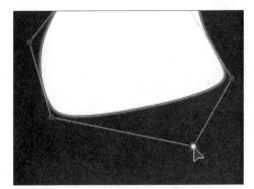

Figure 12.16 Command-clicking a second time reduces the curvature angle from the default.

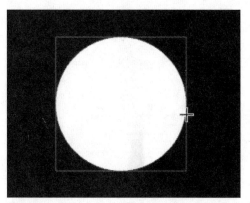

Figure 12.17 Hold down the Shift key while drawing with the Ellipse tool to make a perfect circle.

Drawing Rectangles and Ellipses

Motion includes tools you can use to create rectangular and elliptical shapes quickly without needing to precisely place individual control points

To draw a rectangle:

1. Click the Rectangle tool or press R.

2. Click and drag in the Canvas to draw the rectangle.

✔ Tips

■ Hold down Shift while dragging to make a square.

■ To manipulate the control points, select the Adjust Control Points tool.

To draw an ellipse:

1. Click the Circle tool or press C.

2. Click and drag in the Canvas to draw the ellipse (**Figure 12.17**).

✔ Tips

■ Hold down Shift while dragging to make a circle.

■ To manipulate the control points, select the Adjust Control Points tool.

■ By default, rectangles and ellipses are Bezier shapes—you can change them to BSplines in the Shape tab of the Inspector, which allows you to manipulate them in different ways.

Using Library Shapes

Motion includes six different simple preset shapes in the Library. You can add these to your project and manipulate them in the same way as shapes you create yourself. And, of course, you can save your own shapes into the Library so that they are available at any time.

To browse shapes in the Library:

1. Reveal the Library (Command-2) and click the Shapes category in the Sidebar area.

2. Select a shape in the File Stack.

   The shape is displayed in the Preview Area (**Figure 12.18**).

To apply a Library shape:

Do one of the following:

◆ Drag the shape from the File Stack to the Layers tab, Canvas, or Timeline.

◆ Select the shape in the File Stack and click the Apply button in the Preview Area.

To save a custom shape into the Library:

1. Select the Shape category in the Library.

2. Drag the shape from the Layers tab to the File Stack of the Library.

   The shape appears in the Library with a user icon attached to indicate it is a user-created preset shape.

✔ Tip

■ You can also save custom shapes to the Favorites and the Favorites Menu folders in the Library.

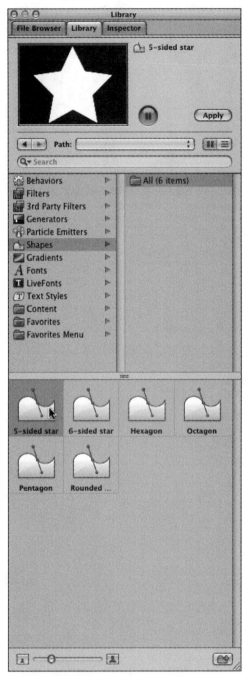

Figure 12.18 Selected shapes are displayed in the Preview Area at the top of the Library pane.

Working with Multiple Shapes

If you want to create a complex illustration, you may find it much easier to build it out of several different shapes—one for each part of the overall drawing (**Figure 12.19**).

You can group each of the shapes together in layers to keep them organized, and you can change their stacking order to change which shapes appear on top in the Canvas. Stacking order is discussed in Chapter 3.

To change how the shapes interact with each other, change opacity and/or blend modes, which are discussed in Chapter 4.

To create transparency inside a shape, add a mask with the Mask tools discussed in "Drawing Masks" later in this chapter.

Figure 12.19 It can be easier to create a complex illustration by using different shapes for each part of the drawing.

Modifying Shapes

You can modify the overall appearance of a shape in many different ways. You can change its Transform properties, such as Position, Rotation, and Scale, just as you would for any other object directly in the Canvas or in the Inspector. You can also use blend modes to change how shapes interact with other objects. And, you can use a shape as a mask for another object.

In addition, shapes have their own unique parameters, such as Fill Color and Outline Width, which you access in the Shape tab of the Inspector. You can view a subset of these parameters and make quick adjustments directly in the Dashboard.

To transform a shape:

Do one of the following:

◆ Select the appropriate tool in the Toolbar (Transform, Anchor Point, Shear), and then make the transform in the Canvas (**Figure 12.20**).

◆ Select the shape, and change the parameters in the Properties tab of the Inspector (**Figure 12.21**). For detailed information on changing object properties, see Chapter 4.

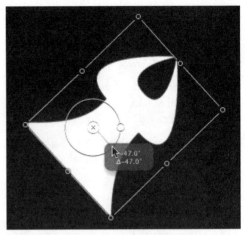

Figure 12.20 You can transform a shape directly in the Canvas just like you can with any object.

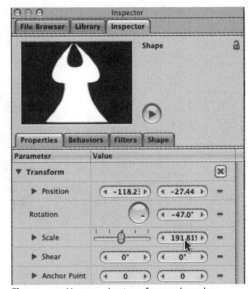

Figure 12.21 You can also transform a shape by changing its parameters in the Properties tab of the Inspector.

MODIFYING SHAPES

Figure 12.22 You can apply any of several blend modes to a shape by Control-clicking it in the Canvas and selecting an action from the drop-down menu.

✔ Tips

- When the Adjust Control Points tool is active, the quickest way to get back to the Select/Transform tool is to press Tab once. Press the Tab key five more times to get back to the Adjust Control Points tool.

- You can also crop, corner pin, and add a drop shadow in either the Canvas or the Inspector.

- If you want to transform multiple objects without changing their relationship to each other, place them all on one layer and transform the layer.

- Because shapes are vector objects, they retain crisp edges when scaled over 100 percent. However, applying Four Corner or Crop rasterizes the object; if you then scale it over 100 percent, you might create blurry or pixilated edges.

To apply a blend mode to a shape:

1. Select the shape.

2. *Do one of the following:*

   ▲ In the Dashboard (press D or F7 to reveal it), select a blend mode from the drop-down menu.

   ▲ In the Properties tab of the Inspector, click the drop-down list of the Blend Mode parameter and select a blend mode.

   ▲ Control-click the shape in the Canvas and select a blend mode from the drop-down menu (**Figure 12.22**). For detailed information on working with blend modes, see Chapter 4.

MODIFYING SHAPES

Modifying Shape Parameters

You modify a shape's parameters in the Shape tab of the Inspector. You can fill the shape with a solid color, a gradient, or make it transparent. You can add an outline and set its color and width. If you don't have an outline, you can choose a feather amount for the edge of the shape.

To modify a shape's parameters:

1. Select the shape.

2. Change the shape's parameters in either the Dashboard or the Shape tab of the Inspector (press F4 to reveal it).

To change a shape's fill:

◆ In the Shape tab, uncheck the Fill check box to make the interior of the shape transparent. Check the Fill check box to fill the shape with a solid color.

✔ Tip

■ Although you can select a Fill color in the Dashboard, you can only change the Fill Mode in the Shape tab of the Inspector.

To change the shape's color:

1. In the Dashboard or the Shape tab, set the Fill Mode to Color (the default).

2. *Do one of the following:*

   ▲ Click the color well and select a new color.

   ▲ Click the Fill Color disclosure triangle and set specific Red, Green, and Blue color channel values (**Figure 12.23**).

✔ Tip

■ You can also Control-click and drag in the color well to quickly choose a color.

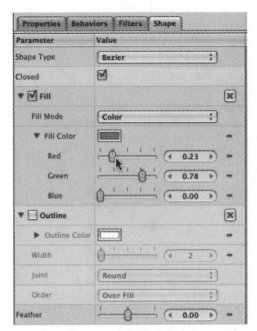

Figure 12.23 You can set specific Red, Green, and Blue values for the fill color of a shape in the Shape tab of the Inspector.

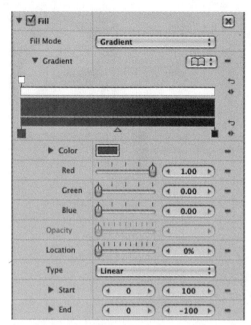

Figure 12.24 You can use the Gradient Editor to fill a shape with a custom gradient.

Figure 12.25 You can feather the edges of a shape, as long as it doesn't also have an outline applied.

To change the shape's gradient:

1. In the Dashboard or the Shape tab, set the Fill Mode to Gradient.

   When you do, the Gradient parameter appears below.

2. Click the Gradient Library button to select a gradient from the Library.

3. Click the disclosure triangle to reveal the Gradient Editor where you can customize a gradient (**Figure 12.24**).

   For details, see Chapter 10.

To adjust the shape's outline:

1. Click the Outline check box in the Shape tab to make an outline around the shape.

   The Outline Color controls work identically to the Fill Color controls discussed in "Modifying Shape Parameters" earlier in this chapter.

2. Set the width of the outline in pixels with the Width parameter.

3. Select a Joint type of Normal, Round, or Bevel.

To adjust the shape's feather amount:

◆ Slide the feather slider from side to side to set a feather amount for the fill (**Figure 12.25**).

✔ Tip

■ Feather only works if the outline is turned off.

Applying Filters to Shapes

Filters can be applied to shapes in the same manner as they are applied to other objects. What is unique about shapes is that they remain editable after the filter is applied, so you can continue to adjust and modify the shape while observing the effect of the filter (**Figure 12.26**).

Figure 12.26 Even with a filter such as the Pixelate filter above applied to a shape, you can manipulate the shape's control points.

To apply a filter to a shape:

Do one of the following:

◆ Drag a filter from the Library onto the shape in the Layers tab, Canvas, or Timeline.

◆ Select the object, then select a filter by clicking the Add Filter icon on the Toolbar.

For details on working with filters, see Chapter 9.

✔ Tip

■ Applying a filter rasterizes a shape, which changes it from a vector object to a bitmapped object. This means that scaling over 100 percent can cause artifacts to appear.

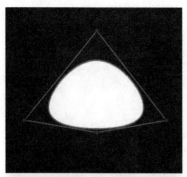

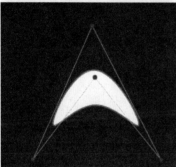

Figure 12.27 You can animate a shape's individual control points so that the shape's form changes over time as the control points move.

✔ Tips

■ When you move the control points at a given frame, Motion sets a keyframe in the Shape Animation parameter which you can view in the Keyframe Editor. All control point adjustments at one point in time are bundled into one keyframe.

■ If you change a corner control point to a curve, the change animates over time between the current keyframe and the prior keyframe.

■ Try not to add or delete keyframes on a shape with animated control points. If you add a control point, the new point does not follow the animation. If you delete a control point, it is removed from the entire animation.

Animating Shapes

Because a shape is an object, you can animate it with behaviors and/or keyframes just as you would other objects. You can make its parameters—such as Position, Rotation, Scale, Outline Width, and so on—change over time.

In addition, you can animate the location of a shape's individual control points so that the *form* of the shape changes over time as the control points move (**Figure 12.27**). You accomplish this by keyframing the individual control points—these keyframes are stored in the Shape Animation parameter.

To learn more about applying behaviors to objects, see Chapter 6; for keyframing objects, see Chapter 7.

To keyframe a shape's control points:

1. Select the Adjust Control Points tool from the Toolbar (or press Tab to cycle through the tools).

2. Select the shape.

3. With the playhead at the beginning of the shape, click the Record button or press A.

4. Move the playhead to the frame for the first change, and move the control points.

5. Move the playhead to the next desired frame and move the control points.

6. Repeat step 5 as needed.

7. Click the Record button or press A to stop recording.

Creating Transparency with Masks

When you create a mask, you tell Motion how to change the transparency of an object. The information about the level of transparency in different regions of an image is called an alpha channel. The alpha channel is stored as grayscale information, with white indicating full opacity, black indicating full transparency, and shades of gray partial transparency (**Figures 12.28** and **12.29**).

One way to create a mask is to draw it on top of an object. Remember, the tools you use to draw a mask work identically to the tools for drawing shapes—you create control points that are connected with either Bezier splines or BSplines, and you can adjust, modify, and animate the resulting mask just as you would a shape. The main difference between the two is that you must apply a mask to an object, while a shape is an object in and of itself. In fact, you can apply a mask to a shape to cut out part of the shape.

However, you can create masks in other ways as well. For instance, the Apply Image Mask command lets you select one of the attributes of one object to act as a mask for another object, and certain blend modes use an object's brightness (luma) or transparency (alpha) information to create transparency. Also, several filters called *keying* filters are designed specifically to create transparency in an image based on color and brightness values.

Figure 12.28 In this image, a mask has been applied to remove the sky. The edge of the mask is feathered where the sky meets the wave.

Figure 12.29 Here's what the mask itself, otherwise known as an alpha channel, looks like: white pixels are visible (opaque), black pixels are invisible (transparent), and gray pixels are partially visible. Press V to toggle between a view of the image and the mask.

Drawing Masks

You draw masks using the Mask tools in the Toolbar—the tools are identical to the tools for creating shapes—the only difference is that you need an object on which to draw the mask.

To draw a mask:

1. Select the object to mask.

2. Select one of the following tools from the Mask tool group in the Toolbar:
   - ▲ Rectangle Mask (Option-R)
   - ▲ Circle Mask (Option-C)
   - ▲ Bezier Mask (Option-B)
   - ▲ BSpline Mask (Option-B)

3. Draw the mask on the object.

4. To complete the mask, *do one of the following:*
   - ▲ Click the first control point.
   - ▲ Press C or Return to join the last control point to the first.
   - ▲ Double-click to place the last control point and join it to the first.

   The mask is applied to the object, and appears underneath the object in the Layers tab and the Timeline (**Figure 12.30**).

✔ Tips

- Although shapes can be open or closed, masks can only be closed.

- You can copy or move masks to other objects by clicking and dragging in the Layers tab (hold down Option to copy) or by using the standard Cut, Copy, and Paste operations.

- To see the alpha channel created by the mask, select View > Channels > Alpha or press V to toggle between the current view and the alpha channel view.

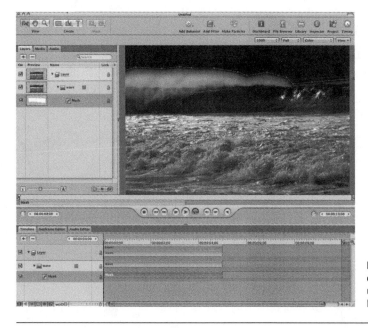

Figure 12.30 Once applied to an object, the mask appears underneath the object in the Layers tab and the Timeline.

Modifying Mask Parameters

Masks can be repositioned, rotated, scaled, and reduced in opacity; in addition you can move their anchor points just like you do with shapes and other objects by manipulating them directly in the Canvas or by using the Properties tab of the Inspector. For details, see Chapter 4.

The Object tab of the Inspector (that becomes the Mask tab when you select a mask) contains four parameters specific to masks, three of which are also available in the Dashboard.

Shape Type lets you convert the method for drawing the mask to Bezier, BSpline, or Linear. Linear creates straight lines between control points.

Mask Blend Mode includes four choices for how the mask interacts with the object's alpha channel. These choices are useful when you are applying multiple masks to an object.

Add, the default, adds to any other masks already present (**Figure 12.31**).

Subtract cuts out the masked area (**Figure 12.32**).

Replace uses the mask to completely replace the object's alpha channel (**Figure 12.33**).

Intersect makes any areas that are not part of all overlapping masks transparent (**Figure 12.34**).

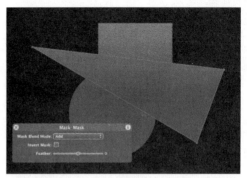

Figure 12.31 When masks are set to the default Add mode, you can see all of them.

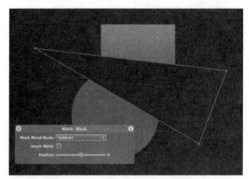

Figure 12.32 Subtract makes the mask itself transparent.

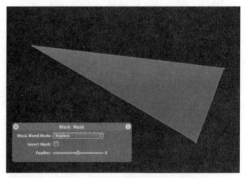

Figure 12.33 Replace mode makes the mask take over, ignoring all other masks.

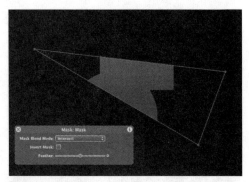

Figure 12.34 Setting a mask blend mode to intersect reveals only the area inside the mask that overlaps with other masks.

Invert Mask swaps the transparent and opaque areas of the object.

Feather softens the edge of the mask—positive values feather by moving outside the mask; negative values soften inside the mask.

To modify mask parameters:

1. Select the mask.

2. Press F4 to reveal the Mask tab of the Inspector.

3. Modify the parameters as you like.

✔ Tips

- Switching from Bezier to BSpline can dramatically change the shape of the mask.

- Don't confuse the Mask Blend Mode parameter with blend modes you can apply to any object. The Mask Blend Mode parameter is specific to how masks interact with each other and the object to which they are applied. Blend modes control how the object interacts with other objects beneath it in the stacking order.

- *Rotoscoping* is the process of animating a mask in order to remove a moving object from a background. When rotoscoping an object, it's often useful to create several masks for different parts of the object in order to more easily mask areas that move in different ways.

- Feathering a mask can make the object blend in better with the background.

Applying Filters to Masks

Just as with shapes and other objects, you can apply filters to masks. The thing to keep in mind is that the filter is being applied to the alpha channel—the grayscale image that determines levels of transparency—and not to the object itself. Therefore the filter affects the grayscale mask, not the object (**Figure 12.35**).

Although you can apply any filter to a mask, there are also two categories of filters, Keying and Matte, that are designed specifically for creating and adjusting masks by applying them to objects. These are discussed in "Using Masks and Keys" later in this chapter.

To apply a filter to a mask:

Do one of the following:

◆ Drag a filter from the Library to the mask in the Layers tab or the Timeline.

◆ Select the mask and then choose a filter by clicking the Add Filter icon in the Toolbar.

Filters appear in the Layers tab nested under the mask to which they are applied (**Figure 12.36**).

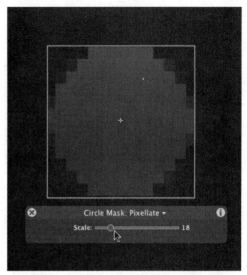

Figure 12.35 Filters that are applied to masks affect only the transparency of the mask, not the object.

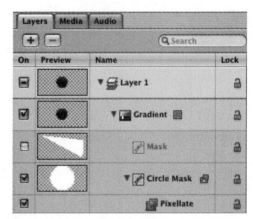

Figure 12.36 Filters that are applied to masks appear in the Layers tab under the mask.

Animating Masks

You can animate masks either with behaviors or keyframes in the same manner as other objects—that is, you can adjust their various parameters, such as Position, Rotation, Scale, and Feathering so they change over time. You can find detailed descriptions of how to work with behaviors and keyframes in Chapters 6 and 7 respectively. Remember, when you animate a mask, you animate the regions of transparency for the object without animating the object itself.

Just as you can animate the control points of shapes, you can animate the control points of masks to make the shape of the mask change over time. This process is called *rotoscoping* when you use it to isolate a moving element from its background. A word of warning—even with the advanced BSpline masking tool and the real-time feedback capabilities of Motion, rotoscoping can be tedious, and it is a skill that takes practice to develop. So if you are new to rotoscoping, take your time, and read "Some Rotoscoping Tips" before you start.

Some Rotoscoping Tips

◆ Work at full resolution (View > Resolution > Full) in order to get precise alignment of your mask.

◆ Often BSpline masks are easier to work with when rotoscoping because of their ability to quickly and precisely change curves by moving control points.

◆ Use multiple masks to isolate different elements of the subject that move in different ways—for instance, for a person, you might create separate masks for the arms, legs, head, and torso.

◆ Try to create just enough control points to make an accurate mask—the more control points you have, the more work you'll have to do to adjust them at each keyframe.

◆ Although Motion interpolates between keyframes to animate the mask, often you may find yourself tweaking the mask on every single frame of an animation. For an NTSC video clip, that's almost 30 frames a second!

◆ To cut down on the number of keyframes, find points in the video clip where the subject changes the type of movement and set your first keyframes there. Then, set keyframes halfway between existing keyframes. Continue to apply new keyframes halfway between existing ones until the mask accurately follows the subject.

◆ Keyframes are stored in the Shape Animation channel; you can view and adjust them in the Keyframe Editor.

To rotoscope an object:

1. Move the playhead to the frame where the mask should begin, and draw a mask (or multiple masks) to isolate the subject (**Figure 12.37**).

2. Enable recording by clicking the Record button or by pressing A.

3. Move to a new location where the mask no longer aligns with the subject and adjust the masks.

4. Repeat step 3 as many times as needed to accurately track your subject.

5. Click the Record button or press A to stop recording.

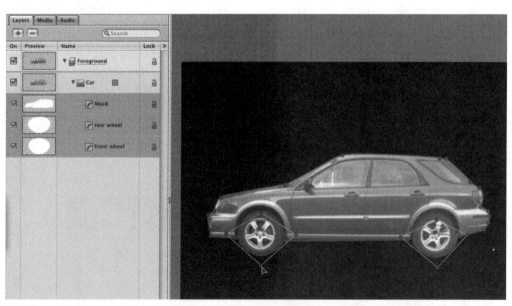

Figure 12.37 To rotoscope objects, start by drawing masks to isolate the subject from the background.

ANIMATING MASKS

Applying Image Masks

Image masks offer another alternative for creating transparency by using properties of one object to mask another. Image masks are very flexible because the object that is used as the source of the mask can be a graphic, a movie, a shape, text, or even a particle system. In addition, you can choose whether to base the mask on the alpha channel, the color channels, or the luma information of the source object. If the source object is animated, as with a video clip or a particle system, then the mask is also animated.

To apply an image mask, you first add it to the object to be masked, and then you tell it what object to use as the source for the mask.

To apply an image mask:

1. Select the object to be masked.

2. Choose Object > Add Image Mask, or press Shift-Command-M.

   The image mask appears below the object in the Layers tab and Timeline.

3. Click the mask in the Layers tab or Timeline to select it.

4. Reveal the Image Mask tab of the Inspector (press F4).

5. Drag the object that serves as the mask into the Image well.

   The alpha channel of the source object masks the object with the image mask applied, and the source object becomes inactive (**Figure 12.38**).

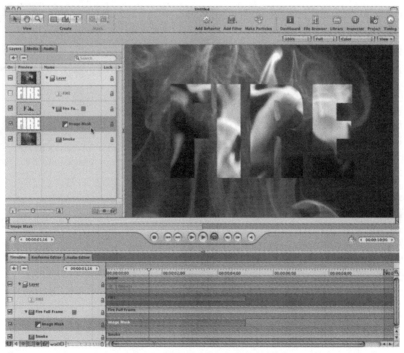

Figure 12.38 Here an image mask is applied to the fire clip, and the text is the source for the image mask. When you drag an object into the image mask well, the object itself is automatically made inactive—notice the check box next to the text object is unchecked.

✔ Tips

- You can set the source object for the mask by dragging it to the Image well in the Dashboard; you can even drag it directly onto the Mask row in the Layers tab or Timeline.

- When selecting a source object to drag to the Image well, be sure not to let go of the mouse—if you do, you select the object and the mask parameters are no longer available.

- Once you apply an image mask, you can draw other masks on the object to further isolate the effect of the image mask.

To modify an image mask:

Change the following parameters in the Dashboard or the Image Mask tab of the Inspector:

- **Frame** (Inspector only) sets the first frame of an animated source object.

- **Hold Frame** (Inspector only) chooses just one frame from an animation to use as the mask.

- **Offset** (Inspector only) changes the x and y position values of the mask relative to the object that it is masking (**Figure 12.39**).

- **Wrap Mode** (Inspector only) is useful if the mask source object is smaller than the object being masked. This property has three settings: *None* is the default, *Repeat* tiles the object to fill the mask, and *Mirror* reverses *and* tiles the object to fill the mask (**Figure 12.40**).

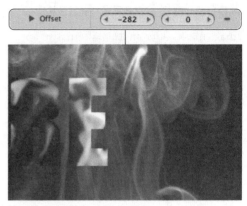

Figure 12.39 Offset changes the x and y position values of a mask.

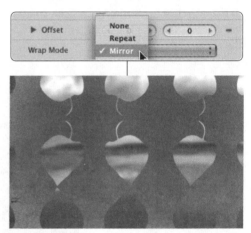

Figure 12.40 Mirror reverses and tiles a mask source object.

APPLYING IMAGE MASKS

Figure 12.41 Luminance makes the brightest areas the most opaque and the darkest areas the most transparent.

◆ **Source Channel** determines how to create the mask. *Alpha* is the default and uses the alpha channel of the source object to determine the transparency of the masked object. *Red, Green,* and *Blue* use the grayscale information for the respective color channel. *Luminance* uses the overall brightness information, with the brightest areas being the most opaque and darkest areas the most transparent (**Figure 12.41**).

◆ **Mask Blend Mode** sets how the mask interacts with the object's alpha channel and is discussed in "Modifying Mask Parameters" earlier in this chapter.

◆ **Invert Mask** reverses transparent and opaque areas.

◆ **Stencil** ensures that any changes to the source object's original parameters are respected in the mask. To have the mask based on default values, uncheck the check box.

The Set Matte Filter

The Set Matte filter in the Matte filter category works almost just like an image mask. Apply it by dragging it from the Library to an object or selecting it from the Add Filter icon on the Toolbar. In the Dashboard there's a Matte Source well, which works just like the Image well for an image mask. You can choose the Matte Channel, which works just like the Source Channel.

The Set Matte filter has three additional options: you can invert the matte, stretch it, and composite it over other objects.

Applying Filters to Image Masks

Any filters applied to an object used as a source for an image mask are passed through to the mask, but you can also apply filters directly to the image mask so that they only affect the grayscale information in the mask and not the underlying object. For example, if you are using an image mask based on an object's brightness, you could use a color correction filter to increase the opacity of the mask without affecting the underlying object (**Figure 12.42**).

To apply a filter to an image mask:

Do one of the following:

◆ Drag a filter from the Library to the image mask in the Layers tab.

◆ Select the image mask in the Layers tab or Timeline and choose a filter from the Add Filter icon in the Toolbar.

The filter appears nested underneath the image mask to which it has been applied. For more information on working with filters, see Chapter 9.

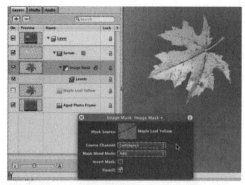

Figure 12.42 Here we are using the luminance of the leaf to create a mask. Because the leaf wasn't very bright, we added a Levels filter to the image mask to increase the brightness, and therefore opacity, of the mask without affecting the leaf object.

Applying Behaviors to Image Masks

Although you can't apply a behavior directly to an image mask, you can apply it to the object that is the source of the mask. For example, you could apply a Throw behavior to animate text that is used as a mask (**Figure 12.43**).

For more on behaviors, see Chapter 6.

Figure 12.43 You can apply behaviors to an object that is the source of a mask. Here the Throw behavior is being applied to text that is being used as a mask.

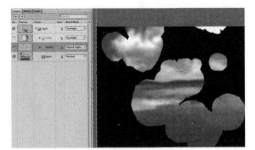

Figure 12.44 Stencil Alpha uses the alpha channel of the object to mask objects beneath it.

Masking with Blend Modes

Although most of the blend modes discussed in Chapter 4 cause overlapping objects to interact with each other without creating any specific areas of transparency, you'll find the Stencil and Silhouette blend modes useful for manipulating the alpha or luma information in an object to create a mask.

To create a mask with a blend mode:

1. Select the object to which you want to apply the blend mode.

2. *Do one of the following:*

   ▲ Choose Object > Blend Mode and select a Stencil or Silhouette blend mode.

   ▲ Select a Stencil or Silhouette blend mode from the Properties tab in the Inspector (press F1 to reveal it).

   ▲ Control-click the object in the Layers tab, Canvas, or Timeline and select one of the following Stencil or Silhouette blend modes:

   Stencil Alpha uses the alpha channel of the object to mask objects beneath it (**Figure 12.44**).

   Stencil Luma uses the luminance information from the object to create a mask.

continues on next page

Silhouette Alpha creates transparency values based on the alpha channel, with full opacity being black like a shadow instead of white (**Figure 12.45**).

Silhouette Luma works like Silhouette Alpha, but makes the selected object transparent based on how bright it is, with full brightness being black.

✔ Tip

■ For the blend mode you choose to have an effect, at least one overlapping object must be beneath the selected object.

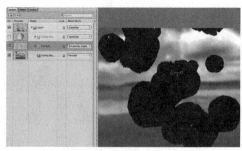

Figure 12.45 Silhouette Alpha works just the opposite of Stencil Alpha.

Alpha on Fire

You can use the Stencil and Silhouette blend modes in conjunction with other blend modes.

For example, the QuickTime movies in the Fire category of the Library's Content element were filmed against a black background and do not have an alpha channel. This makes it difficult to composite them against another object.

Although you could use a Screen blend mode to knock out the black background, the result is that some of the darker elements of the fire may get removed as well. Instead, apply the Silhouette Luma blend mode to the fire to create a "shadow" of the fire, with the brighter areas being the most black. Then duplicate the fire and set the blend mode of the upper copy to Add.

Using Masks and Keys

Sometimes a subject is shot against a blue or green background; the filmer's intention is to later remove the background to composite the subject into a different scene. The process of removing the background is called *creating a key, pulling a key,* or just *keying.*

To create a convincing key, you need a properly lit shot to begin with, coupled with the skillful and patient application and adjustment of filters. Motion includes several filters in the Key and Matte categories to help you create a clean key. By combining these filters with masks, you can produce a convincing key.

The process of keying footage is complex and beyond the scope of this book, but I'll outline the general steps and the tools in Motion that you can use to create your key.

Normally, the first step is to create a *garbage mask,* which very roughly isolates the subject to be keyed so that you don't have to worry about lighting falloff or extraneous materials at the edges of the frame.

Second, you apply the appropriate *keying filter* and carefully adjust the parameters. Sometimes you have to create copies of the object, mask different areas, and use different keying settings on each area.

Third, after you establish the basic key, you might create a *holdout mask* to fill any holes in the mask.

Fourth, you may apply several *filters* so you can work on the edges of the mask to smooth it out, make it tighter, or expand it, or you may remove color from the background that has *spilled* onto the subject.

To create a garbage mask:

1. Use the mask drawing tools to draw a rough mask around the subject (**Figure 12.46**).

2. If necessary, keyframe the control points so that the mask doesn't cut into the subject on any frame of the shot.

To apply a keying filter:

Do one of the following:

◆ Drag the appropriate filter from the Keying subcategory of the Filters category in the Library onto the video clip in the Layers tab, Timeline, or Canvas.

◆ Select the video clip and then choose one of the following keying filters from the Add Filter icon in the Toolbar:

Blue Green Screen is designed specifically for subjects shot against a blue screen or green screen.

Color Key works well for background colors other than green or blue, as long as there isn't much of the same color in the foreground subject.

Lumakey creates a mask based on brightness values, so if the background is very bright or very dark, it is a good filter to try.

Primatte RT is a more sophisticated blue screen or green screen keyer with many more controls.

Spill Suppressor neutralizes background color that appears on the edges of the foreground subject by tinting it. You can use this after applying one of the above keying filters**.**

Figure 12.46 The first step in creating a garbage mask is drawing a rough mask around the subject.

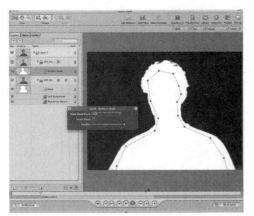

Figure 12.47 To create a holdout mask, draw a Bezier or BSpline mask inside the subject to isolate the areas that shouldn't have transparency.

To create a holdout mask:

1. Duplicate the video clip.
   The duplicate appears above the original clip.

2. Delete the mask from the duplicate clip.

3. Draw a Bezier or BSpline mask inside the subject, isolating the areas that shouldn't have transparency (**Figure 12.47**).

4. Adjust the Feather parameter to blend the holdout mask into the lower mask.

To fine-tune the key:

◆ Apply and adjust any of the following filters as needed:

   Spill Suppressor from the Keying category; this is described above.

   Matte Choker in the Matte category; this widens or narrows the semitransparent edges of the mask.

   Channel Blur in the Blur category; you can set this to blur the alpha channel.

USING MASKS AND KEYS

13

WORKING WITH TEXT

Just look at the beginning of any feature film, any TV ad, any weekly sitcom—text treatments are everywhere. The way that text is formatted and animated can establish an emotional tone, support a message, and emphasize specific content. Whether it's a slow tracking blur of an elegant font for a luxury car ad or the frenetic bouncing of a children's film title, text is a major component of motion graphics. And, not surprisingly, it's a major component of Motion. With the ability to use both system fonts and animated LiveFonts, parameters to adjust every aspect of a text object, and over 100 behaviors designed specifically to animate text, there's no limit to text design and animation with Motion. And of course you can use the behaviors, keyframing, and filters explored in earlier chapters with text objects as well.

This chapter has two parts. First, I explore how to create and format text objects—how to preview and apply different fonts and text styles, how to format with the Dashboard and the Inspector, and how to save modified text parameters as styles. I also show you how to make two animated text effects: by creating a Type On effect and by animating text along a customized path. In the second part, I describe Motion's deep and powerful text animation tools, the Text Animation and Text Sequence behaviors. I also touch on the other Motion behaviors discussed in Chapter 6—keyframing parameters and using filters.

Creating Text

With Motion, you have the option of either creating text directly in the Canvas or using the Text Editor in the Inspector.

To create text in the Canvas:

1. Select the layer that you want to contain the text object.

   If you don't select a layer, Motion creates a new layer for the text.

2. In the Toolbar, click the Text tool, or press T.

   The pointer turns into an Insertion icon.

3. *Do one of the following:*

   ▲ Click in the Canvas where you want the text to be located.

      A flashing vertical line appears at the insertion point.

   ▲ Click and drag in the Canvas to draw a custom margin box for the text.

4. Type your text.

5. Press Enter, Esc, or click the Select/Transform tool in the Toolbar.

Figure 13.1 Use the Type layout method for text on a single line.

Figure 13.2 With the Text tool selected, click and drag a control point on the bounding box to resize the custom margin that contains the text.

✔ Tips

■ When you are done typing, you must press Esc, Enter, or click the Select/Transform tool—you can't use the keyboard shortcut Shift-S because you are still in text-entry mode. If you do, you just type a capital S!

■ If you are adding a short line of text, use the click and type method. When you are typing, Motion continues to enter text along the same line unless you press Return. This is the *Type* layout method (**Figure 13.1**).

■ If you are adding a block of text, use the click and drag method to create a custom margin to contain the text. This is the *Paragraph* layout method. To adjust the size of the custom margin, drag a control point *while the Text tool is still selected* (**Figure 13.2**). If the Select/Transform tool is active, dragging a control point changes the scale of the text object.

■ You can switch between layout methods in the Layout pane of the Text tab of the Inspector, discussed next.

■ If you want to reedit the text, double-click it to enter text editing mode rather than selecting the Text tool from the Toolbar.

To create text with the Text Editor:

1. Click the Text tool or press T and click in the Canvas.

   Clicking in the Canvas creates a blank text object.

2. Open the Text tab of the Inspector by clicking the Inspector tab and then the Text tab, or by pressing F4.

3. If it's not already active, click the Format pane (**Figure 13.3**).

4. Click in the Text Editor at the bottom of the Format pane and enter your text.

✔ Tips

- You can also edit existing text in the Text Editor by simply selecting the text first—you don't need to be in text edit mode.

- Usually it's more convenient to add text directly to the Canvas. However, the Text Editor is convenient if you have a lot of text to enter or you need to edit existing text that isn't currently visible in the Canvas—perhaps it's off screen, and will animate on screen at a later frame.

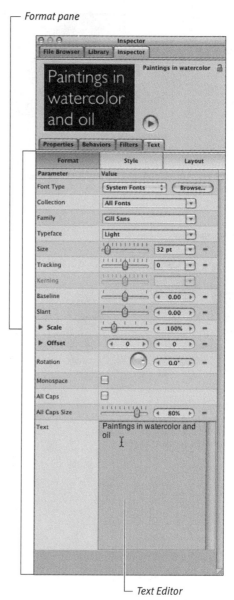

Format pane

Text Editor

Figure 13.3 The Format pane of the Text tab in the Inspector.

Manipulating Text Objects

When you add text, it appears as an object contained in a layer in the Layers tab and in the Timeline (**Figure 13.4**).

Because text is an object, you can manipulate it like other objects in Motion: you can change its Position, Rotation, Scale, Blend Mode, and other basic properties directly in the Canvas or in the Properties tab of the Inspector. For more information on transforming objects, see Chapter 4.

In the Layers tab or the Timeline, you can move text objects into other layers, group them, reorder them, lock them, toggle their visibility, and solo them. These attributes and how to use them are discussed in Chapter 3.

The duration of a text object depends on your Project settings in Motion's Preferences setting for Still Images & Objects (select Motion > Preferences, or Command-, to open them). You can set Motion to add objects at the beginning of the project or at the current playhead location; either way, they last until the end of the project. Or, you can set a custom duration. You can then adjust the location and duration of a text object in the Timeline. Like other objects, text objects can be moved, copied, cut, pasted, duplicated, and deleted. Preferences are discussed in Appendix B and editing objects in the Timeline is discussed in Chapter 5.

Figure 13.4 Text is an object, and appears in both the Layers tab and the Timeline.

Formatting Text

Motion gives you an almost unlimited capability to make your text have a specific look by choosing Font, Typeface, Size, Tracking, Alignment, Justification, Spacing, and other parameters. You can add an outline and a drop shadow to your text, change the color, make it glow, and place it on a path. You can apply preset Styles or LiveFonts from the Library, and you can save your own customized text as a style for future use.

You format text in the same way as you format other objects: by using either the Dashboard for quick access to a small set of key parameters, or by using the context-sensitive Object tab in the Inspector (which becomes the Text tab when you select a text object) for access to all the Text parameters.

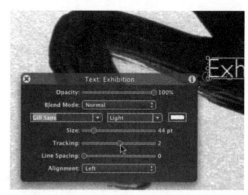

Figure 13.5 Key text parameters are available in the Dashboard.

Formatting text with the Dashboard

When a text object is selected, the Dashboard gives you quick access to nine key parameters: Opacity, Blend Mode, Font Family, Typeface, Color, Size, Tracking, Line Spacing, and Alignment.

To format text with the Dashboard:

1. Select the text object by clicking it in the Canvas, Layers tab, or Timeline.

2. If the Dashboard isn't visible, reveal it by clicking the Dashboard icon in the Toolbar or by pressing D or F7.

3. Use the drop-down menus and sliders to adjust parameters as you desire (**Figure 13.5**).

Figure 13.6 You can use the Mac OS X Color Picker to choose a color.

✔ Tips

- To select a Font Family, click the arrow next to the font family name. Here's the cool part: If you continue to hold down the mouse as you drag down the list, your text updates with each font selection as you drag. This way, you can see what each font looks like before you select it. Really convenient!

- Control-click and hold the color swatch in the Dashboard to quickly select a color. Or, click and release to bring up the Mac OS X Color Picker if you want to sample a color, use a saved color swatch, or view different color options (**Figure 13.6**).

Previewing and Applying Fonts in the Library

You can use the Font category in the Library to select fonts according to subcategories, preview how the fonts will look, and apply them to text objects.

To browse fonts in the Library:

1. Select the Fonts category in the Sidebar area of the Library.

2. Select a Fonts subcategory.

3. Select a font from the File Stack.

   The selected font appears in the Preview Area (**Figure 13.7**).

✔ Tips

■ If you select Icon view for the File Stack, you'll see a thumbnail for each font, which makes it easier to quickly pick a specific look.

■ Motion uses all fonts supported by Mac OS X, including OpenType, Type 1 (or PostScript), and TrueType. Any fonts installed in the system Library or the user Library are available in Motion's Library (and in the Format pane of the Text Inspector, discussed below).

To apply a font from the Library:

Do one of the following:

◆ Drag the font from the File Stack onto the text object in the Layers tab, Canvas, or Timeline.

◆ Select the text object in the Layers tab, Canvas, or Timeline, then select the font in the Font Stack and click the Apply button in the Preview Area.

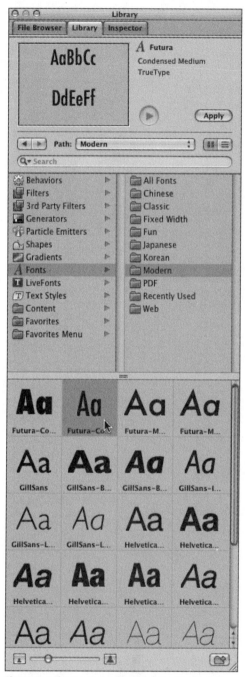

Figure 13.7 If you select a font from the File Stack it appears in the Preview Area.

PREVIEWING/APPLYING FONTS IN THE LIBRARY

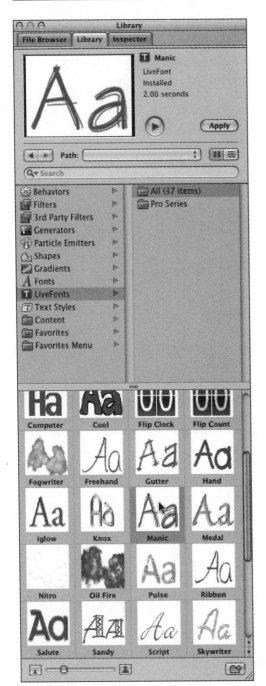

Figure 13.8 Likewise, if you select a LiveFont, it also appears in the Preview Area along with its name and the duration of the animation.

Previewing and Applying LiveFonts

LiveFonts are animated character sets that are part of the LiveType titling application that is bundled with Final Cut Pro HD. The Motion Library includes ten LiveFonts; if you have Final Cut Pro HD installed, the Library includes all the LiveFonts that ship with LiveType.

The process for browsing, previewing, and applying LiveFonts is the same as for system fonts, except that the preview is animated.

Modifying LiveFonts parameters is discussed under Modifying Text Format below.

To preview LiveFonts:

1. Select the LiveFonts category in the Sidebar area of the Library.

2. Select a LiveFont from the File Stack.

   A preview of the selected LiveFont animation appears in the Preview Area, along with the name of the LiveFont and the duration of the animation (**Figure 13.8**).

✔ Tip

■ As with regular fonts, clicking the Icon view button in the Preview Area shows static thumbnails for each LiveFont in the File Stack. This means you can see what they all look like at once.

To apply a LiveFont to a text object:

Do one of the following:

◆ Drag the LiveFont from the File Stack area of the Library to the text object in the Layers tab, Canvas, or Timeline.

◆ Select the text object in the Layers tab, Canvas, or Timeline, select the LiveFont in the File Stack area of the Library, and click the Apply button in the Preview Area.

Previewing and Applying Text Styles

A Text Style is a bundle of preset parameters from the Format and/or Style panes of the Text tab of the Inspector. Motion contains 13 preset Text Styles that you can preview and apply to your text objects. You can modify these Text Styles, create your own custom Text Styles, and save modified or custom Text Styles into the Library for future use. Modifying and saving Text Styles is discussed in "Formatting Text with the Inspector" later in this chapter.

To preview a Text Style:

1. Select the Text Styles category from the Sidebar area of the Library.

2. Select a Text Style in the File Stack.

   The selected Text Style appears in the Preview Area along with the name of the Text Style.

✔ Tip

■ In List view, you can preview each Text Style in the File Stack by using the up and down arrow keys. In Icon view, the thumbnail does not show the Text Style.

To apply a Text Style:

Do one of the following:

◆ Drag the Text Style from the File Stack area of the Library onto the text object in the Layers tab, Canvas, or Timeline.

◆ Select the text object in the Layers tab, Canvas, or Timeline, then select the Text Style in the File Stack area of the Library, and click the Apply button in the Preview Area.

◆ Click the Style pane on the Text tab of the Inspector, and select a Text Style from the drop-down list (**Figure 13.9**).

Using the Style pane is discussed in "Modifying Text Style" later in this chapter.

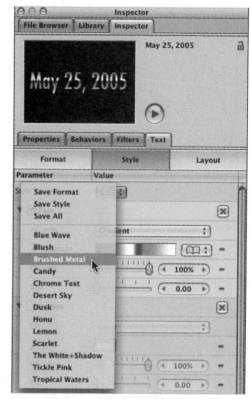

Figure 13.9 To apply a Text Style, simply select the one you want from the drop-down menu in the Style pane.

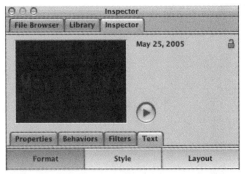

Figure 13.10 The Text tab of the Inspector has three separate panes which contain all of the parameters for a selected text object.

Formatting Text with the Inspector

Although the Dashboard makes it easy to change many critical text parameters, the Text tab of the Inspector contains *all* the parameters of the selected text object. These parameters are separated into three different panes: the Format pane, the Style pane, and the Layout pane (**Figure 13.10**). The Format pane contains basic controls such as Font, Size, and Tracking. The Style pane controls the Fill, Opacity, and Blur of the Face, Outline, Glow, and Drop Shadow of text objects. The Layout pane includes layout controls such as Alignment, Justification, and the option to place the type on a path.

You adjust text parameters with drop-down lists, sliders, dials, and/or value fields, depending on the parameter. For details on working with parameter controls in the Inspector, see "Making Transformations in the Properties Tab" in Chapter 4.

Modifying Text Format

The Format pane of the Text tab contains 15 different parameters for formatting your text object, plus a Text Editor for entering or modifying the text content, as discussed in "Creating Text" earlier in this chapter. Additional parameters appear if you apply a LiveFont to your text object.

You can make adjustments to individual characters or groups of letters, words, or phrases by selecting them with the Text tool, rather than changing the entire selected text object.

Any parameter that has an Animation menu (a dash to the far right) can be animated with either parameter behaviors or keyframes, which are discussed in "Animating Text" later in this chapter.

To show the Format pane:

1. Click the Inspector tab.

2. Click the Text tab.

3. Click the Format button.

✔ Tip

- Instead of steps 1 and 2 above, you can press F4 to immediately reveal the Text tab.

To modify Text Format parameters:

- Adjust each parameter as described below.

  Font Type lets you choose from either System Fonts or LiveType fonts. To browse through all the different options for combinations of Collection, Family, Typeface, and Size, click the Browse button to open the Mac OS X font dialog (**Figure 13.11**).

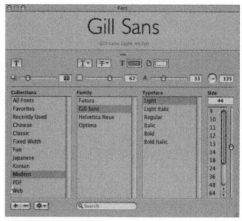

Figure 13.11 To browse through all the different options for font collection, family, typeface, and size, open up the Mac OS X font dialog.

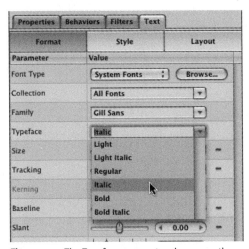

Figure 13.12 The Typeface parameter shows you the available typefaces based on the selected font family.

Collection displays the available collections based on the Font Type selection above.

Family selects the font for the text object. Just as in the Dashboard, if you drag the pointer down the font list with the mouse depressed, your selected text object updates to reflect each font choice.

Typeface displays the available typefaces based on the selected font family (**Figure 13.12**).

Size sets the size of the text.

Tracking sets the spacing between characters at a uniform value.

Kerning sets the spacing between individual letters. To kern letters, select the Text tool and place the insertion point between the letters you want to kern. Use the slider or the drop-down list to adjust the spacing.

Baseline sets the vertical distance of the text from the invisible horizontal line that it rests on by default (**Figure 13.13**).

Slant creates an italic-like slant to text, either forward or backward.

continues on next page

Figure 13.13 Adjusting the baseline of a text object. By selecting an individual letter first, only that letter is affected by the baseline change.

MODIFYING TEXT FORMAT

Scale lets you change the scale of the text either proportionally or non-proportionally. To scale the *x* and *y* values independently, click the disclosure triangle to reveal the controls.

Offset moves the text horizontally and/or vertically relative to its anchor point.

Rotation rotates each character around its base.

Monospace creates a fixed amount of space between each character when selected.

All Caps changes all characters to uppercase. Very handy!

All Caps Size sets the size of the characters, if All Caps has been selected, as a percentage of the original font Size parameter.

✔ Tips

- You can bring up the Mac OS X font dialog anytime a text object is selected by choosing View > Show Fonts or pressing Command-T.

- You can also use the Scale parameter in the Properties tab of the Inspector (or by dragging a control point in the Canvas). The Scale parameter affects the size of the text as an object and is independent of the Size parameter in the Format pane.

- The slider and the drop-down list for the Size parameter only go up to 288 points, but you can enter a higher number directly into the value field.

- Pressing Control-right arrow increases the text kerning one pixel at a time; Control-left arrow decreases the spacing by the same one-pixel increments.

- When kerning text, press the right arrow and left arrow keys to move the insertion point.

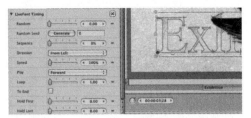

Figure 13.14 If you apply a LiveFont to a selected object, Motion adds the LiveFont Timing parameters to the Format pane.

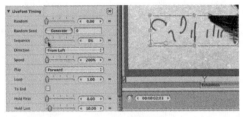

Figure 13.15a When the Sequence parameter is set to 0 percent, each letter starts animating at the same time.

Figure 13.15b When the Sequence parameter is set to values over 100 percent, each letter completes its animation and then there is a delay before the next letters starts its animation.

Modifying LiveFonts

If a LiveFont has been applied to the selected text object, the LiveFont Timing parameters are added to the Format pane (**Figure 13.14**).

To modify LiveFont timing parameters:

1. Select the text object that uses a LiveFont.

2. Select the Format pane of the Text tab of the Inspector.

3. Adjust the parameters as described below.

   Random applies the LiveType animation to each character in a different order, depending on the location of the slider.

   Random Seed generates a new basis for the Random parameter above.

   Sequence controls when the animation starts for each letter. At zero, all letters animate at the same time (**Figure 13.15a**); at 100 percent, the first letter completes its animation before the next letter starts; at values over 100 percent, there is a delay between the animation of each character (**Figure 13.15b**).

   Direction sets the animation across letters to run from From Left, From Right, or Ping Pong (back and forth) across the letters.

   Speed changes the speed of the animation.

   Play sets the animation itself to run Forward, Backward, or Ping-Pong.

   Loop sets how many times the animation plays.

   To End loops the animation continuously for the duration of the text object.

   Hold First sets the number of seconds that the first frame of the animation is displayed before the animation starts.

   Hold Last sets the number of seconds that the last frame of the animation is displayed.

Modifying Text Style

The Text Style pane in the Text tab of the Inspector contains parameters for controlling the Fill, Color, Opacity, and Blur of the text Face. You can also add an Outline, a Glow, and a Drop Shadow, and adjust the parameters for each. And you can change the look of the text by filling it with a gradient, an image, or even a movie.

The Style tab's parameters are divided into four text attributes: Face, Outline, Glow, and Drop Shadow (**Figure 13.16**). Text Style Presets, discussed in "Previewing and Applying Text Styles" earlier in this chapter, are available from this pane. You can choose to make an attribute visible, adjust its parameters, and reset the parameters. Any parameter with an Animation menu icon (the dash on the far right) can be animated with keyframes or behavior parameters.

To show the Style pane:

1. Press F4 to reveal the Text tab of the Inspector (or click the Inspector tab and then the Text tab).

2. Click the Style button.

To apply a Text Style preset:

◆ Choose a preset from the drop-down list (**Figure 13.17**).

To toggle the visibility of a text attribute:

◆ Click the Active check box.
   By default, only the Face attribute is active.

✔ Tips

■ You can't change the parameters of an attribute unless it's active.

■ Making an attribute inactive keeps all the parameter settings in place—it just hides the attribute in the Canvas.

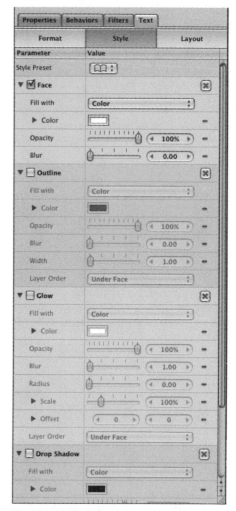

Figure 13.16 The Style tab has four sections, or attributes: Face, Outline, Glow, and Drop Shadow.

Figure 13.17 You can choose a preset text style from the drop-down menu.

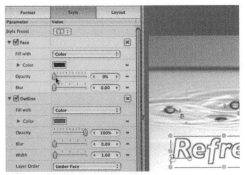

Figure 13.18 You control the opacity of each attribute separately—so, for instance, you could have o percent opacity for the Fill attribute, but still be able to see the letters by setting the Outline opacity to a positive value.

To reset Style parameters for a text attribute:

◆ Click the Reset button for the attribute. The parameters are reset to their default values.

To modify Style parameters:

1. If it isn't checked, click the Active check box for the attribute (Face, Outline, Glow, and Drop Shadow).

2. Adjust the parameters as desired.

All Style attributes have the following three attributes in common.

Fill With lets you choose whether to fill the Face, Outline, Glow, or Drop Shadow with a solid Color, a Gradient, or a Texture. Working with Color, Gradients, and Textures is discussed below.

Opacity sets how opaque the object is and is set by default to 100 percent for all attributes.

Blur sets the amount of blur for the Face, Outline, Glow, or Drop Shadow. By default, it's set to zero for everything but Glow, which is set to 1.

✔ Tip

■ Each Opacity parameter only affects each attribute—for example, you can set the Face opacity to zero and still have an Outline opacity of 100 percent (**Figure 13.18**). By contrast, the Opacity control in the Dashboard and the Properties tab of the Inspector controls the opacity of the entire object: Face, Outline, Glow, and Drop Shadow are all affected.

MODIFYING TEXT STYLE

To change the color of a Style attribute:

1. If it's not already selected, click the Fill With drop-down for the desired attribute and select Color (the default).

2. *Do one of the following:*

   ▲ Click the color well and pick a color with the Mac OS X Color Picker.

   ▲ Control-click the color well and sample a color with the eyedropper (**Figure 13.19**).

   ▲ Click the Color disclosure triangle and set specific Red, Green, and Blue color channel values with the sliders or the value fields (**Figure 13.20**).

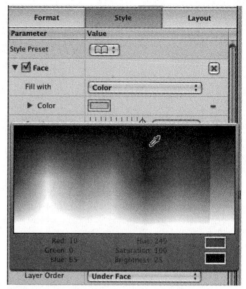

Figure 13.19 To change the color of a Style attribute, Control-click the color well and sample a color with the eyedropper.

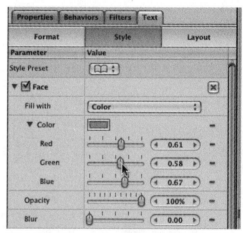

Figure 13.20 You can also change the color of a Style attribute by clicking the Color disclosure triangle and setting specific Red, Green, and Blue color values.

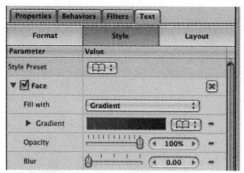

Figure 13.21 When you choose Gradient as the Fill with method, the group of Gradient controls appears. Click the disclosure triangle to reveal them.

Figure 13.22 Gradients presets can be selected from the drop-down menu.

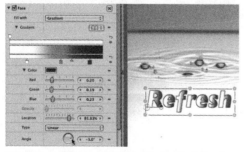

Figure 13.23 The Gradient Editor for text includes the ability to control the angle of the linear gradient.

Adding a Gradient to a Text Object

You can add a gradient to a text object just as you do for other objects that can accept gradients, such as the gradient generator, particle systems and shapes. You can either apply preset gradients or create your own custom gradients.

To add a gradient to a text attribute:

1. In the Style pane of the Text tab of the Inspector, select Gradient from the Fill with parameter.

    The Gradient parameter appears below the Fill with parameter (**Figure 13.21**).

2. *Do one of the following:*

    ▲ Select a gradient preset from the Gradient Library drop-down list (**Figure 13.22**).

    ▲ Click the Gradient disclosure triangle to reveal the Gradient Editor and customize the gradient.

    When customizing a gradient, you can change colors; move, add, and remove color tags and opacity tags; and change the type of gradient to linear or radial. Working with the Gradient Editor is discussed in detail in "Working with Gradients" in Chapter 10.

✔ Tips

■ The Gradient Editor for text includes an additional parameter not found when it is applied to other objects: the ability to control the *angle* of the linear gradient (**Figure 13.23**).

■ If you apply a gradient preset to the text object by dragging it from the Library to the text object, it is only applied to the text's Face attribute.

Adding a Texture to a Text Object

You can use an image or a movie to fill in the Face, Outline, Glow, or Drop Shadow of a text object, which Motion calls a *texture*. You have several options to control the look of the texture.

To add a texture to a text attribute:

1. In the Style pane of the Text tab of the Inspector, select Texture from the Fill with parameter for one of the attributes.

   A set of texture controls appears below the Fill with parameter.

2. If the Texture disclosure triangle is closed, click it to reveal the controls.

3. Click and drag an image or movie from the Layers or Media tab to the image well (**Figure 13.24**).

   The texture appears inside that text's attribute (Face, Outline, Glow, or Drop Shadow) (**Figure 13.25**).

To change the texture:

◆ Drag the new object into the image well. The new object replaces the current one.

To remove a texture:

◆ Click and drag the object out of the well. It disappears in a puff of smoke.

Image well

Figure 13.24 You can add a texture to a text attribute by selecting Texture as the Fill with method, then drag an image or movie from the Layers tab (or Media tab in the Timeline) to the image well.

Figure 13.25 The texture appears within the chosen attribute (in this case, the Face of the text).

Textures have several other parameters as well:

Frame sets the starting frame if the texture is an image sequence or movie.

Hold Frame uses just one frame of an image sequence or movie that you select as the texture.

Offset pushes the image horizontally, vertically, or in both directions inside the text.

Wrap Mode tells Motion what to do if the edge of the image is visible within the text: it can do nothing (the default), it can repeat the image, or it can mirror the image.

✔ Tips

- You may want to use the Offset parameter if you want to use the same image both inside the text and as a background behind the text, but you want to see a different part of the image inside the text without changing the position of the background image.

- For an alternative method of placing an image inside of text, you can use an image mask. See Chapter 12 for a full discussion.

ADDING A TEXTURE TO A TEXT OBJECT

Modifying Attribute-Specific Style Parameters

In addition to the parameters discussed above, there are several parameters that are unique to each attribute:

Outline has a **Width** parameter that sets how wide the outline is in pixels. **Layer Order** determines if the outline is underneath the text face or on top of it (**Figure 13.26**).

Glow has a **Radius** parameter to set the circumference of the glow and a **Scale** parameter to set the size (you can adjust *x* and *y* values independently). **Offset** pushes the glow out from under the text face, and **Layer Order** places the glow either under or over the text face.

Drop Shadow has a **Scale** parameter to adjust its size (you can change *x* and *y* values independently); an **Angle** parameter to adjust its angle relative to the text face; and a **Distance** parameter to set how far the shadow sits along the angle set with the Angle parameter (**Figure 13.27**).

✔ Tip

- The Drop Shadow parameter in the Style pane is different from the Drop Shadow parameter in the Inspector. If you use both, you'll end up with two drop shadows!

Figure 13.26 The Layer Order determines if the outline appears underneath or on top of the face of the text. When the outline is on top, it is fully visible. When it is underneath, it is partially obscured by the face of the text.

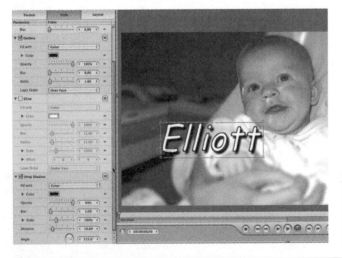

Figure 13.27 The Drop Shadow attribute has Scale, Angle, and Distance parameters, in addition to the other parameters that are common to all attributes: Fill with, Opacity, and Blur.

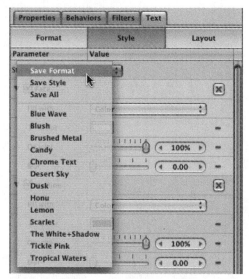

Figure 13.28 When saving a custom text style, you can choose whether to include the parameters from the Format pane, the Style pane, or both.

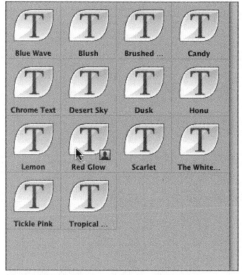

Figure 13.29 Custom styles are available in the Text Styles category of the Library and are denoted by a user icon as seen here with the Red Glow style.

Saving Text Styles

After you make changes to your text in the Format and Style panes of the Text tab to get a specific look, you can save your changes as a Text Style in the Library. This newly created Text Style is then available so you can apply it to other text objects just like the Styles that come with Motion. You can choose to save the values of just the Format parameters, just the Style parameters, or both.

To save a custom Text Style:

1. Select the text object in the Layers tab, Canvas, or Timeline.

2. In the Style pane of the Text tab of the Inspector, click the Style Preset drop-down menu and choose one of the following (**Figure 13.28**):

   ▲ To save just the Format pane parameter values, choose Save Format.

   ▲ To save just the Style pane parameter values, choose Save Style.

   ▲ To save both, choose Save All.

3. In the dialog that appears, type a name for the preset and click Save.

   The custom style is now available in the Text Styles category of the Library (**Figure 13.29**). The user icon identifies it as a user-created custom preset.

Modifying Text Layout

The Layout pane of the Text tab includes parameters for modifying the Layout Method, Alignment, Justification, and Line Spacing. You can create a Type On effect that causes letters to appear one at a time, and you can place text on a path from this pane as well.

To show the Layout pane:

1. Reveal the Text tab of the Inspector by pressing F4 and clicking the Text tab, or click the Inspector tab and then the Text tab (**Figure 13.30**).

2. Click the Layout button.

To change the Layout Method:

◆ Choose one of the following methods from the drop-down list.

Type is the default selection and creates a single line of text.

Paragraph creates a *custom margin*, which is a box to which the text conforms. You can also create a custom margin by clicking and dragging with the text tool in the Canvas. If Paragraph is selected, then the Margin sliders at the bottom of the Layout pane become active. You can adjust the custom margin with these sliders, or by selecting the Text tool (press T to reveal it) and dragging the control points in the Canvas (**Figure 13.31**).

Path activates the Path Options group of parameters for choosing and modifying a Path Shape. See "Creating Text on a Path" below.

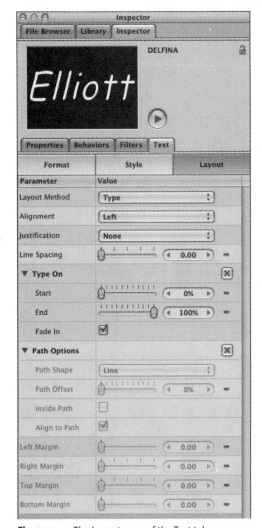

Figure 13.30 The Layout pane of the Text tab.

To change the alignment:

◆ Choose Left (default), Center, or Right from the Alignment drop-down list.

To change the justification:

◆ Choose None (default), Partial, or Full from the Justification drop-down list.

To change the line spacing:

◆ On the Line Spacing parameter, drag the slider, scrub the Value Field, or click the Value Field and enter a value.

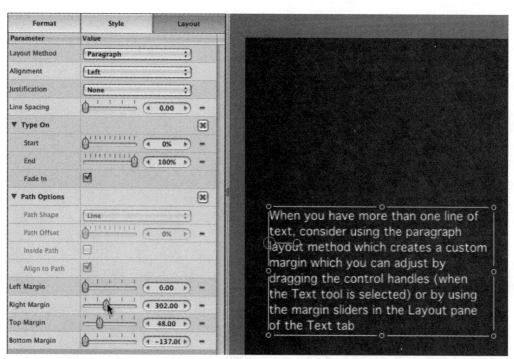

Figure 13.31 As an alternative to dragging the control points in the Canvas, you can set the custom margin size by dragging the sliders in the Layout pane. You need to have Paragraph selected as the Layout Method. As opposed to working in the Canvas, you do not need to have the Text tool active when changing the custom margin with the sliders.

MODIFYING TEXT LAYOUT

Creating a Type On Effect

By animating the Type On parameters, you can create the effect of characters popping onto the Canvas as if they were being typed or you can have them fade on for a softer effect.

To create a Type On Effect:

1. Position the playhead at the beginning of the text object.

2. Click the Record button or press A.

3. In the Type On parameter group of the Layout pane, set the End value to 0 percent.

   The text disappears.

4. Move the playhead to the location where you want the animation to end.

5. Set the End value to 100 percent.

6. Click the Record button or press A to stop recording.

✔ Tips

■ When you play the project, the text appears to fade on one character at a time (**Figure 13.32**). To have each letter pop on as if it were typed, uncheck the Fade In check box.

■ An alternative method of creating a Type On effect by using a behavior is discussed in "Using Text Animation Behaviors" later in this chapter.

■ For more information on recording keyframes, see Chapter 7.

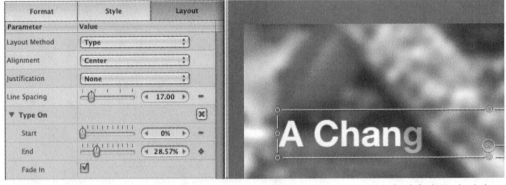

Figure 13.32 When you apply a Type On effect, text appears to fade one character at a time by default. Uncheck the Fade In check box to have each character pop on as if it were being typed.

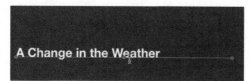

Figure 13.33 The path for a text object becomes visible and editable when you select the Text tool.

Figure 13.34 Controls points have Bezier handles that you use to adjust the shape of the path.

Figure 13.35 Control points are smooth by default, but you can make a hard corner by control-clicking and selecting Smooth.

Creating Text on a Path

Using the Layout pane, you can create and modify a path for your text. You can animate the text along the path by keyframing the Path Offset parameter.

To create text on a path:

1. Choose Path for the Layout Method parameter.

2. In the Path Options group, choose one of the following for a Path Shape:
   ▲ **Line** is the default, and it creates a short straight line.
   ▲ **Loop** creates a circular path.

To add a control point:

◆ Option-click anywhere along the path.

To change the shape of the path:

1. Click the Text tool in the Toolbar or press T and click the text object.
   The path, along with its control points, becomes visible in the Canvas (**Figure 13.33**).

2. Click and drag the control points to change the shape of the path. Control points that are not end points have Bezier handles that you can use to adjust the shape of the curve as it passes through the point (**Figure 13.34**).

To change a control point from Bezier to linear:

◆ Control-click the point and select Linear.
   Instead of curving through the point, the path makes a hard corner (**Figure 13.35**). To go back to Bezier, Control-click and select Smooth.

To remove a control point:

◆ Control-click the point and select Delete Point.

To lock a control point:

◆ Control-click the point and select Lock Point.

Locked points can't be moved.

To disable a control point:

◆ Control-click and select Disable Point. When you do, a disabled point still appears on the Canvas, but the path no longer travels through it. To enable it again, Control-click it and choose Enable Point.

✔ Tip

■ More information on working with control points can be found in Chapter 12.

To change the location of the text along a path:

◆ Change the value of the Path Offset parameter.

See "Animating Text on a Path" later in this chapter for how to animate this parameter to make the text move along the path.

✔ Tip

■ You can set a negative value for the Path Offset parameter by dragging in the value field.

To align text to the path:

◆ Check the Align to Path check box. The check box is checked by default. To force text characters to remain at their original orientation, uncheck the box (**Figure 13.36**).

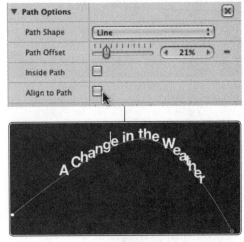

Figure 13.36 By unchecking the Align to Path check box, each character retains their original orientation regardless of the shape of the path.

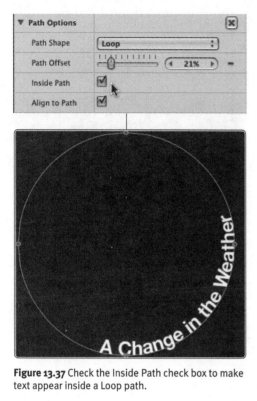

Figure 13.37 Check the Inside Path check box to make text appear inside a Loop path.

To have text appear inside a Loop path:

◆ Select Loop for the Path Shape, and check the Inside Path check box (**Figure 13.37**).

✔ Tips

■ You can only modify control points when the Text tool is active.

■ Once text is on a path, you can still modify it by changing any of the Format, Style, or Layout parameters. You can also still edit the text itself with the Text tool.

■ If the edited text becomes too long for a Line path, click and drag the end point to extend the line. Hold down Shift to constrain the extension horizontally.

■ You can move more than one control point at a time by first Shift-clicking to select them. To move the entire path, switch back to the Select/Transform tool by pressing Enter and dragging the text object.

Animating Text on a Path

To animate text along a path, you keyframe the Path Offset parameter.

To animate text on a path:

1. Position the playhead at the beginning of the text object.

2. Click the Record button or press A.

3. In the Path Offset parameter, drag the slider or enter a value to position the text at the beginning of the path.

4. Move the playhead to the location where you want the animation to end.

5. In the Path Offset parameter, drag the slider or enter a value to position the text at the end of the path (**Figure 13.38**).

6. Click the Record button or press A.

   When you play the project, the text moves along the path.

   For more information on working with keyframes, see Chapter 7.

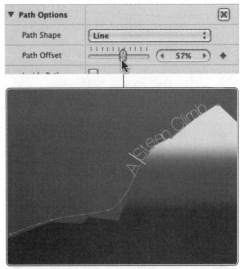

Figure 13.38 By setting keyframes for the Path Offset parameter, you can animate the text along a path.

Animating Text

The variety and control with which you can animate text in Motion is nothing short of fantastic. We have already seen two simple examples above: creating a Type On effect and moving text along a path, both of which are accomplished by keyframing specific Text Layout parameters. And although you can certainly keyframe most of the Text tab and Properties tab parameters of text objects, you can use *behaviors* to animate many different parameters at once without setting a single keyframe.

You can animate a text object, just like any other object, with the Basic Motion, Simulation, and Parameter behaviors discussed in Chapter 6. However, Motion includes two categories of behaviors just for animating text: Text Animation and Text Sequence. The Text Animation category creates basic Crawls, Scrolls, Type Ons, and Tracking effects. Plus, it includes the very powerful Sequence behavior for creating custom animations. The Text Sequence category contains a large number of preset effects that use the Sequence behavior to animate Position, Format, and Style parameters across characters.

ANIMATING TEXT

Using Text Animation Behaviors

The Text Animation category includes seven different behaviors. Six of them are basic effects such as Crawls and Scrolls. The seventh, Sequence, a seemingly innocuous little behavior that doesn't even do anything when you first apply it, is actually a powerful tool for animating parameters so that they affect different parts of a text object at different times.

To browse and preview Text Animation behaviors:

1. Reveal the Library by clicking the Library tab or by pressing Command-2.

2. In the Sidebar area, click the Behaviors category.

3. Click the Text Animation subcategory.

    A list of behaviors appears in the File Stack.

4. Select a behavior in the File Stack.

    A preview of the behavior's animation along with its name and a short description appear in the Preview Area (**Figure 13.39**).

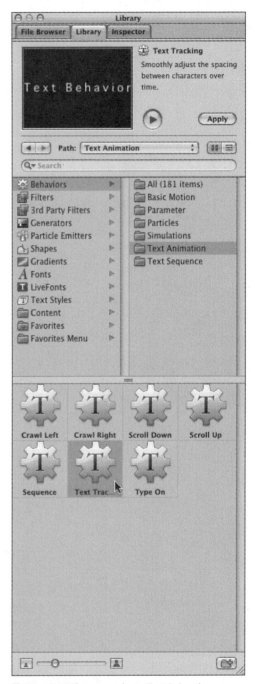

Figure 13.39 When you select a Text Animation behavior, it appears in the Preview Area along with its name and a short description.

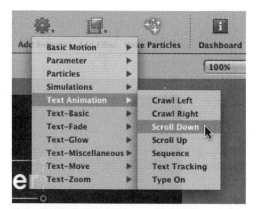

Figure 13.40 To apply a Text Animation behavior, click the Add Behavior icon in the Toolbar and select a behavior from the fly-out menu.

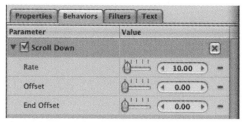

Figure 13.41 You can adjust the parameters for text animation behaviors in the Behaviors tab.

To apply a Text Animation behavior:

1. Select the text object in the Layers tab, Canvas, or Timeline.

2. *Do one of the following:*

   ▲ Drag the behavior from the File Stack in the Library onto the text object in the Layers tab, Canvas, or Timeline.

   ▲ Click the Add Behavior icon in the Toolbar and select a Text Animation behavior from the drop-down, fly-out menu (**Figure 13.40**).

To modify Text Animation behaviors:

◆ Adjust the parameters in the Behaviors tab as desired (**Figure 13.41**).

✔ Tips

■ Crawl Left, Crawl Right, Scroll Up, and Scroll Down all have the same three parameters: **Rate** is the movement in pixels per second; **Offset** sets the starting position of the animation; and **End Offset** sets the number of frames before the end of the text object's duration that the object stops.

■ Even though the value range of the sliders for each of these three parameters is limited to between 0 and 100, you can enter a lower or higher value in the Value field by scrubbing or typing.

continues on next page

USING TEXT ANIMATION BEHAVIORS

- To delay the start of a Text Animation behavior, trim its in point in the mini-Timeline or the Timeline (**Figure 13.42**).

- To stop a Text Animation behavior before the end of the text object duration, use the End Offset parameter rather than trimming—if you trim the out point of the behavior, the text jumps back to it's starting condition. However, for Type On, you *can* trim the out point to speed up the animation.

- The Tracking behavior expands or contracts the spacing between characters based on the Alignment parameter setting in the Layout pane. For example, if you want the text to expand or contract from the center, choose Center for the Alignment setting.

- Text Animation behaviors can be modified, moved, trimmed, copied, pasted, reordered, and more, just like other behaviors. For more information on working with behaviors, see Chapter 6.

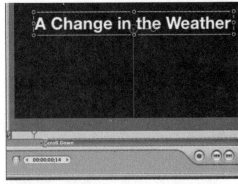

Figure 13.42 By trimming the in point of a text animation behavior, you delay the start of the animation

USING TEXT ANIMATION BEHAVIORS

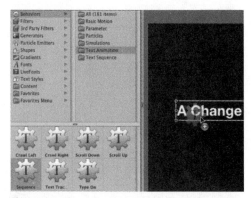

Figure 13.43 To apply a Sequence behavior to a selected text object, simply drag it from the File Stack in the Library to the text object in the Canvas.

A Change in the Weather

Figure 13.44 When you apply the Sequence behavior, the two solid vertical lines identify the selection range, which is the region that is currently animating. The distance between the two solid lines and the two outer, softer lines indicates the range over which the animation tapers off.

Using the Sequence Behavior

With the Sequence behavior, you choose parameters to animate, and the animation occurs on each letter at a different point in time—in other words, the animation *sequences* through the text. You can animate any of the Format and Style parameters that have an animation menu such as Rotation, Color, Size, Outline Width, or Drop Shadow Distance, as well as the Position parameter from the Properties tab. You can change how the animation sequences through the text object—for example, forward, backward, or randomly.

Once you create a custom sequence animation, you can save it as a preset in the Library for future use. In fact, all of the behaviors in the Sequence Behavior category are just that—customized Sequence behaviors.

To apply the Sequence behavior:

Do one of the following:

◆ Drag it from the File Stack in the Library onto the text object (**Figure 13.43**).

◆ Select the text object and choose the Sequence behavior from the Add Behavior icon in the Toolbar

A box appears around the text object along with four vertical white lines (**Figure 13.44**). The two solid lines represent the selection range, which is the range that is currently receiving the full effect of the animation; the two softer lines represent the range over which the animation falls off.

Adding and Animating Parameters for the Sequence Behavior

Nothing happens when you first add the Sequence behavior, because you need to choose the parameters you wish to animate.

To add a parameter to the Sequence behavior:

1. Click the Behavior tab of the Inspector (or press F2).

2. Click Add in the Parameter row and select a parameter from the drop-down fly-out menu (**Figure 13.45**).

   The selected parameter appears above the Parameter row (**Figure 13.46**).

3. Set a value for the parameter.

   Once you add a parameter and set a value, the animation animates from its original default value to the new value you set and back to the default again within the selection range (**Figure 13.47**).

✔ Tip

- You can add as many parameters as you like—by choosing a mix of parameters and values, you can create very different effects (**Figure 13.48**).

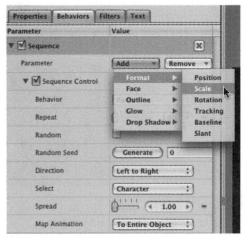

Figure 13.45 To add a parameter to the Sequence behavior, click Add in the Parameter row and select the parameter you want.

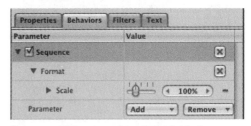

Figure 13.46 When you add a parameter to the Sequence behavior, it appears just above the Parameter row.

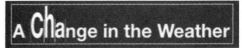

Figure 13.47 Parameters animate from their default values to the new value and back to the default value. In this example, the Scale y parameter animates from the original value up to a larger value and back down again.

Figure 13.48 By adding multiple parameters to the Sequence behavior and assigning new values, you can create complex animations. Here, Scale, Rotation, Opacity, Tracking, and Blur are all animating across the text object.

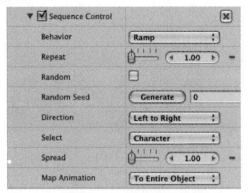

Figure 13.49 The Sequence Control parameters allow you to fine-tune exactly how the animation unfolds.

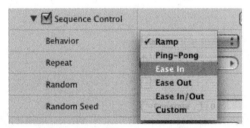

Figure 13.50 To change the behavior of the sequencing animation, choose an option from the Behavior parameter drop-down menu.

Modifying the Sequence Behavior

Once you have added parameters to the Sequence behavior and set values for those parameters, you can modify how the animation unfolds with the Sequence Control parameters (**Figure 13.49**). You can turn the sequencing animation off; you can choose how the animation moves through the text—whether it affects individual characters, words, lines, or the entire object at once—and you can map the animation to keyframed parameter values.

To turn off the Sequence behavior:

◆ Click the Active check box next to the Sequence Control group.

To change the behavior of the sequencing animation:

◆ Click and choose one of the following options from the Behavior parameter drop-down menu (**Figure 13.50**).

  Ramp is the default and moves the animation through the text object at a steady rate.

  Ping-Pong causes the animation to move forward and backward through the text based on the number that you set in the Repeat parameter. Repeat must be set to at least 2 for Ping-Pong to have any effect.

  Ease In causes the animation to start up slowly, then proceed through the text at a steady rate.

  Ease Out causes the animation to slow down as it comes to the end.

  Ease In/Ease Out causes the animation to start up slowly and slow down toward the end.

  Custom allows you to set keyframes to determine how the animation moves through the text over time. See "Using the Custom Option for the Behavior Parameter" later in this chapter.

To repeat the sequence animation:

◆ Set a value for the number of repetitions with the Repeat parameter.

To randomize the sequence animation:

◆ Click the Random check box.

To change the random sequence animation:

◆ Click the Generate button for the Random Seed parameter.

To change the direction of the sequence animation:

◆ Select Left to Right or Right to Left from the Direction parameter drop-down list.

If Random is selected, this parameter has no affect.

To change the selection range for the sequence animation:

◆ Click and choose one of the following options from the Select parameter drop-down menu.

Character is the default and animates a character at a time.

Word animates whole words at a time.

Line animates full lines of text at a time.

All changes the animation for each character so that instead of moving from default value to new value and back to default value, the animation starts immediately at the new value for all characters, and animates each character to the default value.

Custom allows you to set custom start and end points for the animation range that you can then keyframe to change over time (**Figure 13.51**).

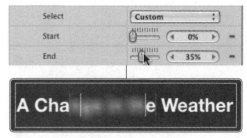

Figure 13.51 By choosing the Custom Behavior in the Sequence Controls, you can set the start and end points for the animation range. You can then keyframe the range to change over time.

Figure 13.52 The Spread parameter affects the range over which the animation tapers off. Here, the Position Y parameter animates to drop each letter down, and the spread is set so that 2 letters on each side of the letter that has reached the new value are either starting to animate or finishing the animation.

✔ **Tip**

■ To have the text object start at the new value and animate to the default value rather than animating from the default value, to the new value, and back to the default value, change the Select parameter from Character to All.

To change the falloff range of the sequence animation:

◆ Adjust the Spread parameter value.

✔ **Tip**

■ Use the soft white lines in the Canvas as a guide to the width of the spread. A setting of zero means that each selection area completely finishes its animation before the next selection area starts. Higher values overlap the animation so that it spills over into neighboring selection, meaning that the selection range to the left hasn't quite finished animating, and the range to the right has already started to animate (**Figure 13.52**).

MODIFYING THE SEQUENCE BEHAVIOR

Using the Custom Option for the Behavior Parameter

I know, it's getting confusing: there are behaviors, there are parameters, there are parameter behaviors—and now, there is a Behavior parameter! Well, the Behavior parameter is a parameter that is only located in the Sequence Control group of the Sequence behavior, nowhere else—does that help? Maybe not.

At any rate, if you set the Behavior parameter to Custom, a new Location parameter appears below it that allows you to keyframe exactly how the sequencing animation moves through the text object. If you want the animation to only affect the first three letters or to move halfway through the text and then move backward, the Custom Behavior parameter can do the job.

To use the Custom Behavior parameter:

1. Select Custom from the Behavior parameter drop-down in the Sequence Control group.

   The Location parameter appears (**Figure 13.53**).

2. Move the playhead to the beginning of the text object.

3. Click Record or press A.

4. Change the Location parameter value to move the selection range to the area on the text object where you want the animation to begin.

5. Move the playhead to the location for the next desired keyframe.

6. Change the Location parameter to move the selection range to the next area of text.

7. Repeat steps 5 and 6 as desired.

8. Click Record or press A to stop recording.

   The animation now follows the direction of the keyframed selection range.

   For details on using keyframes, see Chapter 7.

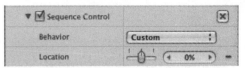

Figure 13.53 When you select Custom for the Behavior parameter, a new parameter called Location appears. You animate this parameter to change the location of the animation range.

Using Map Animation with Keyframed Parameters

When you add a parameter to the Sequence behavior, normally you set a value and the animation moves from the default value to that value and back to the default over the selection range (unless you change the Select parameter to All, in which case it moves from the set value to the default). However, you can also keyframe the parameter to move to multiple specific values. When you do so, you can choose whether the keyframes get mapped across the duration of the entire object, or to each individual selection range.

To keyframe a parameter:

1. Place the playhead at the beginning of the object.

2. Click Record or press A.

3. Set the value for the parameter.

4. Move the playhead to the location for the next keyframe.

5. Set the next value for the parameter.

6. Repeat steps 4 and 5 as needed.

7. Click Record or press A to stop recording.

To choose a Map Animation option:

◆ Select one of the following options from the Map Animation drop-down list.

To Entire Object is the default and maintains the keyframed animation timing as you created it, but it sequences through the text as the animation progresses.

For example, if you keyframe the Position parameter to move up 30 pixels over 2 seconds and then down 60 pixels over the next 3 seconds, the first few letters move up, and wherever the selection range happens to be at 2 seconds, that letter moves up 10 pixels. As the animation progresses, letters start moving down, and the last letter moves down by 30 pixels (**Figure 13.54**).

To Selection forces the full animation to be squeezed into the selection range and repeated for each selection.

Using the same example as above, the first letter moves up 10 pixels and then down 30 pixels, then the second letter moves up 10 pixels and down 30 pixels, and so on as the selection range moves through the text object (**Figure 13.55**).

✔ Tip

■ To Selection only works if you have a keyframed parameter.

Figure 13.54 When Map Animation is set to Entire Object, that animation is applied across every character. In this case the animation is set to have each letter move upwards and then downwards—but with Entire Object chosen, the first few letters only move up, and the last letters only move down.

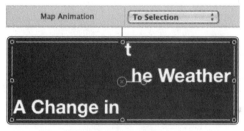

Figure 13.55 When Map Animation is set to To Selection, the entire animation occurs on each selection range. Here, the selection range has animated to the middle of the text object, and the characters currently in the selection range complete the full animation—they each move up, then down.

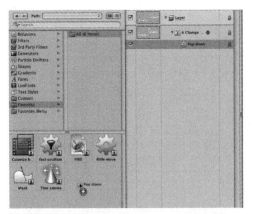

Figure 13.56 To save a modified Sequence behavior, such as Pop down here, drag it from the Layers tab or the Timeline to the Favorites folder, Favorites Menu folder, or one of the Text Sequence folders in the Library.

Saving a Modified Sequence Behavior

After you spend a lot of time adding parameters and modifying values to create the perfect text sequencing animation, you surely will want to be able to save all your settings to apply to other text objects. No problem—just give the modified sequence behavior a name and add it to the Library.

To save a modified Sequence behavior:

1. Rename the behavior in the Layers list or the Timeline (this isn't required, but it is a good idea so you can identify it later).

2. Drag the behavior from the Layers tab or the Timeline to the Favorites folder, Favorites Menu folder, or one of the Text Sequence folders in the Library (**Figure 13.56**).

   The preset appears in the File Stack with a small user icon attached to indicate that it's a user-created custom preset.

✔ Tips

■ You can create your own folders for storing preset behaviors (and filters, particle emitters, text styles, shapes, gradients, and generators, for that matter). See Chapter 8 for more information.

■ What you saved is a Text Sequence behavior, just like the ones discussed below, but with your own special settings.

Using Text Sequence Behaviors

There are over 140 different Text Sequence behaviors in Motion's Library—enough to keep you busy experimenting for quite awhile!

As discussed above, all of these behaviors are actually presets created by applying the Sequence behavior and animating various Format and Style parameters (some have additional behaviors applied as well, such as Simulation behaviors). Therefore, you can modify them by adding and removing parameters and adjusting the Sequence Control parameters.

These behaviors work pretty much like other behaviors discussed in Chapter 6, except that, when applied, they do not last for the duration of the object. Instead, they are designed to have a short impact: the text bounces in or flies out, for example.

To browse and preview Text Sequence behaviors:

1. Reveal the Library by clicking the Library tab or pressing Command-2.

2. Click the Behaviors category in the Sidebar area and then click the Text Sequence subcategory.

   Seven folders appear in the File Stack area (**Figure 13.57**).

3. If you are in Icon view, double-click a folder. If you are in List view, either double-click the folder or click the disclosure triangle.

4. Click a behavior to select it.

   An animation of the behavior plays in the Preview Area.

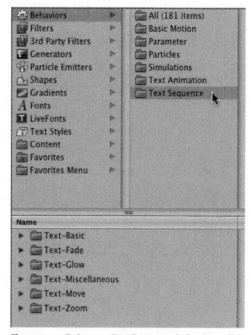

Figure 13.57 To browse Text Sequence behaviors, click the Behaviors category in the Sidebar and then click the Text Sequence subcategory to reveal seven folders in the File Stack.

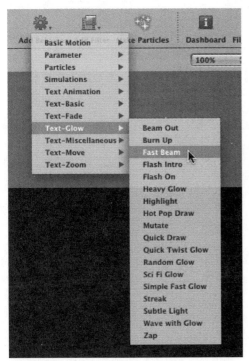

Figure 13.58 You can choose a Text Sequence behavior by clicking the Add Behavior icon in the Toolbar.

To apply a Text Sequence behavior:

1. Select the text object to receive the behavior.

2. *Do one of the following:*

   ▲ Drag the Text Sequence behavior from the File Stack of the Library onto the text object in the Layers tab, Timeline, or Canvas.

   ▲ Choose the Text Sequence behavior from the Add Behavior icon in the Toolbar (**Figure 13.58**).

USING TEXT SEQUENCE BEHAVIORS

397

Modifying Text Sequence Behaviors

Unlike the Sequence behavior discussed in the Text Animation behaviors section, when you apply a Text Sequence behavior, it already has a preset animation in place. This means you can use it as is, or you can immediately tweak the Sequence Controls directly in the Dashboard— all of them are available. If you want to add or remove parameters, use the Inspector.

Figure 13.59 You can modify text sequence behaviors by adding more parameters and then setting values for them.

To modify the Sequence Control parameters of a Text Sequence behavior:

Do one of the following:

◆ In the Dashboard (press D or F7 to reveal it), adjust each parameter as desired.

◆ Open the Behavior tab of the Inspector (press F2 to reveal it) and adjust the parameters there.

   Every Sequence Control parameter is available on the Dashboard. For detail on each parameter, see "Modifying the Sequence Behavior" earlier in this chapter.

To add a new parameter to a Text Sequence behavior:

◆ In the Behavior tab, click the Add button on the Parameter row and select the parameter to add (**Figure 13.59**).

To remove an existing parameter from a Text Sequence behavior:

◆ In the Behavior tab, click the Remove button on the Parameter row and select the parameter to remove.

✔ Tip

■ To change the duration of a Text Sequence behavior, trim the out point in the mini-Timeline or Timeline. See Chapter 5 for more information on editing in the Timeline.

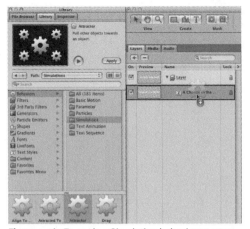

Figure 13.60 To apply a Simulation behavior to a text object, drag it from the File Stack of the Library onto the text object.

Using Basic Motion and Simulation Behaviors with Text Objects

Although the Text Animation and Text Sequence behaviors are designed specifically to animate text, you can use the other behaviors on text objects as well. The Basic Motion and Simulation behaviors work with text almost the same way they work on other objects (discussed in Chapter 6), but because text is made up of individual characters, behaviors that normally only affect other objects (such as Attract, Repel, and Vortex) affect the individual characters in a text object—which can create some interesting effects.

To apply a Basic Motion or Simulation behavior to a text object:

Do one of the following:

- ◆ Drag the behavior from the File Stack of the Library onto the text object in the Layers tab, Canvas, or Timeline (**Figure 13.60**).

- ◆ Select the text object and then select the behavior from the Add Behavior icon in the Toolbar.

See Chapter 6 for detailed information on how to work with these behaviors.

✔ Tips

- In general, Simulation behaviors use the object's anchor point as the focus of forces, so changing the anchor point location can dramatically impact the animation (**Figure 13.61**).

- Many behaviors have an Affect Objects option, which is checked on by default (and in fact, the Affect Objects parameter for certain behaviors, such as Edge Collision, is *only* available when the behavior is applied to a text object). In the case of text objects, this property causes each character to be affected by the behavior. If you want the entire text object to be affected as a whole, uncheck this parameter.

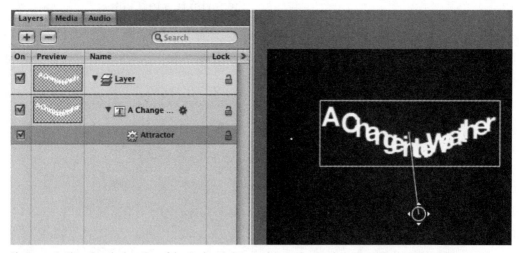

Figure 13.61 Changing the location of the Anchor Point can change the way behaviors play out. Here, the Attractor behavior causes the individual letters to move towards the anchor point, which has been moved down below the text object.

Animation menus

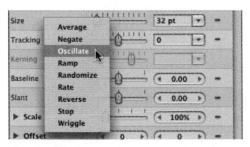

| Properties | Behaviors | Filters | Text |
| Format | Style | Layout |

Parameter	Value
Font Type	System Fonts ⬍ (Browse...)
Collection	All Fonts ▾
Family	Helvetica Neue ▾
Typeface	Bold ▾
Size	32 pt ▾ —
Tracking	0 ▾ —
Kerning	▾
Baseline	◀ 0.00 ▶ —
Slant	◀ 0.00 ▶ —
▶ Scale	◀ 100% ▶ —
▶ Offset	◀ 0 ▶ ◀ 0 ▶ —
Rotation	◀ 0.0° ▶ —
Monospace	☐
All Caps	☐
All Caps Size	◀ 80% ▶ —

Figure 13.62 Any parameter that has an animation menu can by animated with parameter behaviors or keyframes.

Size	32 pt ▾ —
	Average
Tracking	Negate 0 ▾ —
	Oscillate
Kerning	Ramp ▾
	Randomize
Baseline	Rate ◀ 0.00 ▶ —
Slant	Reverse ◀ 0.00 ▶ —
	Stop
▶ Scale	Wriggle ◀ 100% ▶ —
▶ Offset	0 ◀ 0 ▶ —

Figure 13.63 To apply a parameter behavior to the parameter of a text object, Control-click the name of the parameter and then choose the parameter behavior to apply.

Using Parameter Behaviors with Text

You can apply Parameter behaviors to the parameters of text objects the same way you apply them to other objects in Motion. You can apply them to any parameter in the Inspector that has an animation menu— this means parameters of object properties in the Properties tab, like Position, Scale and Rotation; parameters of other behaviors applied to the object in the Behaviors tab (including other parameter behaviors!); parameters of applied filters in the Filters tab; and of any parameters in the Text tab, whether they are Format, Style, or Layout parameters. As long as the parameter has an Animation menu (**Figure 13.62**), it can be animated with a Parameter behavior (or with keyframes, which are discussed in the next section).

For a detailed discussion of working with Parameter behaviors, see Chapter 6.

To apply a Parameter behavior to the parameter of a text object:

1. Select the text object.

2. Choose a parameter in the Inspector that has an Animation menu.

3. Control-click the name of the parameter and choose the parameter behavior to apply (**Figure 13.63**).

Keyframing Text

Just as with Parameter behaviors discussed above, you can keyframe any parameter of a text object or of an effect applied to a text object, such as a filter or behavior, that has an Animation menu in the Inspector. You can set keyframes using the Record button or by using the Animation menu, and you can modify the keyframes in the Keyframe Editor. Two examples of setting keyframes on Text tab parameters using the Record method are discussed earlier in this chapter: creating a Type On effect, and animating text on a path.

For a discussion of when to use keyframes and when to use behaviors, see Chapter 6.

Figure 13.64 Some filters, such as the Distortion filter seen here, get clipped by the bounding box of the text object.

Figure 13.65 Other filters, such as Light Rays seen here, are able to expand beyond the text objects' bounding box.

Adding Filters to Text

Because text is an object, you can add filters just like you do with other objects in Motion. Drag the filter from the Library onto the text object or select it from the Add Filter icon in the Toolbar. Filters are discussed in Chapter 9.

✔ Tips

- The effect of some filters, such as Tiling and Distortion, is restricted to the bounding box of the text. Other filters, such as Light Rays and Zoom Blur, are able to expand beyond the bounding box (**Figures 13.64** and **13.65**).

- You can still edit text with filters applied. It may be easier to use the Text Editor at the bottom of the Format pane of the Text tab of the Inspector than to edit in the Canvas when filters are applied.

- You can also apply masks to text objects. See Chapter 12 for information on working with masks.

WORKING WITH AUDIO

Often neglected, audio is an integral part of most motion graphics projects, whether it is music that sets an emotional tone, narration that tells a story, or sound effects that enhance an animation.

Motion has two parts of its interface dedicated to working with audio: an Audio tab in the Project pane and a full-featured Audio Editor in the Timing pane.

Using these tools, you can import audio files with different formats and adjust the volume (*level*) and balance (*pan*) of each to create an optimal combination (*mix*) of your audio elements. In addition, you can view a representation of the change in the audio level over time (called a *waveform*), and you can set markers that you can use as you move, trim, and slip audio tracks to line up with visual cues. You can also keyframe audio to change levels and pan over time—for example, to create cross fades or to lower the music level when the narrator is speaking. Then you can use the Master Controls to adjust the overall level and pan of the entire audio mix. You can even keyframe audio levels in real-time with Motion's Record Animation feature.

Adding Audio

You can add many different types of audio files to Motion, including AIFF, WAV, MP3, AAC, and QuickTime audio (MOV). Motion supports sample rates up to 48 KHz, and bit depths up to 24 bits. When you add an audio file, Motion converts the file based on its own internal format of 44.1 KHz and 16 bits for built-in audio (CD quality).

When you add QuickTime movies to Motion, the audio and video components are both added by default, but you can override this behavior to add just the audio (see the last tip on the next page for how to do this).

To preview an audio file:

1. Navigate to the file in the File Browser.

2. *Do one of the following:*

   ▲ Click the file.

   It begins to play immediately. Press Pause in the Preview Area to stop playback.

   ▲ Double-click the file to launch the Play window and click the Play button (**Figure 14.1**).

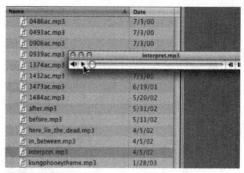

Figure 14.1 To preview an audio file, double-click it to launch the Play window. Then just click the Play button.

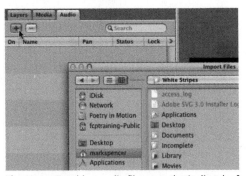

Figure 14.2 To add an audio file, go to the Audio tab of the Project pane, click the Add button, find the file you want, and then click the Import button in the lower right corner.

To add an audio file:

Do one of the following:

◆ Select the audio file in the File Browser and click the Import button in the Preview Area.

◆ Drag the audio file from the File Browser to either the Project pane (any tab), the Canvas, or the Timeline.

◆ In the Audio tab of the Project pane (press Command-6 to reveal it), click the Add button (+), browse to the file in the dialog, and click Import (**Figure 14.2**).

✔ Tips

■ Audio files appear in the Media and Audio tabs of the Project pane and in the Timeline.

■ Audio files do not appear in the Layers tab or the Canvas.

■ If you don't see the audio track in the Timeline, click the Show/Hide Audio button near the bottom left.

■ If you add the audio file to the Media tab, it is imported into the project, but it isn't available to play or manipulate until you drag it from the Media tab to the Canvas or Timeline. You can use the Media tab to store a collection of selects that you can then go to as you build your project, instead of digging back through the File Browser.

■ Playback quality may not be as high with compressed formats such as MP3 and AAC.

■ You can't use rights-protected AAC files in Motion.

■ To add just the audio track from a QuickTime movie, drag the file from the File Browser to the Audio tab of the Project pane.

ADDING AUDIO

Manipulating Audio Files

You can cut, copy, paste, duplicate, and delete audio files just as you do with other objects in Motion. The only difference is that you select audio files in the Audio tab of the Project pane.

Figure 14.3 To cut an audio file, simply Control-click the file and choose Cut from the menu.

To cut an audio file:

1. Select the audio file in the Audio tab.

2. *Do one of the following:*

   ▲ Choose Edit > Cut.

   ▲ Control-click the file and choose Cut from the shortcut menu (**Figure 14.3**).

   ▲ Press Command-X.

To copy an audio file:

1. Select the audio file in the Audio tab.

2. *Do one of the following:*

   ▲ Choose Edit > Copy.

   ▲ Control-click the file and choose Copy from the shortcut menu.

   ▲ Press Command-C to copy the file to the Clipboard for pasting.

To paste an audio file:

1. Select the Audio tab.

2. *Do one of the following:*

   ▲ Choose Edit > Paste.

   ▲ Control-click an empty area and choose Paste from the shortcut menu.

   ▲ Press Command-V.

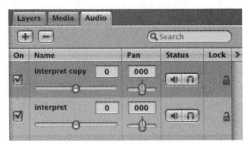

Figure 14.4 A duplicate audio file appears above the original in the Audio tab.

To duplicate an audio file:

1. Select the audio file in the Audio tab.

2. *Do one of the following:*

   ▲ Choose Edit > Duplicate.

   ▲ Control-click the file and choose Duplicate from the shortcut menu.

   ▲ Press Command-D.

   The duplicate appears above the original file in the Audio tab (**Figure 14.4**).

To delete an audio file:

1. Select the audio file in the Audio tab.

2. *Do one of the following:*

   ▲ Choose Edit > Delete.

   ▲ Control-click the file and choose Delete from the shortcut menu.

   ▲ Click the Delete button (−) at the top of the Audio tab.

MANIPULATING AUDIO FILES

Working with Audio Tracks

Each audio file appears as a track in the Audio tab of the project pane (**Figure 14.5**). You can select tracks for playback, turn tracks on and off, adjust their levels and panning, lock, and rename them. You can also keyframe the volume and pan of individual tracks to change over time as described in "Keyframing Audio" later in this chapter.

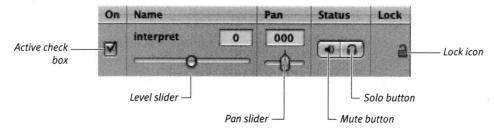

Figure 14.5 An audio track in the Audio pane.

Figure 14.6 To play back a track, select it in the Audio tab and then press the Play audio track button in the Audio Editor.

To play back a selected track:

1. Select the track by clicking it in the Audio tab.

2. In the Audio Editor (press Command-9 to reveal it), press the Play audio track button (**Figure 14.6**).

   Only the selected track plays—the Canvas does not update.

✔ Tip

- When you click Play in the Canvas or press the spacebar, the full project plays, including the Canvas and all audio tracks that are active and not muted.

To turn off an audio track:

- ◆ Click the Active check box at the left side of the track.

  When an audio track is turned off, it isn't included in the rendered output.

✔ Tip

- You can also turn off an audio track using the Active check box in the Timeline. If you don't see the audio track in the Timeline, click the Show/Hide Audio button in the bottom left corner.

To mute an audio track:

Do one of the following:

- ◆ Click the Mute button.

- ◆ Control-click the track and select Mute from the shortcut menu.

✔ Tips

- A muted track is silent during playback, *but it is still included when you export the project.*

- To turn muting off, click the Mute button again.

- You can mute or unmute while the project is playing.

To solo an audio track:

Do one of the following:

◆ Click the Solo button (**Figure 14.7**).

◆ Control-click the track and select Solo from the shortcut menu.

✔ Tips

■ All tracks that are not soloed are silent during playback, *but they are included when you export the project.*

■ To unsolo, click the Solo button again.

■ You can solo or unsolo while the project is playing.

■ You can solo more than one track at a time. If you have many audio tracks, it can be faster to solo a few tracks than to mute the others.

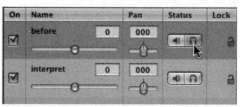

Figure 14.7 Clicking the Solo button turns off all other tracks (but they will still play when exported). You can solo more than one track at a time.

To adjust the level of an audio track:

◆ Drag the Level slider in any one of the following locations:

▲ The Audio Track tab of the Inspector (press F4 to reveal it).

▲ The Audio tab of the Project pane (press Command-6 to reveal it).

▲ The Dashboard (press D or F7 to reveal it).

▲ The Audio Editor in the Timing pane (press Command-9 to reveal it).

✔ Tips

■ In every location except the Dashboard, you can also enter a specific value in the Value field.

■ All audio levels consider the original level of the imported audio as zero. Therefore, a level of zero for one track may sound much louder or softer than a different track at the same zero level.

■ As you raise or lower the level, the change is represented in decibels (dB) relative to the starting value.

■ See "Using the Master Track" later in this chapter for setting the overall level of all the audio tracks mixed together.

To adjust the panning of an audio track:

◆ Drag the Pan slider in any one of the following locations:

▲ The Audio Track tab of the Inspector (press F4 to reveal it).

▲ The Audio tab of the Project pane (press Command-6 to reveal it).

▲ The Dashboard (press D or F7 to reveal it).

▲ The Audio Editor in the Timing pane (press Command-9 to reveal it).

✔ Tips

■ In every location except the Dashboard, you can also enter a specific value in the Value field.

■ The default pan is set to zero, meaning audio plays equally to both left and right channels. Moving the slider to the left shifts the balance to the left channel; moving it right shifts it to the right. At the end values, –100 is all the way left and +100 is all the way right (**Figure 14.8**).

To lock a track:

◆ Click the Lock button in the Audio tab.

✔ Tip

■ You can still turn locked tracks off and on, but you can't change their Level, Pan, Mute, or Solo properties. You also can't move, trim, or keyframe a locked track.

To rename a track:

◆ Double-click the track's name in the Audio tab and type a new name.

✔ Tip

■ Changing a track's name does not affect the name of the source media.

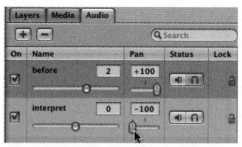

Figure 14.8 Moving the slider to the left shifts the audio balance, or pan, to the left channel; moving it right shifts the balance to the right channel. Here, –100 indicates that the audio is panned all the way to the left.

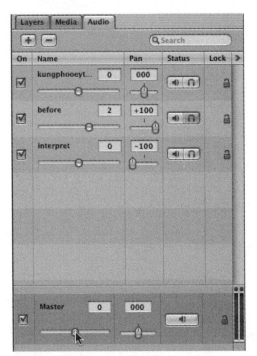

Figure 14.9 The Master audio track, located at the bottom of the Audio tab, lets you set the overall level and pan for the entire mix.

Using the Master Track

The Master audio track is located at the bottom of the Audio tab (**Figure 14.9**). Once you have created your mix by adjusting levels and pans for individual tracks, you can use the Master track to set the overall level and pan for the entire mix. The Master track includes a pair of level meters that indicate the current level while the project is playing. The level meters also warn you if the overall volume ever goes high enough to cause *clipping*, or digital distortion. You can turn off or mute all tracks at once with the Master track. You can also keyframe the Master level and volume controls to change over time, as described in "Keyframing Audio" later in this chapter.

To turn off the Master track:

◆ Click the Active check box on the left side. Click it again to turn the Master track back on.

✔ Tip

■ When the Master track is turned off, all audio is silenced, and it *is not* included when you export the project.

To mute the Master track:

◆ Click the Mute button. Click it again to unmute.

✔ Tip

■ When the Master track is muted, all audio is silenced, but it *is* included when you export the project.

To set the Master level:

◆ Drag the Master level slider left to decrease or right to increase the level.

✔ Tip

■ The Master level adjustment gets combined with the level adjustments for individual tracks for the final level output.

To set the Master pan:

◆ Drag the Master pan slider to the left or right.

✔ Tip ·

■ The Master pan control combines with the individual track pan settings—if a track is set to pan hard left, and the Master is set to pan hard right, the track ends up being silent.

USING THE MASTER TRACK

Too Hot!

Digital audio has a fixed volume threshold, and when the volume exceeds that threshold, it gets clipped, or immediately distorted. If one or both of the red dots at the top of the level meters (located with the Master track in both the Audio tab and in the Audio Editor) lights up during playback, it means your combined overall audio level is too high (**Figure 14.10**). These *clipping indicators* warn you by lighting up at the offending frame(s); they stay lit until you click them. If this happens to you, there are several solutions:

1. Lower the level on the individual track(s). By soloing tracks, you can identify if there is one offender, or if it's a result of several tracks playing together.

2. Lower the Master level.

3. Keyframe the level on either individual tracks or the Master.

Figure 14.10 If the audio level goes high enough to be clipped, the clipping indicators at the top of the level bars light up for the offending track(s).

No matter what approach you take, the goal is to make sure that the clipping indicators don't ever light up when you play the project.

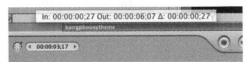

Figure 14.11 When you move an audio clip in the mini-Timeline, a tooltip displays the new in and out points as well as the change from the original location.

Editing Audio

Similar to the way you work with video, you can move, trim, and slip audio using the mini-Timeline or the full Timeline. The Audio Editor lets you trim and slip audio using the audio waveform as a guide. Trimming refers to changing the duration of an audio clip, and slipping refers to changing what section of audio plays for a given duration and location. These operations, as they apply to objects in general, are discussed in "Editing Objects in the Timeline" in Chapter 5. Audio *scrubbing* allows you to hear the audio as you drag the playhead through the clip. By turning on Audio Scrubbing, you can more easily identify where to move, trim, or slip a clip.

To move an audio clip:

1. Select the track in the Audio tab.

2. In the mini-Timeline or the Timeline, click and drag the audio to the new location.

   A tooltip indicates the new in and out points and the change from the original location (**Figure 14.11**).

✔ Tips

- By default, audio clips (and other objects) are placed either at the beginning of the project or at the current playhead location, depending on your selection in the Project section of Motion's preferences (Motion > Preferences or Command-,).

- If you want to move the audio to a specific frame, place the playhead at that frame, then either drag while holding the Shift key to snap to the playhead, choose Mark > Move Selected In Point, or press Shift-[(left bracket).

To trim the in or out point of an audio clip:

1. Select the track in the Audio tab.

2. In either the mini-Timeline, the Timeline, or the Audio Editor, *do one of the following:*

   ▲ Click and drag the in point or out point.

   A tooltip indicates the new location and change.

   ▲ Move the playhead to the location for the new in point or out point and press I for in point or O for out point.

✔ Tip

■ If you don't remember the keyboard shortcuts, you can find them in the Mark menu.

To slip an audio clip:

1. Select the track in the Audio tab.

2. *Do one of the following:*

   ▲ In the mini-Timeline or Timeline, hold down the Option key, and then click and drag on the audio clip.

   The pointer changes to a slip icon, and a tooltip indicates the new in and out points and the change.

   ▲ In the Audio Editor, click and drag the object bar.

   A highlight shows which section of the audio waveform is between the in and out points (**Figure 14.12**).

✔ Tip

■ Before you can slip a clip, you must trim it so that there is media beyond the in point or out point.

Highlighted region

Figure 14.12 Slipping a clip in the Audio Editor. The highlighted region indicates what portion of the audio is included for playback. Note that moving the bar only changes the portion that plays, not the location of the audio clip in the Timeline.

EDITING AUDIO

Figure 14.13 Click the Audio Scrubbing button in order to hear audio as you click-drag the playhead.

To turn on Audio Scrubbing:

◆ In the Audio Editor, click the Audio Scrubbing button at the bottom left corner (**Figure 14.13**). Click again to turn it off.

✔ Tip

■ With audio scrubbing enabled, you can hear the audio as you drag the playhead through the clip.

Using Markers with Audio

Markers, covered in "Using Markers" in Chapter 5, can be extraordinarily useful for timing visual effects to audio cues. Markers that you set in the Timeline are visible in both the Keyframe Editor and the Audio Editor. By using the audio waveform and audio scrubbing to identify audio cues, you can add markers to audio clips and align them with markers in either video clips or the overall Timeline (**Figure 14.14**). Make sure that snapping is enabled (View > Snap or press N) to make it easy to align markers to clips or other markers.

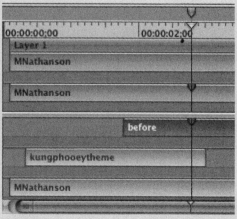

Figure 14.14 By using markers you can precisely align an audio cue, such as a downbeat, with a visual cue.

Keyframing Audio

By changing the audio level over time with keyframes, you can fade in and fade out an audio track; "duck" the audio of a music track so that the level drops when a voice-over comes on and picks up again when it finishes; or cross-fade between two audio tracks. You can also keyframe the pan control to create the sensation of audio moving from one speaker to another. You can apply these keyframes to individual tracks and/or the Master track.

When you keyframe audio, you are using the same tools you use when animating parameters of objects such as Position, Scale, or Rotation. In fact, you are "animating" the level or pan controls. As with other parameters, you can either set keyframes manually or record them on the fly.

On difference from graphic and video objects is that the curves that get created when you keyframe level and/or pan parameters appear in the Audio Editor as opposed to the Keyframe Editor. But you work with these curves in similar ways.

A full discussion of keyframing can be found in Chapter 7. Here we focus on those processes that are specific to keyframing audio.

Figure 14.15 The Audio Editor contains four rows of controls that give you options for playback, play range, levels, and pan.

Keyframing in the Audio Editor

The Audio Editor is the third tab in the Timing pane, and you can reveal it by clicking its tab or by pressing Command-9. On the left side of the Audio Editor are four rows of controls (**Figure 14.15**).

Playback controls allow you to play the audio without playing back the video portion of your project. Pressing Play here will play the full audio clip, regardless of the location of the in and out points.

Play range lets you set the play range—using this control is the same as setting the in and out points of the audio by trimming.

Level controls let you adjust the volume up or down.

Pan controls let you adjust the audio mix between left and right channels.

The right side of the Audio Editor contains the audio waveform and the keyframe graphs for level and pan, which by default are horizontal dotted lines that overlap each other (**Figure 14.16**). Along the bottom is a Zoom slider and a Zoom/Scroll bar that work just like the ones in the Timeline, discussed in Chapter 5.

You set keyframes for level and pan in the Audio Editor in the same manner as you set them for other parameters in the Keyframe Editor—by Option-clicking the appropriate curve, or by using the Animation menu of the Inspector.

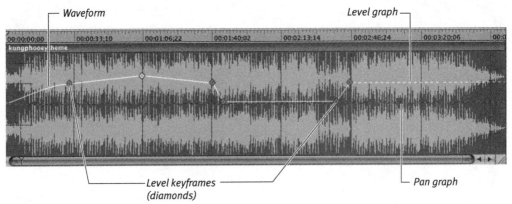

Figure 14.16 The Audio Editor lets you see the waveform for the audio, along with graphs for keyframing volume and pan.

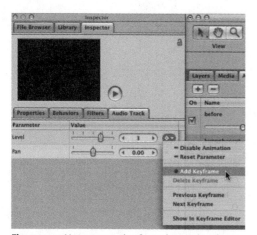

Figure 14.17 You can set a keyframe by moving the playhead to the location where you want the keyframe. Then in the Audio Track tab of the Inspector, click the Animation menu and select Add Keyframe.

To set level and pan keyframes in the Audio Editor:

◆ Option-click the level or pan curve at the location for the keyframe. Drag up or down to set the value.

The first number in the parentheses next to the keyframe is the time location, and the second is the value of the level or pan control.

✔ Tips

■ If the level and pan curves overlap, turn off the one you aren't working on by clicking the check box to the left of the parameter name.

■ Alternatively, you can set a keyframe by moving the playhead to the location for the keyframe; then in the Audio Track tab of the Inspector, click the Animation menu and select Add Keyframe (**Figure 14.17**).

■ Although the keyframe Interpolation options are grayed out when you Control-click a keyframe, you can add and adjust Bezier handles to audio keyframes by Command-dragging the keyframe.

Recording Keyframes

As an alternative to setting keyframes manually, you can automate the process by using the Record button and making level or pan adjustments in real-time as the project plays.

To record audio keyframes on the fly:

1. Click the Record button.

2. Click the Play button in the Canvas or press the spacebar to begin playback.

3. In the Audio tab of the Project pane, the Audio Track tab of the Inspector, or the Audio Editor, drag the level or pan slider as the project plays.

4. Click the Record button to stop recording.

✔ Tip

■ Recording keyframes can create a large number of keyframes, making it difficult to make adjustments to the curve. You can reduce the number of keyframes by clicking the Animation menu in the Keyframe Editor (not the Audio Editor), and selecting Reduce Keyframes from the drop-down menu (**Figure 14.18**).

■ For more details on working with keyframes, see Chapter 7.

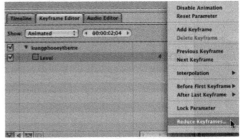

Figure 14.18 You can reduce the number of keyframes after recording them by clicking the Animation menu in the Keyframe Editor and selecting Reduce Keyframes.

Keeping in Sync

If you have a lot of objects, layers, and effects in your project, it may not play back in real-time. When this happens, you can tell Motion to either skip video frames in order to keep the audio in sync with the video, or simply pause audio playback so that the video plays every frame as fast as possible.

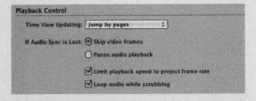

Figure 14.19 Choose how you want Motion to behave if it can't keep realtime audio and video playback in sync.

Open up Motion's Preferences (Motion > Preferences or Command-,) and click the Project icon. Under Playback Control, select an option for If Audio Sync is Lost: either Skip video frames or Pause audio playback (**Figure 14.19**).

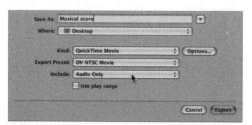

Figure 14.20 To export just the audio from your project, select Audio Only from the pop-up menu in the Export sheet.

Exporting Audio

If you want to export only audio from your project, you export a QuickTime movie with only the audio option selected.

To export audio from Motion:

1. Check the Active check box in the Audio tab for all tracks you want to export.

   Tracks that aren't checked won't be exported. However, remember that muted tracks are exported, unless they have the Active box unchecked.

2. Choose File > Export.

3. Select a name and location for the file in the dialog that appears.

4. In the same dialog, under the Include drop-down, select Audio Only (**Figure 14.20**). If you wish, click the Options button for additional options.

5. Check the Use play range check box if you only want to export the play range.

6. Click Export.

   The QuickTime movie with only audio is saved in the location you specified with the name you gave it.

15

USING TEMPLATES

One of the easiest ways to get started with Motion is to use a *template*. Motion ships with over a dozen different template collections, and each collection contains anywhere from two to five royalty-free templates based on the collection design. Templates contain preanimated graphics, text, and backgrounds. By replacing media elements and otherwise customizing a template, you can quickly create a unique and professional-looking project. You can also create your own templates and add them to the Template Browser for future use.

Creating Projects from Templates

Motion has a dedicated Template Browser for browsing and previewing the templates in the different collections (**Figure 15.1**). When you open a template from the Template Browser, Motion creates a new project based on the selected template.

To browse templates:

Do one of the following:

◆ When Motion first launches, click Start with a Template from the Welcome screen.

◆ Choose File > Open Template.

◆ Press Shift-Command-O.

✔ Tip

■ You can tell Motion to automatically open the Template Browser upon launching by changing the At Startup setting to Browse Templates in the General section of Motion's preferences (Motion > Preferences).

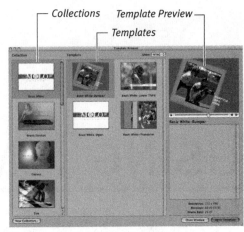

Collections   Template Preview
Templates

Figure 15.1 Motion's Template Browser

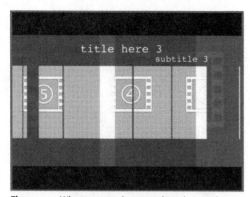

Figure 15.2 When you apply a template, it contains placeholder objects with various effects applied to them.

To create a project from a template:

◆ Select a template from the Template Browser and click Open Template.

Motion creates a new project file that contains all of the animated template elements as placeholders (**Figure 15.2**).

✔ Tip

■ You can have multiple projects open in Motion at the same time. If you already have a project open when you open a template, the new project opens in front of the old one. You can navigate among open projects using the Window menu.

Template Media and Effects

Perhaps you really like a particular movie or graphic in a template, but you don't want to create a whole new project from the template—you just want that media file.

No problem, just check the Content category in the Library: the various graphics and movies used in the templates are contained in its subject-based folders.

If you like a particular look in a template that was created with a behavior, mask, filter, keyframed animation, or other effect, you can save the effect and use it in your own project.

Customizing Templates

When you open a template, you'll find that the objects it contains are *placeholder* files named Replace with various effects such as masks, behavior, keyframes, and filters applied (**Figure 15.3**). You can customize the template by replacing the placeholder media with your own content in two ways: you can *exchange* each object individually, or you can *replace* all copies of an object that were created from the same source at once.

You can then modify the project just like you would any regular project by changing the text, adjusting parameters of existing effects, removing elements, or adding new elements.

To exchange objects in a template:

1. Drag the new object from the File Browser onto the object to be replaced in the Layers tab or the Timeline.

2. When the exchange pointer (a hooked arrow) appears, release the mouse.

To replace all instances of an object:

1. Select the object on the Media tab of the Project pane (press Command-5 to reveal the Media tab).

2. On the Media tab of the Inspector (press F4 to reveal it), click the Replace Media File button (**Figure 15.4**).

3. Browse to the file you want to use in the Choose replacement for dialog and click Open.

   Every copy of the object that was created from the imported media file is replaced at once. For more information, see "Replacing Media" in Chapter 3.

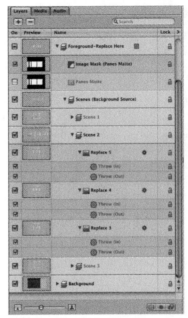

Figure 15.3 The placeholder objects are named Replace in the Layers tab. You customize the template by replacing the placeholders with your own content.

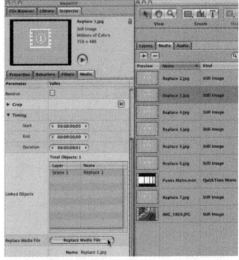

Figure 15.4 To replace all instances of an object, click the Replace Media File button in the lower-left corner of the Media Tab in the Inspector.

CUSTOMIZING TEMPLATES

Figure 15.5 When creating a new template, be sure to name it, choose a collection, choose a format, and decide if you want to create a QuickTime preview.

Figure 15.6 Voila! Your new template appears in the Template Browser.

Creating a New Template

If you know you will be working with a particular project design repeatedly and you will just be updating elements like text and graphics, you can save your own project as a template. Each time you need a variation of the same project, just open and modify the template.

You can also organize the Template Browser by adding and deleting your own collections.

To create a new template:

1. Design your project.

2. Choose File > Save as Template.

3. In the dialog that appears, type a name for the template (**Figure 15.5**).

4. Choose a collection.

   If you don't already have any custom collections, click the New Collection button, name the new collection, and click Create.

5. Choose a format.

6. Uncheck the Create QuickTime Preview check box if you don't want to create a QuickTime preview.

7. Click Save.

   Your template is now available in the Template Browser (**Figure 15.6**).

✔ Tips

- Choose generic object names for your template. For instance, if you have a lower-third text element that changes based on the name and title of a new person each time, use Name and Title. For a background element, name it Background.

- Create different templates for different resolutions. If you know you need NTSC, PAL, and HD versions of the project, create a template for each.

- Collect all template-based media files into one location. If you move media files to different folders on your hard disk after creating the template, Motion is not able to find them and shows them as offline. By consolidating all media to be used in a template, you reduce the likelihood that you'll accidentally move the media later.

- Custom templates are saved into /Home/ Library/Application Support/Motion/ Templates. Because they are simply Motion project files, they can be easily shared with others (although any media in the template appears as offline if you don't share it as well).

- Templates that shipped with Motion are stored in the Users/Shared folder.

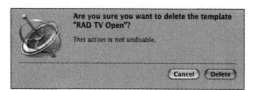

Figure 15.7 Click Delete in the confirmation dialog if you're sure you want to get rid of the template forever.

To add a collection to the Template Browser:

1. Press Shift-Command-O to open the Template Browser.

2. Click the New Collection button and type a name for the collection.

To delete a collection or a template from the Template Browser:

1. Select the collection or the template in the Template Browser and choose Edit > Delete or press Command-Delete.

A confirmation dialog appears (**Figure 15.7**).

2. Click Delete.

CREATING A NEW TEMPLATE

EXPORTING A PROJECT

16

As you design a Motion graphics project, you may find that you want to post a draft version to the Web for a client in a remote location to review. And when the project is complete, you'll want to share your masterpiece, whether by tape for a television station, by DVD, or via a Web site.

Motion makes it easy to export your project in a variety of formats to suit your needs. When you get ready to export, you can choose the type of export, use one of Motion's presets, or create your own presets. When you export your project, you create a self-contained file (or a series of files) that you can then share with others.

You can also export using a separate, dedicated application called Compressor that ships with Apple's Pro applications, including Motion. Compressor allows you to create a batch of exports: you can continue to work in Motion while Compressor handles the exporting.

This chapter covers the basics of exporting projects and using Compressor.

Exporting a Project

You manage the exporting process by making selections in the Export sheet. These selections determine the format of the exported file.

To export a project:

1. Choose File > Export, or press Command-E.

   The Export sheet appears (**Figure 16.1**).

2. In the Save As box, type a name for the exported file(s).

3. In the Where field, navigate to the location where you want to save the file(s).

4. In the Kind field, choose whether to export a QuickTime movie, an image sequence, or a still image.

   You can also click the Options button to opens the Export Options dialog.

5. In the Export Preset field, select a predefined group of export settings.

   The content of this list changes based on what you selected in the Kind field. You can also create your own preset, as discussed in "Working with Export Presets" later in this chapter.

6. If you have selected QuickTime movie in the Kind pop-up, you then have the choice of whether to include the video, the audio, or both using the Include pop-up menu.

Figure 16.1 The Export sheet gives you options for exporting your project.

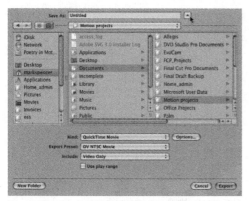

Figure 16.2 To reveal a full browser window in the Export sheet, simply click the down arrow at the top of the sheet.

7. Check the Use play range check box if you want to export only the frames within the play range.

If you leave this unchecked, the full project duration is exported.

8. When you are finished making your choices in this dialog, click the Export button to start the export process.

✔ Tips

- Click the down arrow at the top of the Export sheet to reveal a full browser window (**Figure 16.2**).

- If you export an image sequence, Motion creates a still image file for every frame of your project and appends a sequential number to the filename. You can tell Motion to use a specific number of digits by adding a pound symbol enclosed in brackets after the filename in the Save As field. For example, Filename[###] appends three digits, such as Filename001, Filename002, and so on.

Working with Export Presets

You can view the details of the different default export presets in the Presets section of Motion's Preferences. You can create a new preset based on an existing preset, create your own preset from scratch, and delete presets. You can choose between using either the Export sheet or Preferences for these operations.

The presets for each export type are listed here.

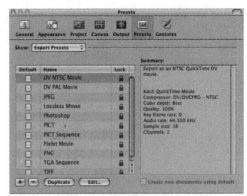

Figure 16.3 When you choose a preset, Motion displays a description of its settings.

◆ QuickTime movie presets:
DV NTSC, DV PAL, Lossless, Pixlet

◆ Image sequence presets:
PICT, TGA

◆ Still image presets:
JPEG, Photoshop, PICT, PNG, TIFF

To view preset settings:

1. Open Motion's Preferences by choosing File > Preferences or by pressing Command-, (comma).
   The Presets dialog appears.

2. Click the Presets button from the icon list at the top of the Presets dialog.

3. In the Show field, choose Export Presets.

4. In the detailed list below the Show field, click on the name of a preset.

   When you do, a description of the preset's settings appears on the right side (**Figure 16.3**). When an export preset is chosen as a default (by checking the Default check box), it will automatically be selected in the Export dialog.

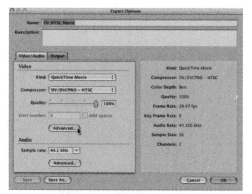

Figure 16.4 Clicking the Advanced button brings up additional options for creating an export preset based on an existing preset.

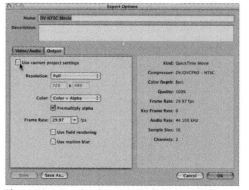

Figure 16.5 To make changes in the Output tab, be sure to uncheck the Use current project settings check box.

To create an export preset based on an existing preset:

1. Choose File > Export or press Command-E and select a preset.

2. Click the Options button.
   The Export Options dialog appears.

3. In the Video/Audio tab, make the changes you want.
   Click the Advanced buttons for additional options (**Figure 16.4**).

4. Click the Output tab.
   If you want to make changes here, uncheck the Use current project settings check box (**Figure 16.5**).

5. After you have adjusted the Video/Audio and Output tabs, type a name for the preset in the Name field at the top of the Export Options dialog.

6. Enter a description in the Description field if you desire.

7. Click Save As to save your export options.

8. Click OK to return to the Export dialog
   You can see that this new preset is now available in the Export Preset pop-up.

✔ Tips

- You can also use the Presets section of the Preferences to duplicate and modify an existing preset.

WORKING WITH EXPORT PRESETS

To create a new preset:

1. In the Presets section of the Preferences window, choose Export Presets from the Show field.

2. Click the Add Preset button (+) at the bottom left (**Figure 16.6**).

3. In the resulting Export Options dialog, choose your setting..

4. Give your new preset a name and description and click OK.

To delete a custom preset:

◆ Select the preset in the Preset section of the Preferences window and click the Delete Preset (–) button.

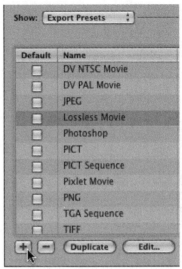

Figure 16.6 Click the Add Preset button (the plus sign) to start creating a new preset.

Why Leave If You're Coming Back?

Another handy reason for exporting is to export certain project elements so you can bring them right back into the project. Why would you want to do this?

To simplify a project. If you have a very complex project with many layers, objects, and effects, you can export a subset of elements and bring them all back in as one file. For example, if you have a complex animating background and you know you won't need to change it, make all the non-background layers inactive (by unchecking the Active check box in the Layers tab) and export the background. You can then import the file you just exported, turn all non-background layers back on, and make all of the original background objects inactive because you can now use the exported/reimported version instead.

To improve performance. When you replace many complex elements with a single rendered file, Motion no longer needs to calculate all the filters, behaviors, motions paths, and so on. As a result, playback performance can improve dramatically.

To create Library content. Do you have a great animation you want to use again? Export it and then add it to the Library. Now it's available every time you use Motion.

Where's My Alpha?

If you want your exported movie or image sequence to have an alpha channel so you can composite it in another application, you need to take care of a couple of things:

1. First make sure your background opacity is set to 0% in Project Properties (Edit > Project Properties or Command-J) (**Figure 16.7**).

   Note: Changing the background color and opacity in the Preferences dialog only affects *new* projects, not the current project.

2. Then, in the Video/Audio pane of the Export Options dialog (choose File > Export, and then click the Options button), select a Compressor type that supports an alpha channel, such as Animation (**Figure 16.8**)

3. Click the Advanced button to bring up the QuickTime Compression Settings dialog. Under the Depth selection, choose Millions of Colors +.

4. And finally, in the Output tab of the Export Options dialog, make sure the Premultiply alpha check box is checked so you can mix semi-transparent pixels with your background color.

If you follow these steps you should get an alpha channel when you export.

Note: If your destination is Final Cut Pro HD or DVD Studio Pro, you do not need to worry about any of these steps except for the background opacity (step 1). Either application imports the Motion project file itself, which always contains an alpha channel. See Chapter 17 for more information.

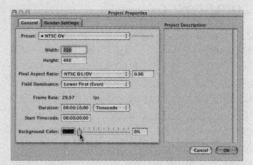

Figure 16.7 To make sure that your exported movie or image sequence has an alpha channel, first be sure to set the background opacity to 0%.

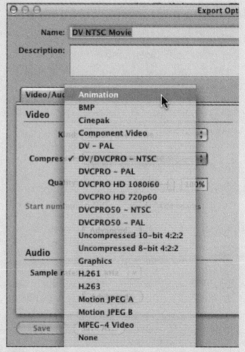

Figure 16.8 You'll also need to select Animation for the Compressor type in the Video/Audio tab of the Export Options dialog.

Exporting with Compressor

Compressor is a separate application that ships with Motion (and Final Cut Pro HD and DVD Studio Pro). It is designed specifically to export projects into different formats. Many more presets are available in Compressor than in Motion's Export command, and you can set up a batch, with multiple different files to be exported in multiple formats, which Compressor then exports automatically. Because Compressor works on a temporary copy of your project file, you can continue to work on your project while Compressor is running.

Figure 16.9 You can view the details about the preset by clicking the Summary button.

To export a project using Compressor:

1. Choose File > Export using Compressor, or press Shift-Command-E.

   The Compressor Export Options dialog appears.

2. Choose an export preset from the pop-up menu.

   Click the Summary button to view the preset details (**Figure 16.9**).

3. In the Include field, choose whether to include video, audio, or both.

4. Check the Use play range check box if you want the exported project to be limited to frames within the play range.

5. In the Output section, either use the current project settings, or uncheck this check box and choose your own settings.

6. Click the Export button.

   Compressor launches and displays the Batch and Presets windows (**Figure 16.10**).

Figure 16.10 Once you click Export, Compressor launches and presents you with the Batch and Presets windows.

Figure 16.11 The Batch Monitor application provides information on the progress of each job you submitted to Compressor.

7. Choose a destination and an output file name or accept the defaults.

8. If you want, you can add more presets for the same project to the batch by clicking the Presets button at the top of the Batch window and choosing options from the menu.

9. Click the Submit button.

   Compressor springs into action, exporting each item in the batch. It launches another application called Batch Monitor that displays the progress of the operation (**Figure 16.11**).

10. When Compressor is finished, the Batch Monitor window appears empty. Choose Batch Monitor > Quit.

✔ Tips

■ Checking the Use motion blur check box in the Output section of the Export Options dialog turns on motion blur for exporting even if it is turned off in the project (View > Motion Blur).

■ You can also use Compressor separately from Motion—launch Compressor and drag your Motion project file onto the Batch window.

■ Compressor includes options for preparing files for use in DVD Studio Pro. For more details on using Compressor, choose Help > Compressor Help from the Compressor application.

INTEGRATING WITH APPLE PRO APPS

17

Motion graphics are usually created as part of an overall workflow designed to most efficiently create elements in different applications and integrate them into the final product. For example, you may be editing in Final Cut Pro HD, creating motion graphics in Motion, and building a DVD in DVD Studio Pro.

Apple has integrated their Pro applications with each other so that you can move back and forth between them by embedding Motion project files directly into Final Cut Pro HD and DVD Studio Pro. This integration obviates the need to render out intermediate files—saving time and hard drive space. Plus, when you update the Motion project, the content in Final Cut Pro HD or DVD Studio Pro is updated automatically. Very sweet!

Integrating with Final Cut Pro HD

When working with Final Cut Pro HD and Motion, you can move between applications in either direction: you can create a project in Motion and bring it into Final Cut Pro, or you can export clips in a sequence from a Final Cut Pro HD project into Motion (for example, you might do this to create motion graphics effects on an edited sequence, which would then get automatically updated in Final Cut Pro).

When you export from Final Cut Pro into Motion, all clip in and out points, opacity settings, motion effects clip markers, and blend modes are preserved.

To use a Motion project in Final Cut Pro HD:

1. Launch Final Cut Pro HD.

2. Choose File > Import > Files.

3. Browse to the Motion project file in the File Open dialog and click OK.

    The Motion project file appears in the Browser as an ordinary video clip, and you can add it to Final Cut Pro's Timeline just like any other clip. Any alpha channel information in the Motion project is preserved, so you can freely composite the clip over other clips (**Figure 17.1**).

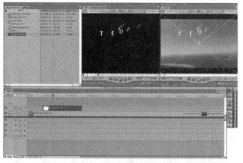

Figure 17.1 You can import a Motion project into Final Cut Pro HD and edit it into a sequence just like a video clip. Here, some animated text create in Motion is composited over some video.

✔ Tips

- You need to render the Motion clip for playback. This is because the project file stays in a lossless format to maintain the alpha channel information, and you need to render it into the codec that you have chosen for your Final Cut Pro HD sequence.

- If your Motion clip has an alpha channel, Final Cut Pro may interpret the alpha incorrectly in which case you'll see ugly stair-stepping or a colored fringe around objects. If this happens, click the Motion project in the Final Cut Pro Browser and choose Modify > Alpha and try Black, White, or Straight.

- You can go back to Motion and make changes that are immediately updated in Final Cut Pro HD. To do so, Control-click on the Motion clip (which is really a .motn project file) in the Timeline and choose Open in Editor from the drop-down menu. The project opens in Motion. Make your changes and switch back to Final Cut—you'll see Motion clip update.

To use Final Cut Pro HD clips in Motion:

1. In the Final Cut Pro HD Timeline, select the clips to export.

2. Choose File > Export > Export to "Motion" Project.

3. In the Export dialog that appears, make the following selections (**Figure 17.2**):

   Save As. Type the name of the Motion file.

   Where. Choose where to save the file. Note that you are actually saving a Motion project file that contains these clips.

   Launch "Motion". When this check box is checked, Motion automatically launches. If it is already running, Motion becomes the active application.

   Embed "Motion" Content. When this check box is checked, the selected clips in Final Cut Pro HD are replaced automatically by the Motion project (**Figures 17.3a** and **17.3b**).

Figure 17.2. When exporting Final Cut Pro HD clips to Motion, you have several choices to make in the Export dialog.

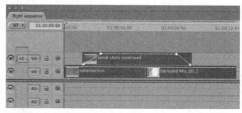

Figure 17.3a Select the clips you want to export to Motion.

Figure 17.3b Once exported, the clips are replaced with the Motion project file.

INTEGRATING WITH FINAL CUT PRO HD

Figure 17.4 The select clips from the Final Cut Pro HD sequence appear in Motion, with tracks, In and Out points, and keyframes intact.

4. Click Save.

The Motion project launches (assuming you left the check box checked), and the clips are reproduced in Motion's Timeline (**Figure 17.4**).

5. Make your desired changes in Motion.

✔ Tips

■ Changes you make to the Motion project are automatically reflected in the Final Cut Pro HD project (if you left the Embed Motion Content check box checked, that is).

■ If you don't want the Motion file to replace the selected Final Cut Pro HD clips, deselect the Embed "Motion" Content check box when you are exporting.

■ As an alternate strategy, duplicate the Final Cut Pro HD sequence before exporting, then select Embed "Motion" Content. That way you get the Motion project into your sequence and you have the original clips as a backup.

Who's Coming Along for the Ride?

So what properties of the selected Final Cut Pro clips are retained in Motion? Here's the list:

◆ Media

◆ Frame rates and in and out points

◆ Markers (clip markers only, not sequence markers)

◆ Motion tab parameters such as Position, Scale, and Rotation

◆ Composite modes (called blend modes in Motion)

◆ Opacity levels

◆ Keyframes set for Motion parameters (both linear and smooth)

◆ Audio media and markers

Integrating with DVD Studio Pro

Motion is a great tool for creating motion menus for DVDs. Similar to how you move between Motion and Final Cut Pro HD, you can import Motion project files directly into DVD Studio Pro, add them to a project, and immediately view them in the Simulator. And any changes you make to the Motion project are immediately reflected in DVD Studio Pro.

To use a Motion project in DVD Studio Pro:

1. Launch DVD Studio Pro.

2. Choose File > Import > Asset and locate the Motion project file.

3. Drag the file from the Asset window to the Menu window and choose how to place it (**Figure 17.5**).

4. The Motion project plays in the Simulator (**Figure 17.6**).

As you make changes to the Motion project, DVD Studio Pro automatically updates to reflect the changes.

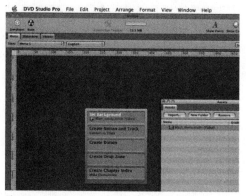

Figure 17.5 When importing a file from Motion to DVD Studio Pro you have four options for placing it.

Figure 17.6 Once imported, your Motion project is immediately available and can be played in DVD Studio Pro's Simulator.

EDITING PROJECT PROPERTIES

Every time you create a project, Motion assigns a set of universal properties such as the codec you will be working in, the frame size, and the duration. You can choose from a list of presets when you first create a project, and you can go back and change these properties at anytime. For example, you may decide you want your project to be longer than what you first anticipated. Or, you may want to change the background color.

Editing these properties is quick and easy via the Project Properties pane. And, if you find that you are regularly changing certain properties of a preset, it's a simple matter to create your own custom preset for future projects. You can even assign a default preset so that when you open a new project Motion assigns it automatically and you can get right to work.

Opening and Editing Project Properties

The Project Properties pane is where you go to create custom project settings or change the current settings. This pane has two tabs: General and Render Settings. The General tab lets you select and modify project presets and change the project duration, the method of displaying time code, and the color and opacity of the background. The Render Settings tab contains two controls for motion blur.

To create a new project with custom project settings:

1. Choose File > New or press Command-N.

   The Select Project Preset pane appears (**Figure A.1**).

2. Choose Custom from the Preset pop-up menu.

   The Project Properties pane appears (**Figure A.2**).

To open the current project's properties:

◆ Choose Edit > Project Properties or press Command-J.

To change settings in the General tab:

◆ Adjust the following settings as you desire:

   Preset. Choose a preset from the pop-up menu (**Figure A.3**). Each preset has its own Width, Height, Pixel Aspect Ratio, and Field Dominance settings. You can modify these settings in the following controls, or you can choose a Custom preset. To create new presets that will appear in the pop-up menu, use the Presets section of the Preferences pane, described in Appendix B.

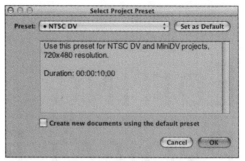

Figure A.1 The Select Project Preset pane lets you choose a Preset or opt to create a custom one.

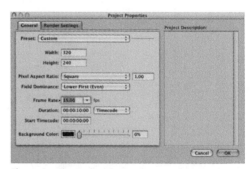

Figure A.2 The Project Properties pane lets you create custom project settings or change the current ones.

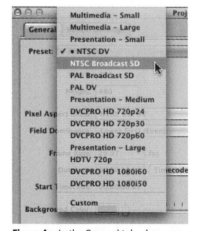

Figure A.3 In the General tab, choose a preset from the pop-up menu.

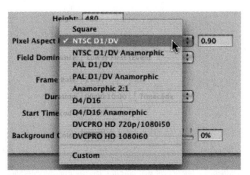

Figure A.4 Using the Pixel Aspect Ratio setting you can determine how to interpret an object based on whether it was created with square or non-square pixels.

Width and Height. Set the frame size of the project and the default output resolution. Note that if you already have objects in the Canvas, changing frame size has no impact on them—essentially it just makes the Canvas area larger or smaller.

Pixel Aspect Ratio. This setting determines how to interpret the object based on whether it was created with square or non-square pixels. Square pixels are used in computer displays, whereas analog televisions use non-square pixels. Choose from the presets in the pop-up menu or enter a custom number in the field to the right of the pop-up (**Figure A.4**).

Field Dominance. For interlaced video, choose Upper or Lower. Your selection should match the field dominance of the device that you will use to output to video. For progressive scan video or film, set the field dominance to None.

Frame Rate. Choose a frame rate from the pop-up menu or enter a custom frame rate. The frame rate should match the final output format (for example, 29.97 for NTSC video, 25 for PAL video, or 24 for film).

Duration. This setting sets the overall length of the project, which is 10 seconds by default. Use the pop-up to decide how to display the timecode: in frames, in traditional timecode notation, or in seconds.

Start Timecode. This setting sets the starting timecode that gets embedded in the timecode track when you export a QuickTime movie.

continues on next page

OPENING AND EDITING PROJECT PROPERTIES

Background Color. This setting sets the background color behind all objects in the Canvas. Click the color swatch to bring up the Mac OS X Color Picker or Control-click to quickly sample a color (**Figure A.5**).

Background opacity. Denoted by the percentage slider to the right of the Background Color setting, this setting determines the opacity of the background color when you are exporting.

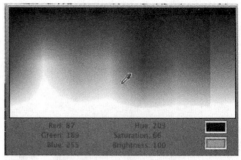

Figure A.5 You can Control-click to quickly sample a color for the background behind objects in the Canvas.

✔ Tips

- Generally, you just need to select a preset and accept all the settings that go along with it. Making changes to the parameters described here can have unintended results.

- It's not necessary to change the frame size if you want to output a different size than the project size—instead, just change the output settings, as described in Chapter 16.

- Background opacity has no impact on how the background color appears in the Canvas as you work.

- If you want to export your project with an alpha channel, you must set the background opacity to zero. When you do so, the alpha channel is premultiplied with the color of the background, which you normally set to black or white, depending on the objects and destination for compositing.

- If you want to change the default background color and opacity for new projects, use the Project section of the Preferences pane (discussed in more detail in Appendix B).

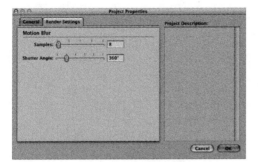

Figure A.6 The Render Settings tab gives you two controls for adjusting motion blur.

To change settings in the Render Settings tab:

◆ Adjust the following settings for Motion Blur as you desire (**Figure A.6**):

Samples. This setting sets the number of samples per pixel that are used to create the effect of motion blur.

Shutter Angle. This setting sets the amount of motion blur.

✔ Tips

■ Higher sample rates can create a higher-quality blur effect, but they also take considerably more processor power to calculate, which may impact playback performance.

■ Motion blur only affects animated objects, not the motion within a QuickTime movie or image sequence.

■ Motion blur is applied globally to all objects in a project. To turn it on or off, choose View > Motion Blur or press Option-M.

SETTING
PREFERENCES

Most applications for Mac OS X have a set
of *user preferences* that determine various
settings for the application. Motion is no
exception—you even open the Preferences
pane with the same standard menu command or keyboard shortcut most Mac OS X
applications use. You access Motion's preferences by choosing Motion > Preferences or
by pressing Command-, (comma).

Motion's preferences are divided into the
following seven different sets of controls,
or *panes*, that tweak how Motion looks
and behaves:

- General pane

- Appearance pane

- Project pane

- Canvas pane

- Output pane

- Presets pane

- Gestures pane

Using the General Pane

The General pane has settings that affect the overall behavior of Motion. It is divided into six sections (**Figure B.1**).

Startup. This section allows you to select what happens when you launch Motion. You can elect for Motion to open the last project or create a new project. You can bypass the Welcome screen. And you can go directly to the Template Browser.

Interface. In this section, you can adjust the amount of time that passes before a Drop Menu appears by using the slider, and you can turn Tooltips on or off with the check box.

File Browser & Library. Use the pop-up menu in this section to choose whether to display folders alphabetically, mixed in with files, or after all the files are listed. You can also turn the preview icons in the Utility window on or off with the Show preview type check box. Another check box lets you decide whether to allow items to play in the Preview window just by selecting them. If you uncheck the check box, you have to press the Play button for playback.

Memory & Cache. In this section, you can set the project cache as a percentage of total available memory.

LiveFonts. In this area, you can choose to cache intermediate LiveFont sizes, decide on the path for storing the LiveFont cache, and delete the LiveFont cache.

3rd Party Plug-ins. In this section, you can click the Choose button to select the location where you store any third-party plug-ins that you might use with other applications, such as After Effects. Plug-ins in the selected path appear in the 3rd Party Filters category of the Library.

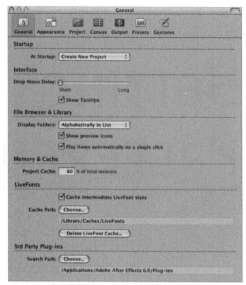

Figure B.1 Use the General pane to change the overall settings for Motion.

Figure B.2 You can change the delay before the drop menu appears.

✔ Tips

- A Drop Menu refers specifically to the multicolored menu of editing options that appears when you drag objects to the Layers tab, the Canvas, the mini-Timeline, or the Timeline (**Figure B.2**).

- Turning off automatic playback in the File Browser & Library area can improve system performance.

- A high Project Cache setting increases the number of frames that can be played back in real-time or rendered for a RAM preview. The tradeoff is that it cuts down on the amount of memory available for other applications that you may be running at the same time, like Final Cut Pro HD or DVD Studio Pro.

- Leaving the caching on (the default) for LiveFonts improves performance when you're working with LiveFonts, but it can create a large cache file as you continue to use more LiveFonts. Consider storing the cache file on a drive other than your system drive, and consider deleting it if it gets too large.

- The path for third-party plug-ins must point to the actual folder, not an alias.

USING THE GENERAL PANE

Using the Appearance Pane

The Appearance pane contains controls for how various parts of the interface look. It has four sections (**Figure B.3**).

Dashboard. Use the slider in this section to set how transparent the Dashboard appears as it floats over the interface.

Thumbnail Preview. If an object has an alpha channel (areas of transparency), the setting in this section determines what you see in the transparent areas in the object's icon in both the Layers tab (**Figure B.4**) and in the Media tab of the Project pane. The default is a checkerboard pattern, but you can select Color from the pop-up menu and then click the color well to open the Mac OS X Color Picker and choose a color.

Timeline. In this section, you can choose whether to display object timebars with just a Name, a Name Plus Thumbnail, or a Filmstrip that shows each frame of an animation in thumbnail form.

Status Bar. This section determines what appears below the Toolbar. By default, only the frame rate appears (during playback), but you can choose to display the color value of the pixel under the pointer and the coordinates of the pointer location. You can choose to display the color value as RGB (Red, Green, and Blue) values, RGB percentages, or as HSV (Hue, Saturation, and Value) values.

✔ Tips

■ Control-click the color well to quickly sample a color for the Thumbnail Preview.

■ If the track height is too small in the Timeline, thumbnails and filmstrips do not appear.

■ Play the project to update the Status bar with any changes.

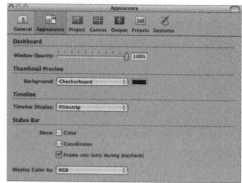

Figure B.3 The Appearance pane lets you tailor the look of the Dashboard, thumbnails, the Timeline, and the Status bar.

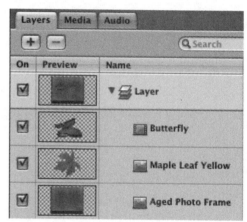

Figure B.4 If an object has an alpha channel, the Thumbnail Preview setting determines what you see in the transparent areas in the object's icon.

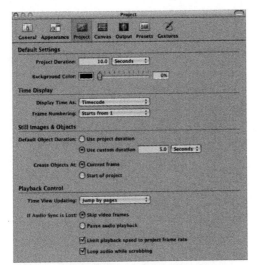

Figure B.5 You use the Project pane to change project-specific attributes. The Default Settings section only applies to new projects and doesn't affect the current project.

Using the Project Pane

The Project pane has four sections that control various aspects specific to your project (**Figure B.5**).

Default Settings. In this section, you can set the default project duration, the background color, and the background opacity for *new* projects.

Default Settings only affect *new* projects. To change the project duration and background of the *current* project, use Project Properties, discussed in Appendix A.

Time Display. In this section you can choose to display time in timecode or frames. If you use frames, you can choose whether the first frame is frame 0 or frame 1.

Still Images & Objects. With the settings in this section, when you add an object to your project that does not have an inherent duration (such as graphics, text, shapes, and generators), you can choose whether the Default Object Duration is the full length of the project or a fixed number of seconds or frames. Create Objects At determines whether objects you add to your projects start at the playhead location or at the beginning of the project.

Playback Control. Use the settings in this section to determine how Motion plays back the project. Time View Updating lets you select what happens when the playhead moves beyond the visible area of the Timeline: you can do nothing, jump to the next section a page at a time, or continuously scroll along—which leaves the playhead static in the middle of the Timeline and moves the Timeline instead.

Audio Sync is Lost lets you choose whether to skip video frames to keep the audio in sync, or just pause the audio so that the video plays every frame as fast as possible. This setting comes into play if your project is complex enough that Motion cannot play back both audio and video in real time.

By unchecking Limit playback speed to project frame rate, you cause Motion to play back your project as fast as your hardware allows, perhaps faster than the project's frame rate.

If you uncheck Loop audio while scrubbing, when you drag the playhead repeatedly over a section of the Timeline, you'll only hear the audio once.

✔ Tips

- You can toggle between timecode and frames at any time by clicking the Location and Duration icons at the bottom of the Canvas.

- If you set Create Objects At Current frame and you set the Object Duration to Use project duration, the object starts at the playhead and extends to the end of the project.

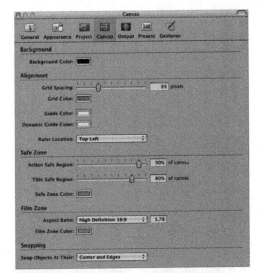

Figure B.6 With the Canvas pane, you change the properties of the various visual aides such as grids, guides, and safe zones.

Using the Canvas Pane

The Canvas pane has five sections of properties that control how the Canvas looks and operates (**Figure B.6**).

Background. This section lets you set the color for the area *outside* of the Canvas.

Alignment. This section lets you set the spacing and color of the grid, the color of guides and dynamic guides, and the location for the rulers.

Safe Zone. In this area, you can set the size of the Action Safe and Title Safe regions and the color of the lines that indicate the regions.

Film Zone. In this area, you can determine the aspect ratio for the film zone from the pop-up. (You can choose from among Anamorphic Scope, Academy Standard, Academy Flat, High Definition, or Custom). This area also lets you choose the color of the film zone lines.

Snapping. In this area, you can set whether objects snap to other objects' centers, edges, or both.

✔ Tips

- To toggle snapping on and off as you work in the Canvas, press N.

- To set the color of the Canvas for the current project, go to Project Properties (Edit > Project Properties or Command-J).

- To show the grid, guides, dynamic guides, or the rulers, use the View button in the Toolbar (**Figure B.7**).

- To show the safe zones, use the View button on the Toolbar or press ' (apostrophe).

- Keep text objects within the Title Safe region and any important action within the Action Safe region to ensure visibility on most consumer TV sets.

- To show the film zone, use the View button on the Toolbar.

- The Film Zone option can be useful if you are working on a project destined for both television and theatrical release. Using this option, you can see the areas that will be cut off.

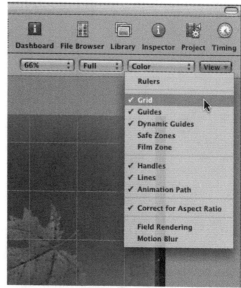

Figure B.7 To show the Grid, Guides, Dynamic Guides, or the Rulers, use the View button in the Toolbar.

Figure B.8 The Output pane lets you change the anti-aliasing method and lets you output your video to an external device.

Using the Output Pane

The Output pane lets you choose an antialiasing method and a video output method (**Figure B.8**).

Antialiasing. In this area, you can choose None, Normal (the default), or Best from the pop-up menu.

Video. If a video device is connected to your computer, it becomes available in the Video Output pop-up, and the Options button also becomes available. Check the Update during playback check box to send each frame to the output device as the project plays. Check Update dynamically on parameter change to see an update on an external monitor as you drag sliders and keyframes.

✔ Tips

■ The None setting for antialiasing can increase performance and decreases render time, but it can also produce jagged edges. The Best setting produces the smoothest edges, but it can slow down playback performance and render times.

■ Turning on an external video device, such as a deck connected by FireWire, slows down Motion's performance. Checking either of the Update check boxes further degrades performance.

■ If your project is destined for television broadcast, it is important to view your project on a monitor. The color space of television is quite different than a computer; the viewable area is different (you can use safe zones, discussed above, to assist with ensuring that your elements are seen); and TVs display interlaced fields that can produce line twitter and other artifacts that you cannot see on a computer screen.

Using the Presets Pane

The Presets pane lets you select and modify presets for both project settings and export settings (**Figure B.9**). Export settings are discussed in Chapter 16.

Show. You can choose either Project Presets or Export presets from the pop-up.

Default. Placing a check in the check box in this column selects a default preset. If you also check the "Create new documents using default check box" at the lower right, all new projects have the preset applied without prompting you.

Summary. The specifics of each preset are listed in this section.

You can duplicate and edit presets with the Project Preset Editor as described in Chapter 16.

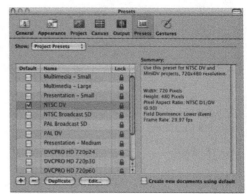

Figure B.9 The Presets pane lets you select and modify presets for both project settings and export settings, depending on what your selection in the Show pop-up menu is.

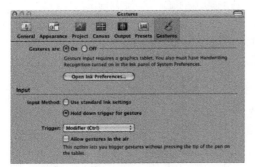

Figure B.10 The Gestures pane lets you set up a graphics tablet you can use with Motion.

Figure B.11 In order to use gestures, you must have Handwriting Recognition turned on in the Ink preferences pane in Mac OS X.

Using the Gestures Pane

If you have a tablet input device attached to your computer, you can use it to control Motion with pen strokes rather than menu commands, mouse clicking, or keyboard shortcuts. You must first turn on Handwriting Recognition in the Ink preferences section of Mac OS X's System Preferences, which you can access from the Gestures pane (**Figure B.10**).

To turn on gestures:

1. Click the On button next to Gestures are.

2. Click the Open Ink Preferences button to launch Mac OS X's System Preferences and turn on Handwriting Recognition in the Ink preferences section (**Figure B.11**).

3. Then, back in Motion's preferences, go to the Gestures pane and click the Open Ink Preferences button.

4. Set the Input settings described here:
   - ▲ **Input Method.** Choose whether to use the Ink preferences settings or to use a trigger. If you choose a trigger, the pen acts like a mouse until you use the trigger to tell Motion that the next movement is a gesture.
   - ▲ **Trigger.** This setting lets you choose whether the trigger is a pen button or the Control key.
   - ▲ *Allow gestures in the air:* If the input method is set to Trigger, checking this check box allows you to draw gestures while holding the pen above the tablet.

For more information on using gestures, see Appendix C of Motion's Help (Help > Motion Help or Command-?).

INDEX

INDEX

INDEX

INDEX

INDEX

INDEX

INDEX

INDEX

THIS BOOK IS SAFARI ENABLED

INCLUDES FREE 45-DAY ACCESS TO THE ONLINE EDITION

The Safari® Enabled icon on the cover of your favorite technology book means the book is available through Safari Bookshelf. When you buy this book, you get free access to the online edition for 45 days.

Safari Bookshelf is an electronic reference library that lets you easily search thousands of technical books, find code samples, download chapters, and access technical information whenever and wherever you need it.

TO GAIN 45-DAY SAFARI ENABLED ACCESS TO THIS BOOK:

- Go to **http://www.peachpit.com/safarienabled**

- Complete the brief registration form

- Enter the coupon code found in the front of this book before the Table of Contents

If you have difficulty registering on Safari Bookshelf or accessing the online edition, please e-mail customer-service@safaribooksonline.com.